CREATED BY **JOSS WHEDON**

BRYAN EDWARD **HILL**   GLEB **MELNIKOV**   ROMAN **TITOV**

ANGEL™

VOLUME TWO **CITY OF DEMONS**

A **BUFFY** † **ANGEL** EVENT

HELLMOUTH

Published by

BOOM!
S T U D I O S™

Series Designer
Grace Park

Collection Designer
Scott Newman

Assistant Editor
Gavin Gronenthal

Associate Editor
Jonathan Manning

Editor
Jeanine Schaefer

Special Thanks to **Sierra Hahn,
Becca J. Sadowsky**, **Nicole Spiegel**,
and **Carol Roeder**

Ross Richie CEO & Founder
Joy Huffman CFO
Matt Gagnon Editor-in-Chief
Filip Sablik President, Publishing & Marketing
Stephen Christy President, Development
Lance Kreiter Vice President, Licensing & Merchandising
Arune Singh Vice President, Marketing
Bryce Carlson Vice President, Editorial & Creative Strategy
Kate Henning Director, Operations
Spencer Simpson Director, Sales
Scott Newman Manager, Production Design
Elyse Strandberg Manager, Finance
Sierra Hahn Executive Editor
Jeanine Schaefer Executive Editor
Dafna Pleban Senior Editor
Shannon Watters Senior Editor
Eric Harburn Senior Editor
Matthew Levine Editor
Sophie Philips-Roberts Associate Editor
Amanda LaFranco Associate Editor
Jonathan Manning Associate Editor
Gavin Gronenthal Assistant Editor

Gwen Waller Assistant Editor
Allyson Gronowitz Assistant Editor
Ramiro Portnoy Assistant Editor
Shelby Netschke Editorial Assistant
Michelle Ankley Design Coordinator
Marie Krupina Production Designer
Grace Park Production Designer
Chelsea Roberts Production Designer
Samantha Knapp Production Design Assistant
José Meza Live Events Lead
Stephanie Hocutt Digital Marketing Lead
Esther Kim Marketing Coordinator
Cat O'Grady Digital Marketing Coordinator
Breanna Sarpy Live Events Coordinator
Amanda Lawson Marketing Assistant
Holly Aitchison Digital Sales Coordinator
Morgan Perry Retail Sales Coordinator
Megan Christopher Operations Coordinator
Rodrigo Hernandez Operations Coordinator
Zipporah Smith Operations Assistant
Jason Lee Senior Accountant
Sabrina Lesin Accounting Assistant

ANGEL Volume Two, June 2020. Published by BOOM!
Studios, a division of Boom Entertainment, Inc. Angel ™
& © 2020 Twentieth Century Fox Film Corporation. All
rights reserved. Originally published in single magazine form
as ANGEL No. 5-8. ™ & © 2019 Twentieth Century Fox
Film Corporation. All rights reserved. BOOM! Studios™
and the BOOM! Studios logo are trademarks of Boom
Entertainment, Inc., registered in various countries and
categories. All characters, events, and institutions depicted
herein are fictional. Any similarity between any of the
names, characters, persons, events, and/or institutions in this
publication to actual names, characters, and persons, whether
living or dead, events, and/or institutions is unintended and
purely coincidental. BOOM! Studios does not read or accept
unsolicited submissions of ideas, stories, or artwork.

For information regarding the CPSIA on this printed
material, call: (203) 595-3636 and provide reference
#RICH – 888951.

BOOM! Studios, 5670 Wilshire Boulevard, Suite 400, Los
Angeles, CA 90036-5679. Printed in USA. First Printing.

ISBN: 978-1-68415-529-3, eISBN: 978-1-64144-695-2

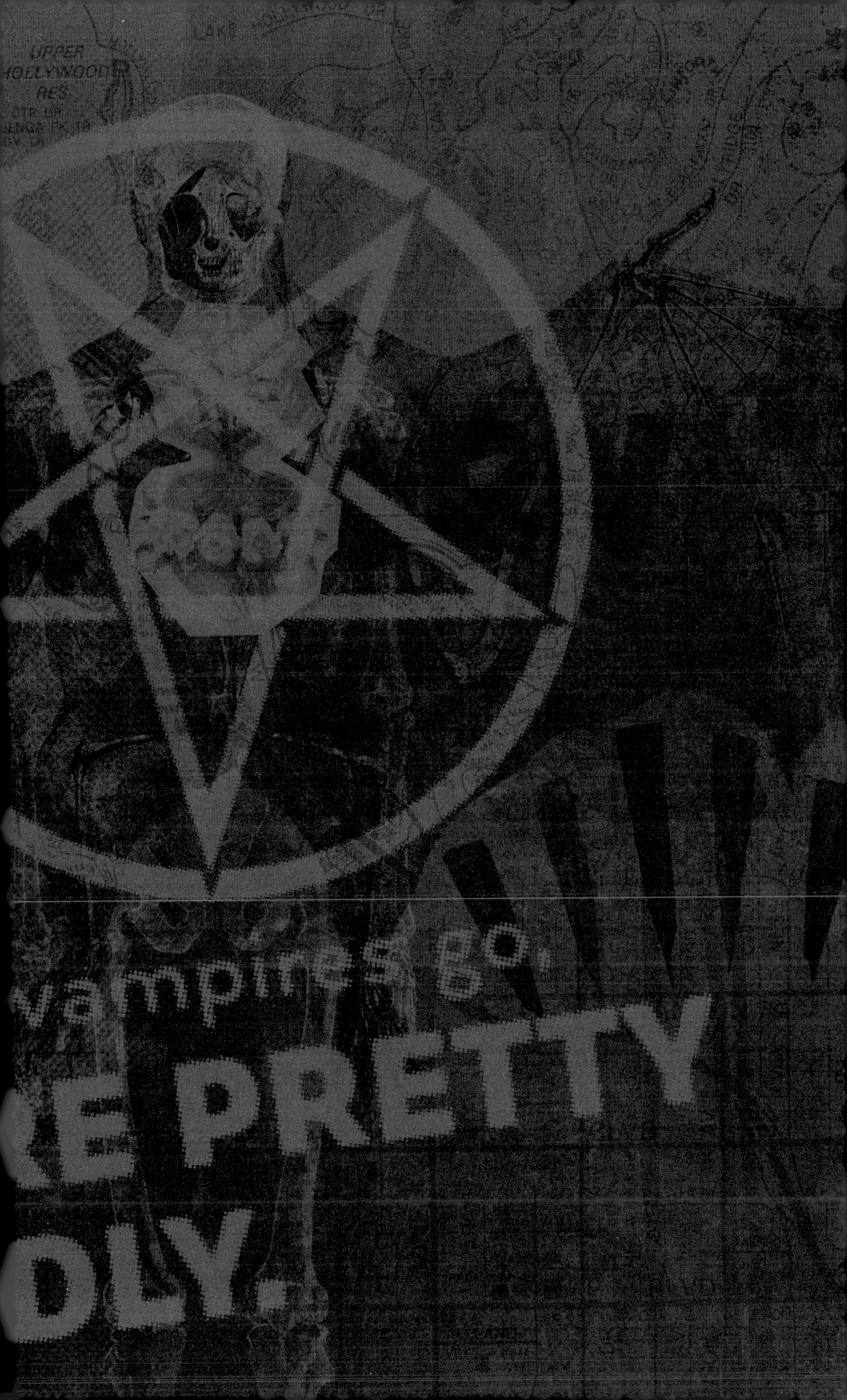
UPPER
HOLLYWOOD
RES
LAKE
vampires &co.
E PRETTY
DLY.

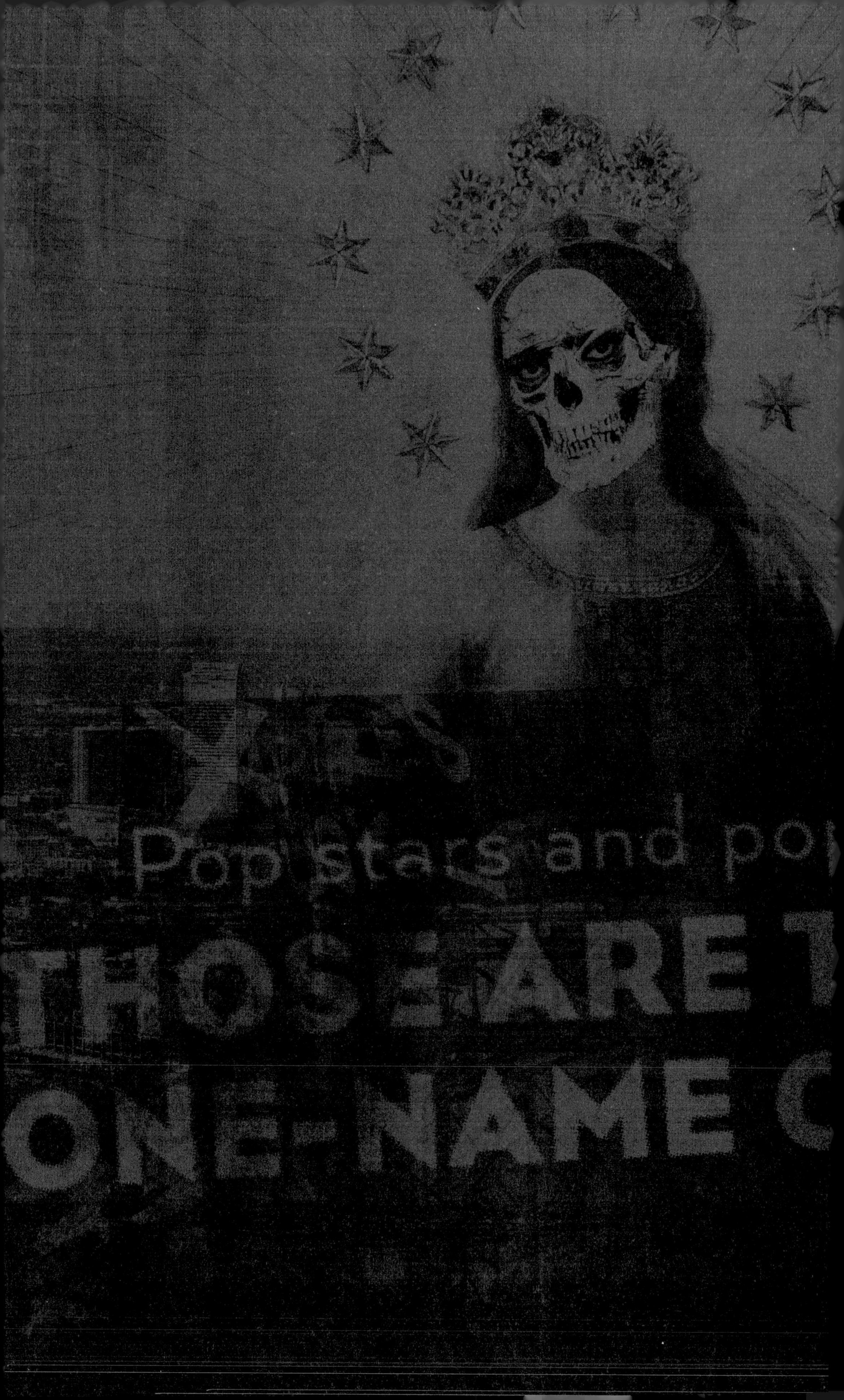
Pop stars and
THOSE ARE
ONE-NAME

Created by
Joss Whedon

Written by
Bryan Edward Hill

Illustrated by
Gleb Melnikov

Colored by
Roman Titov

Lettered by
Ed Dukeshire

Cover by
Dan Panosian

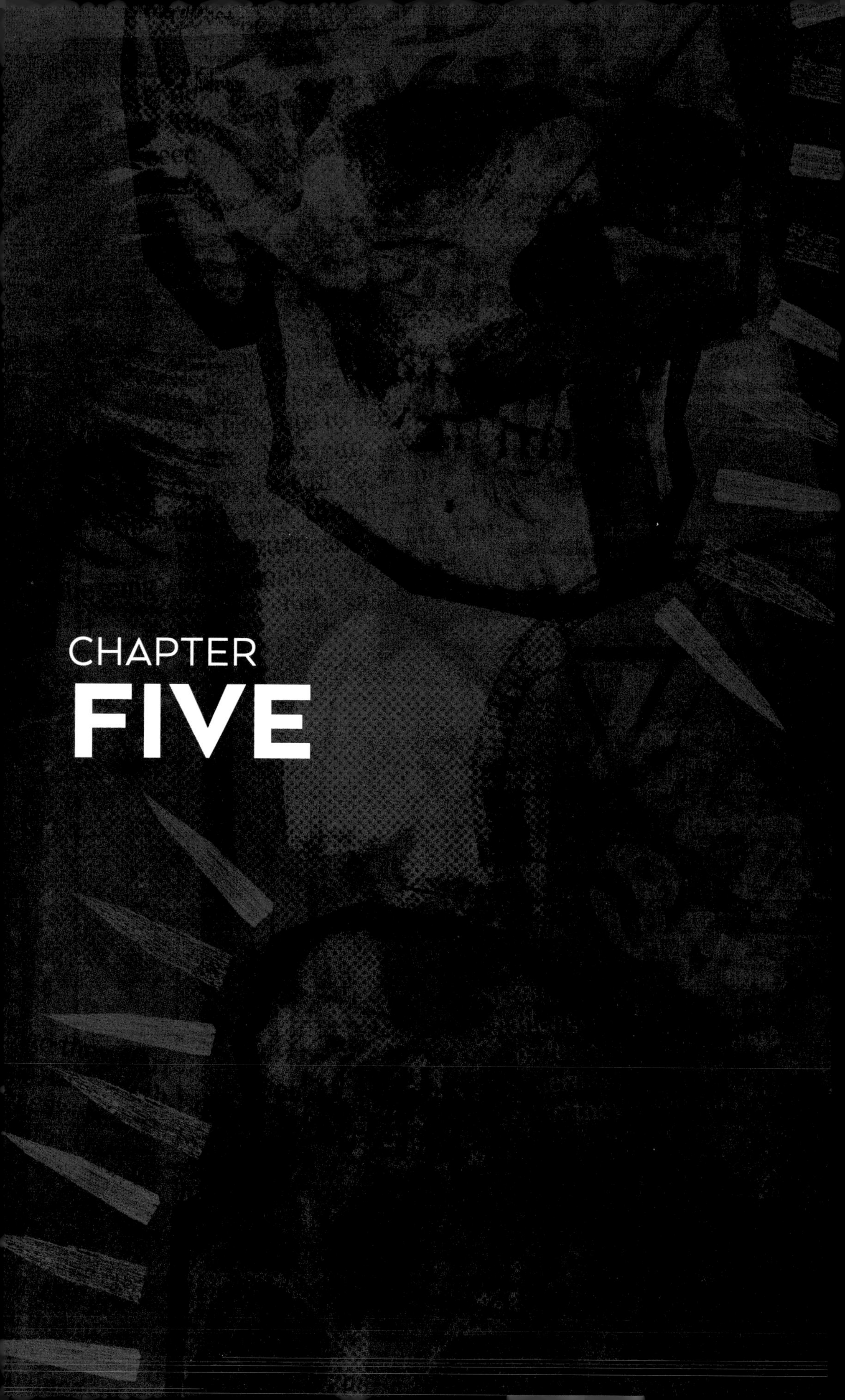

CHAPTER FIVE

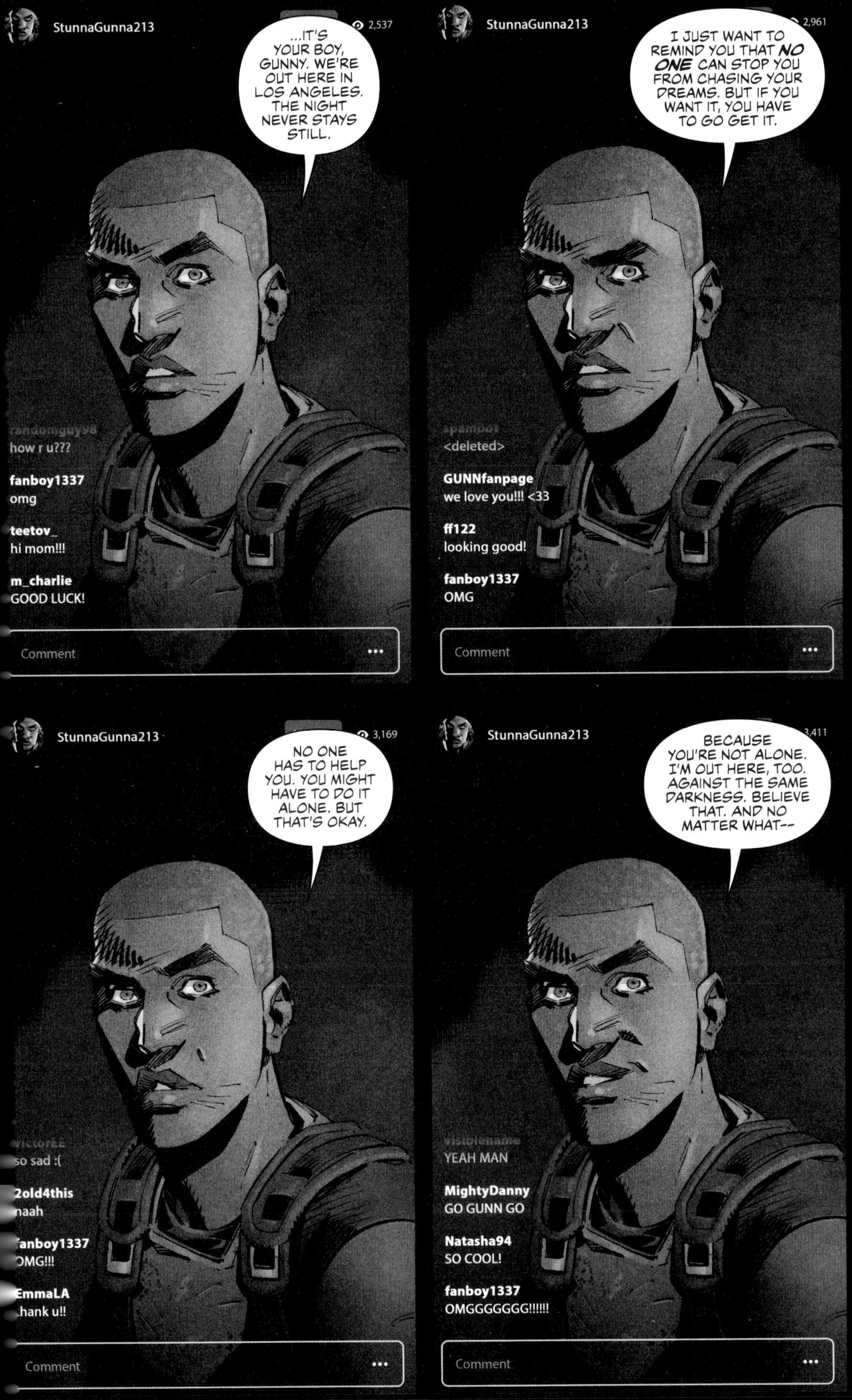
StunnaGunna213
2,537
...IT'S YOUR BOY, GUNNY. WE'RE OUT HERE IN LOS ANGELES. THE NIGHT NEVER STAYS STILL.
how r u???
fanboy1337
omg
teetov_
hi mom!!!
m_charlie
GOOD LUCK!
Comment
StunnaGunna213
2,961
I JUST WANT TO REMIND YOU THAT *NO ONE* CAN STOP YOU FROM CHASING YOUR DREAMS. BUT IF YOU WANT IT, YOU HAVE TO GO GET IT.
<deleted>
GUNNfanpage
we love you!!! <33
ff122
looking good!
fanboy1337
OMG
Comment
StunnaGunna213
3,169
NO ONE HAS TO HELP YOU. YOU MIGHT HAVE TO DO IT ALONE. BUT THAT'S OKAY.
so sad :(
2old4this
naah
fanboy1337
OMG!!!
EmmaLA
thank u!!
Comment
StunnaGunna213
3,411
BECAUSE YOU'RE NOT ALONE. I'M OUT HERE, TOO. AGAINST THE SAME DARKNESS. BELIEVE THAT. AND NO MATTER WHAT--
YEAH MAN
MightyDanny
GO GUNN GO
Natasha94
SO COOL!
fanboy1337
OMGGGGGGG!!!!!!
Comment

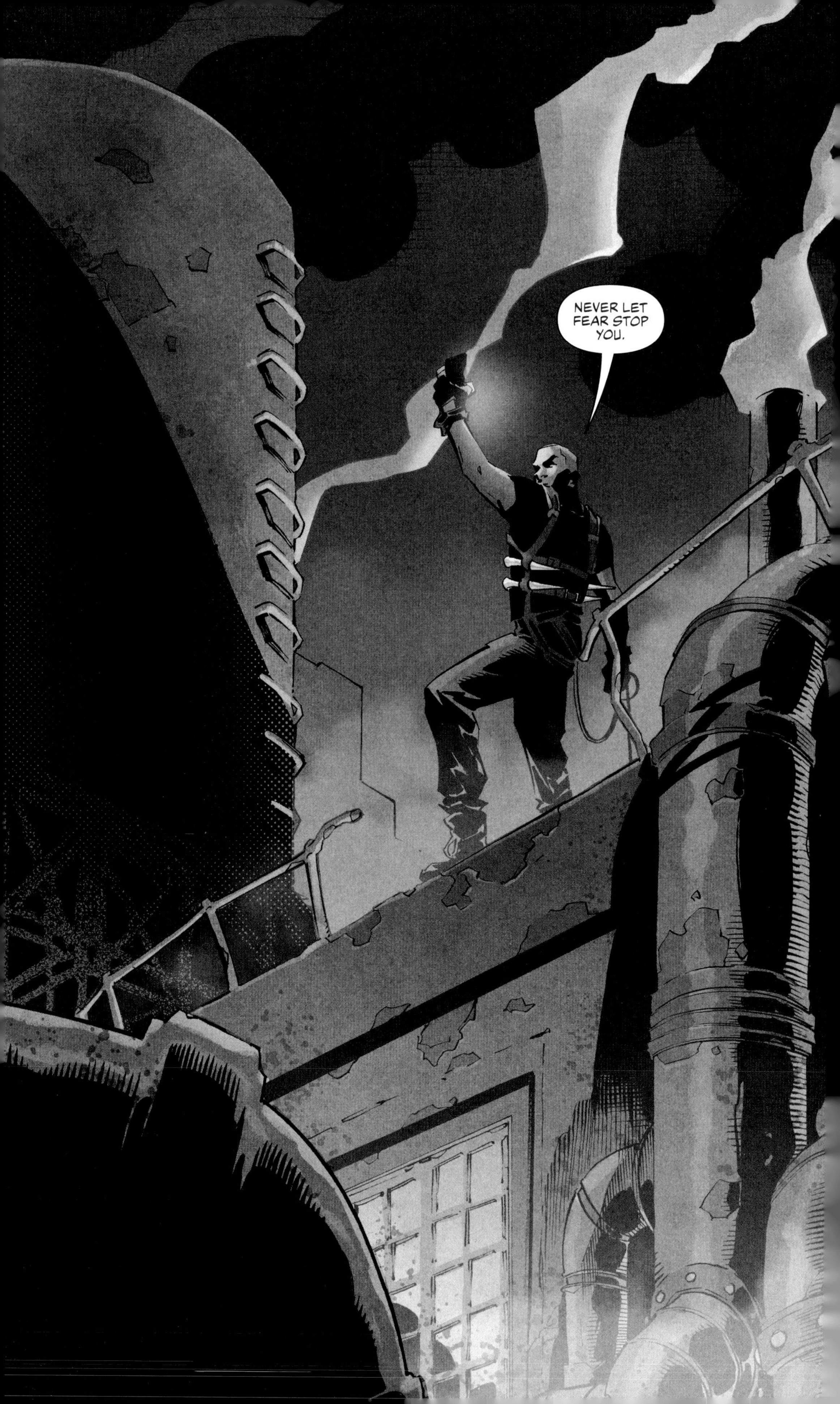
NEVER LET FEAR STOP YOU.

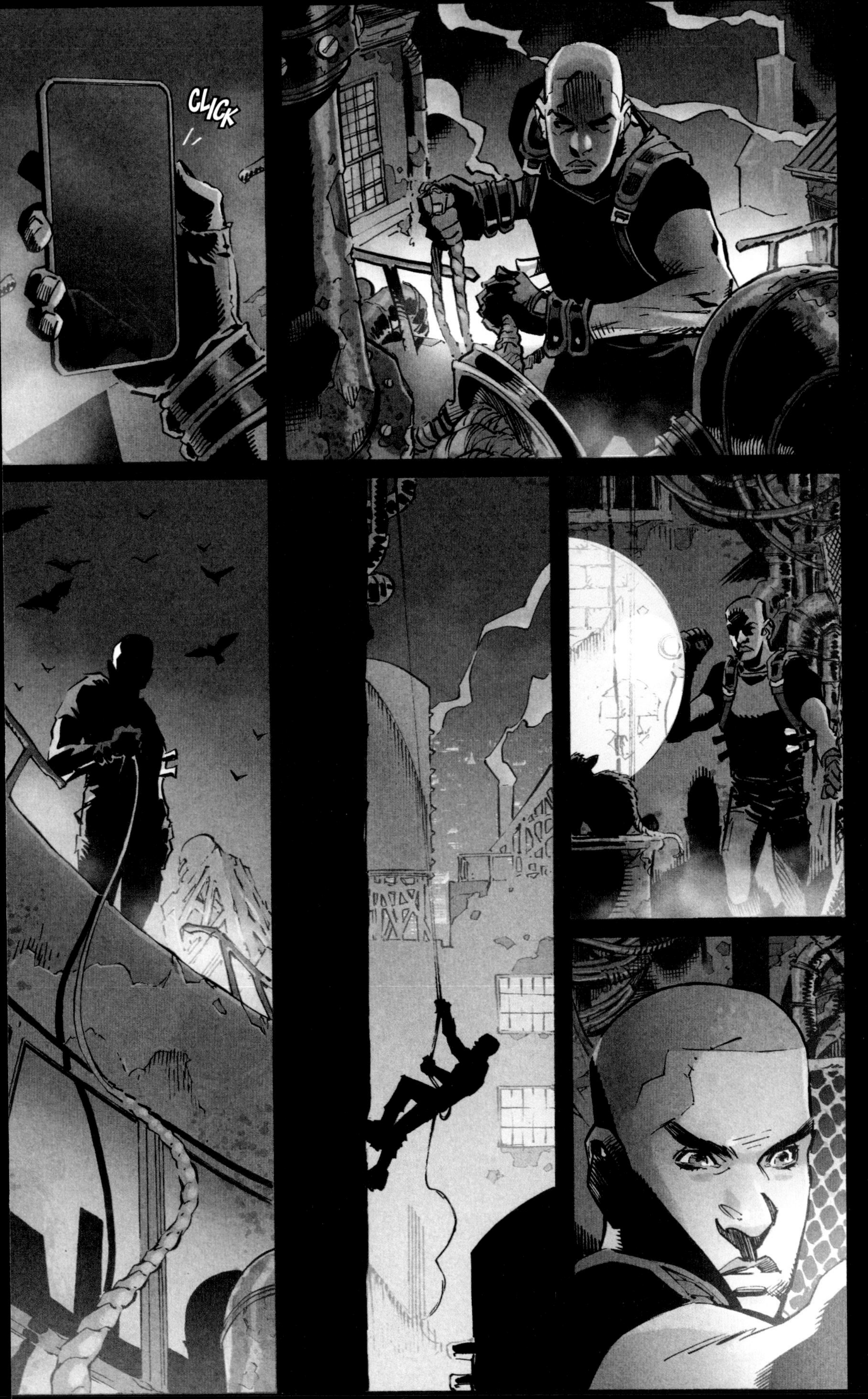
CLICK

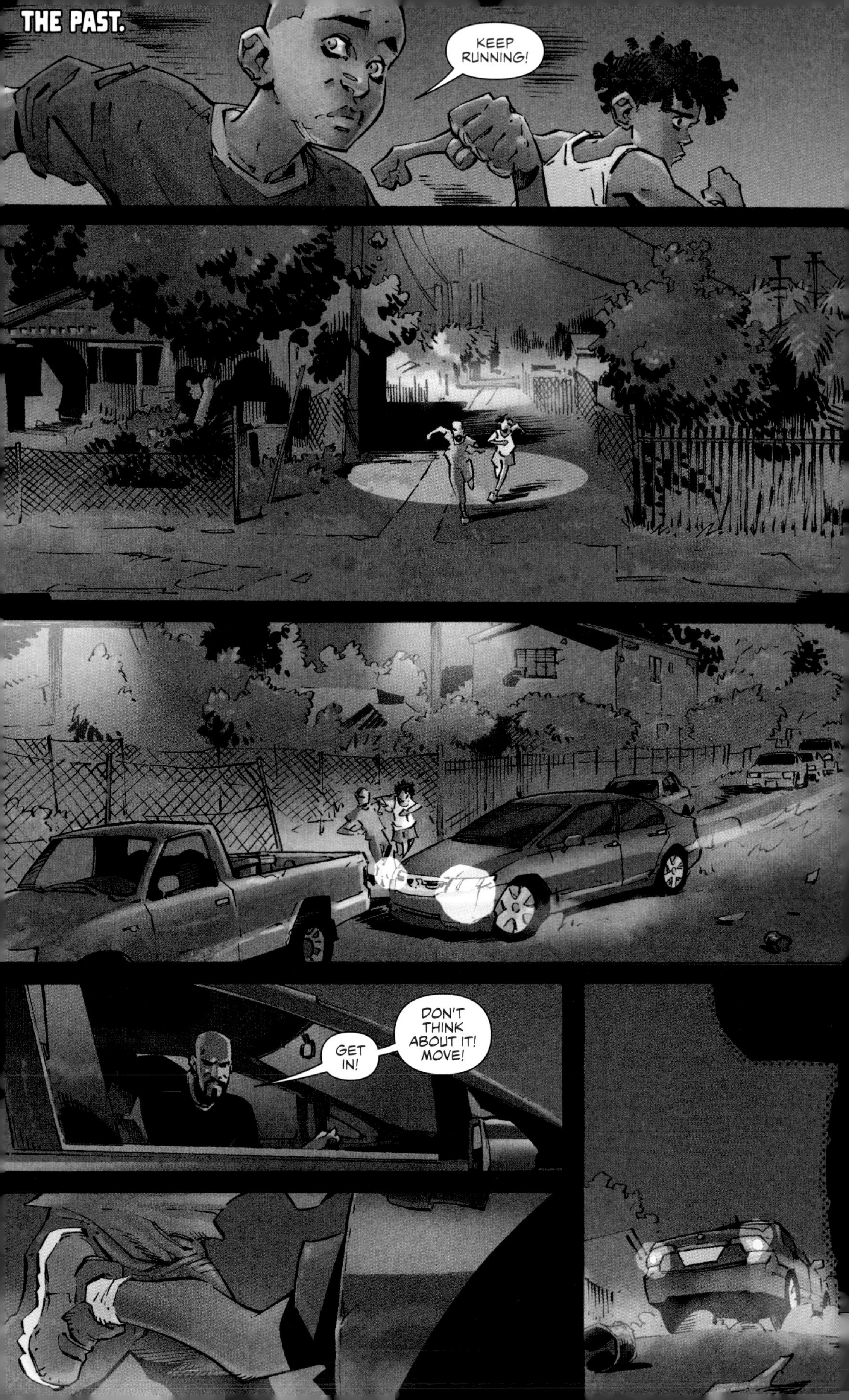
THE PAST.
KEEP RUNNING!
GET IN!
DON'T THINK ABOUT IT! MOVE!

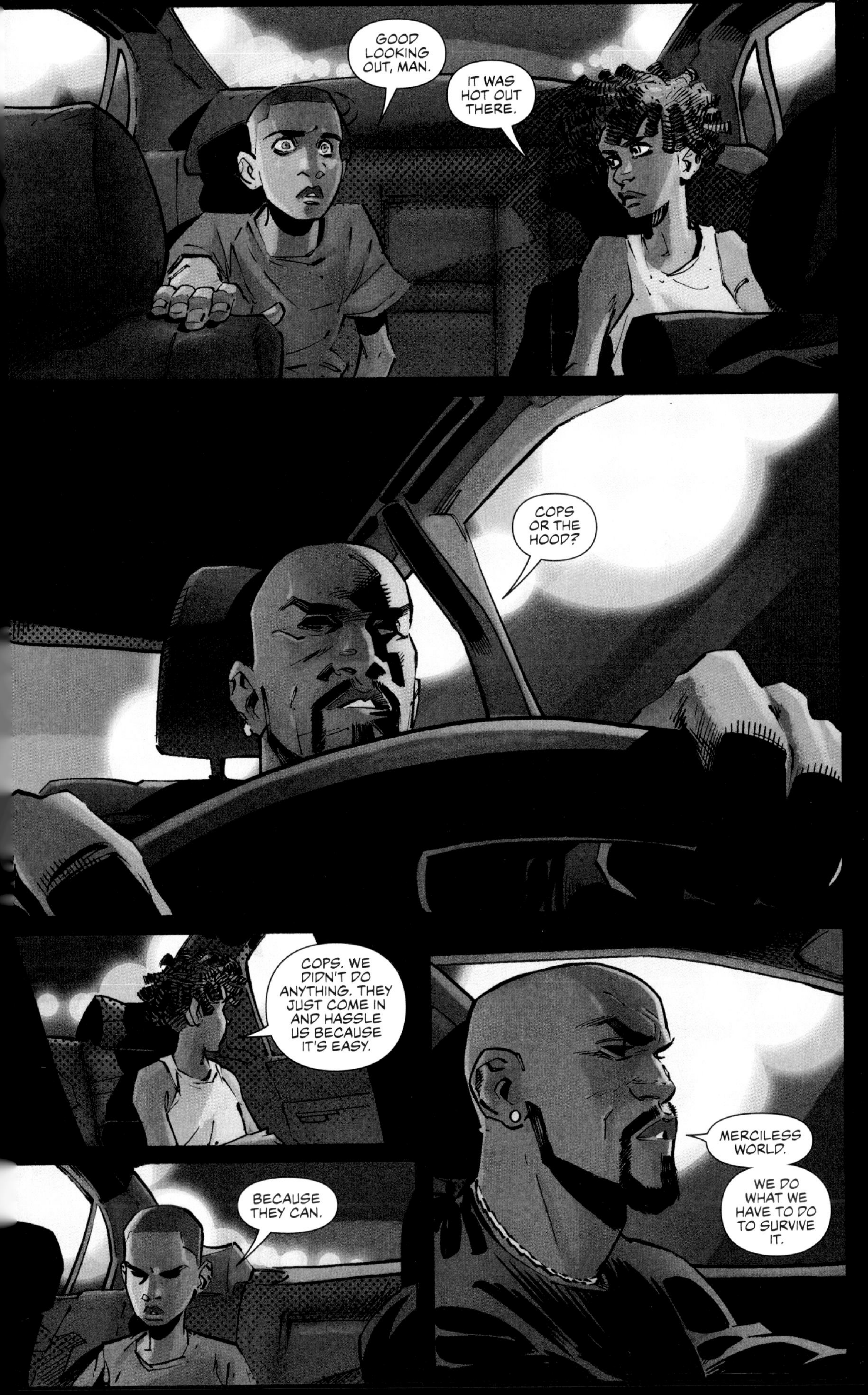
GOOD LOOKING OUT, MAN.
IT WAS HOT OUT THERE.
COPS OR THE HOOD?
COPS. WE DIDN'T DO ANYTHING. THEY JUST COME IN AND HASSLE US BECAUSE IT'S EASY.
BECAUSE THEY CAN.
MERCILESS WORLD.
WE DO WHAT WE HAVE TO DO TO SURVIVE IT.

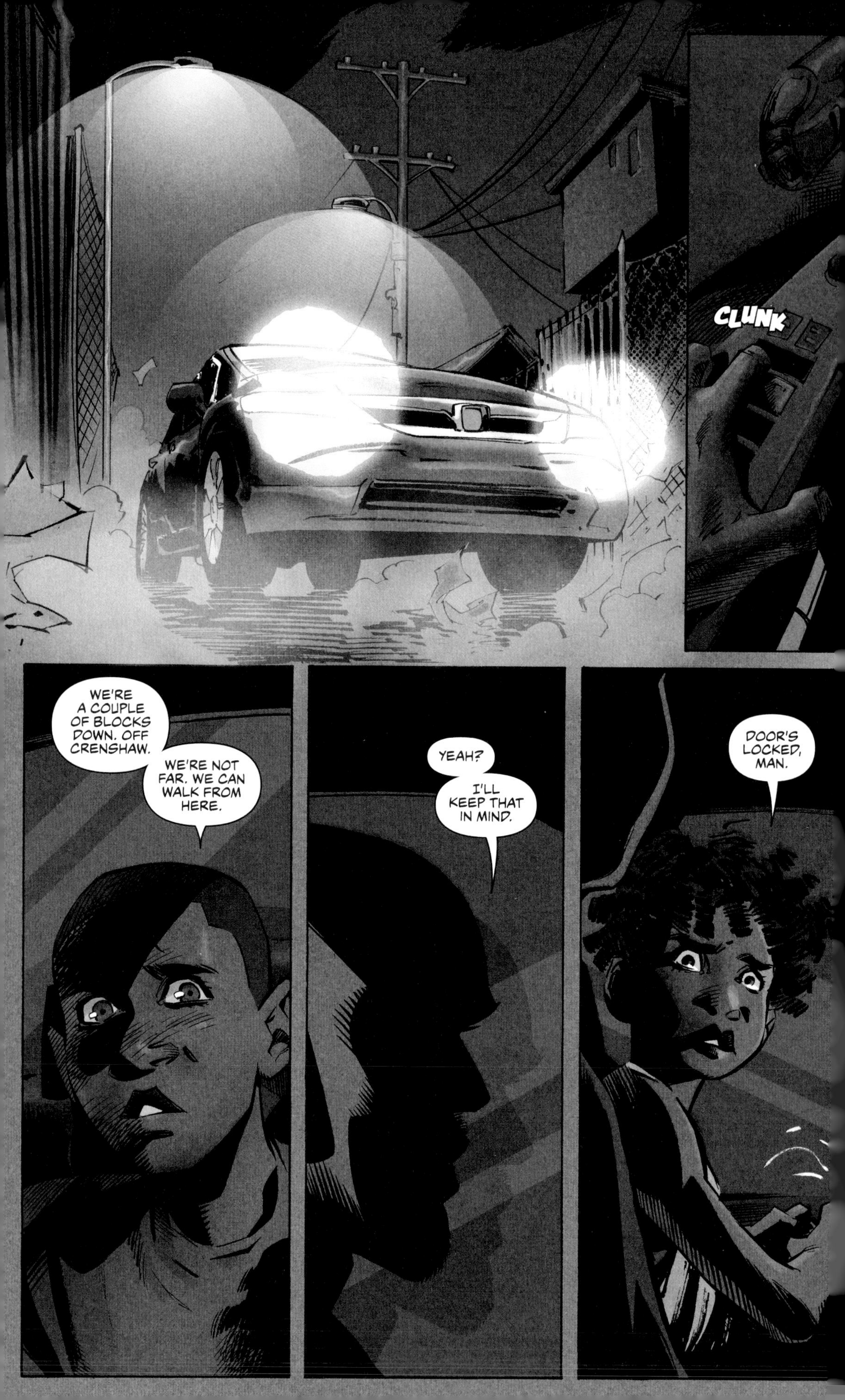
CLUNK
WE'RE A COUPLE OF BLOCKS DOWN. OFF CRENSHAW.
WE'RE NOT FAR. WE CAN WALK FROM HERE.
YEAH?
I'LL KEEP THAT IN MIND.
DOOR'S LOCKED, MAN.

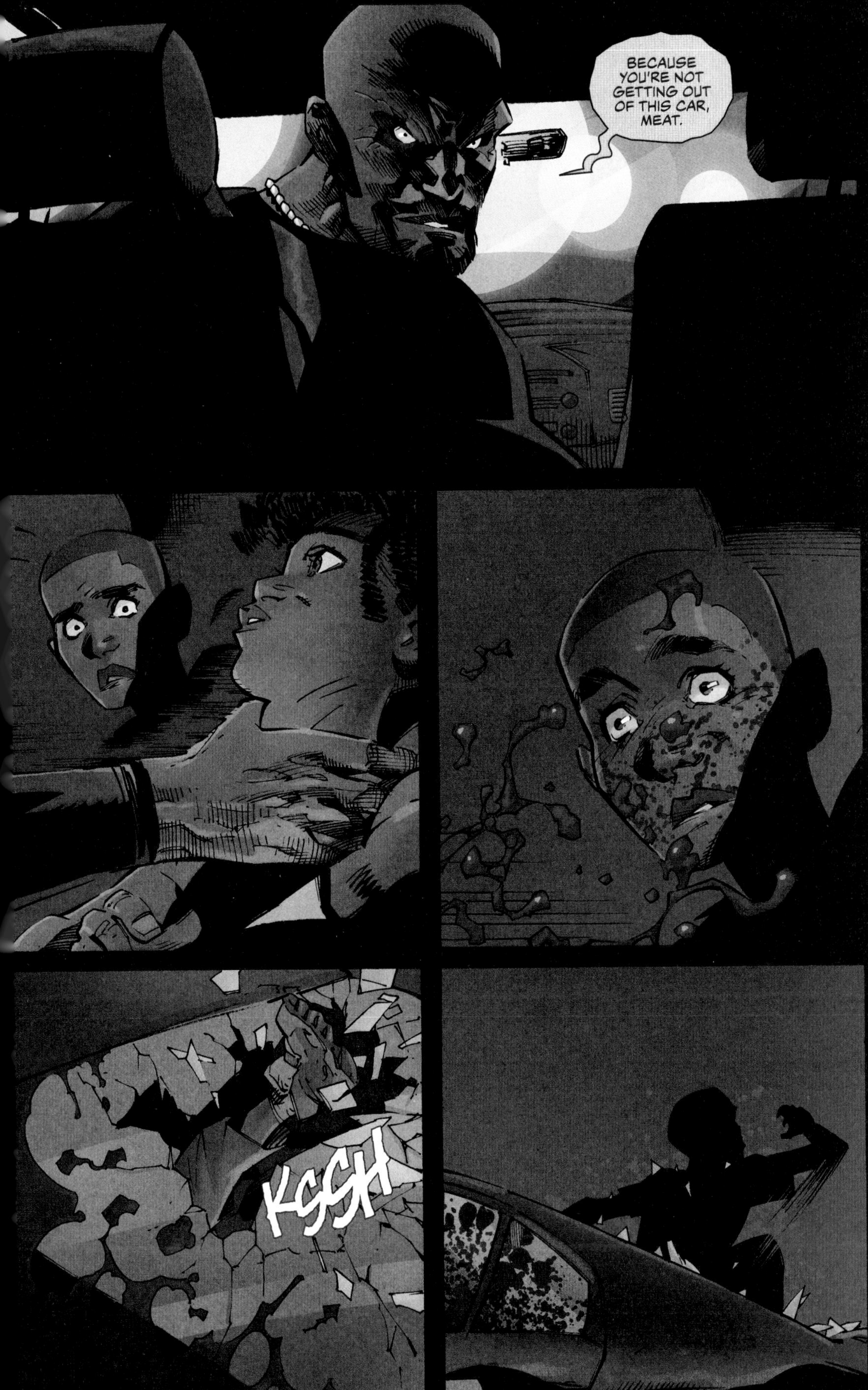
BECAUSE YOU'RE NOT GETTING OUT OF THIS CAR, MEAT.
KSSH

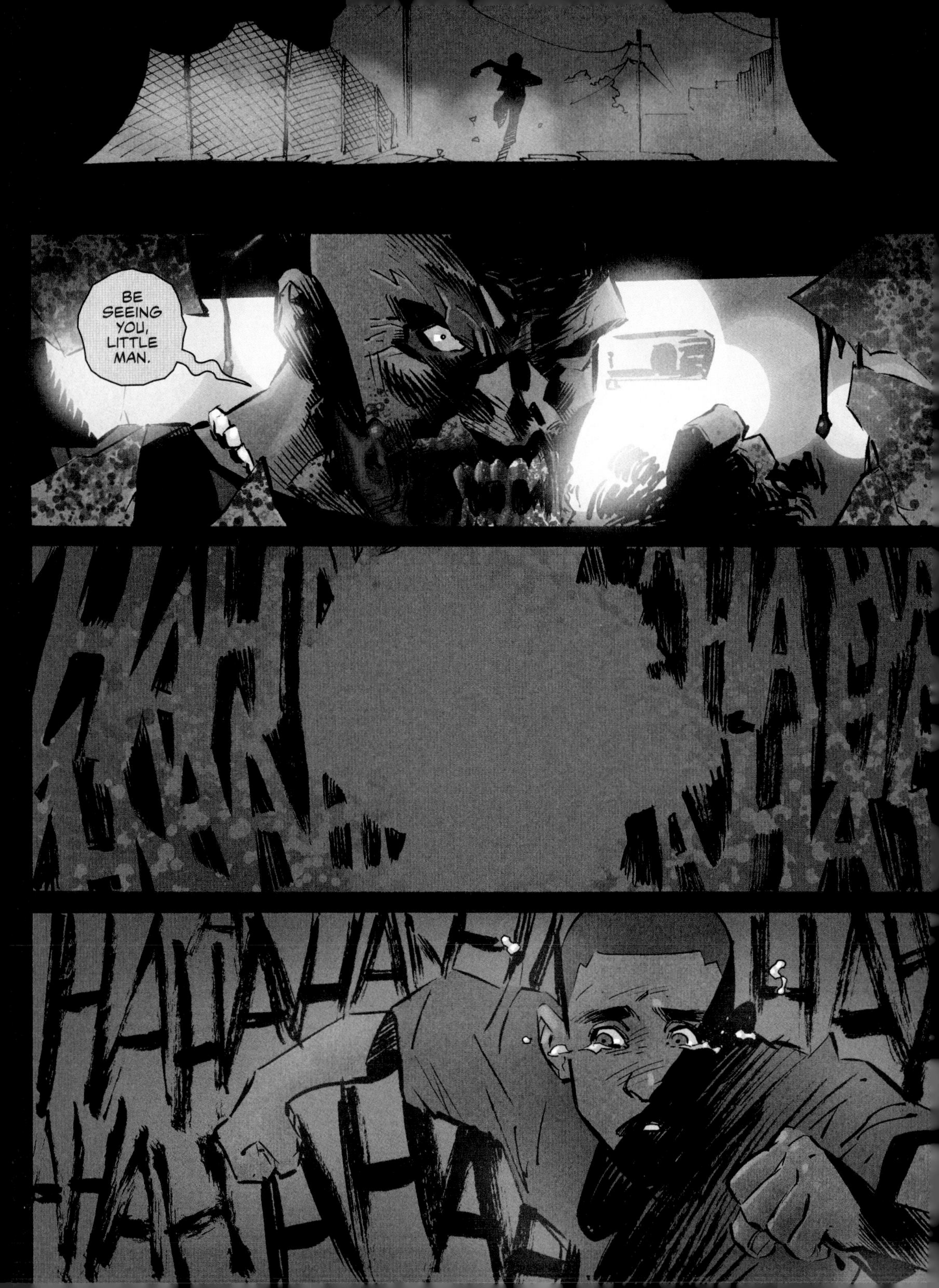
BE SEEING YOU, LITTLE MAN.

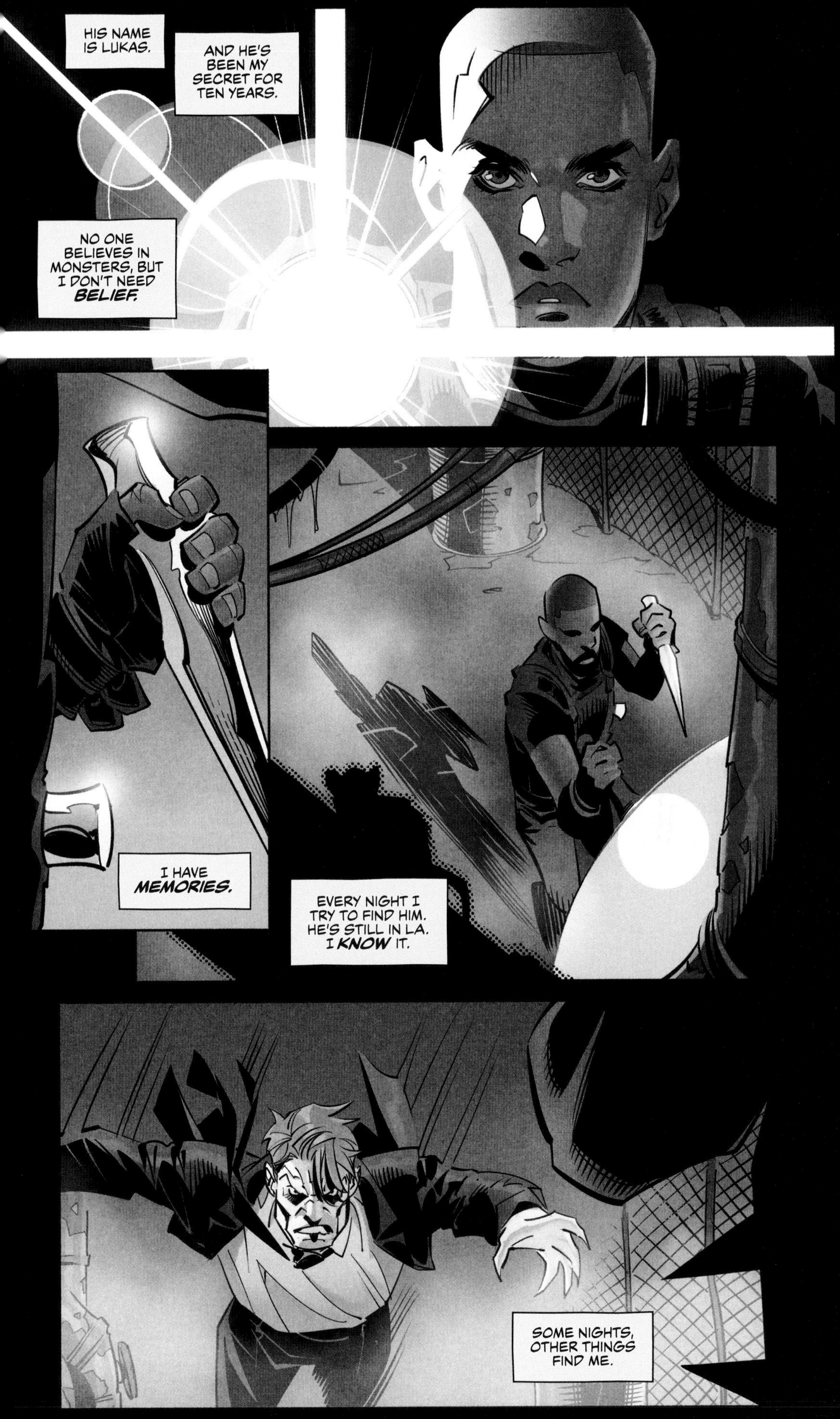

HIS NAME IS LUKAS.
AND HE'S BEEN MY SECRET FOR TEN YEARS.
NO ONE BELIEVES IN MONSTERS, BUT I DON'T NEED BELIEF.
I HAVE MEMORIES.
EVERY NIGHT I TRY TO FIND HIM. HE'S STILL IN LA. I KNOW IT.
SOME NIGHTS, OTHER THINGS FIND ME.

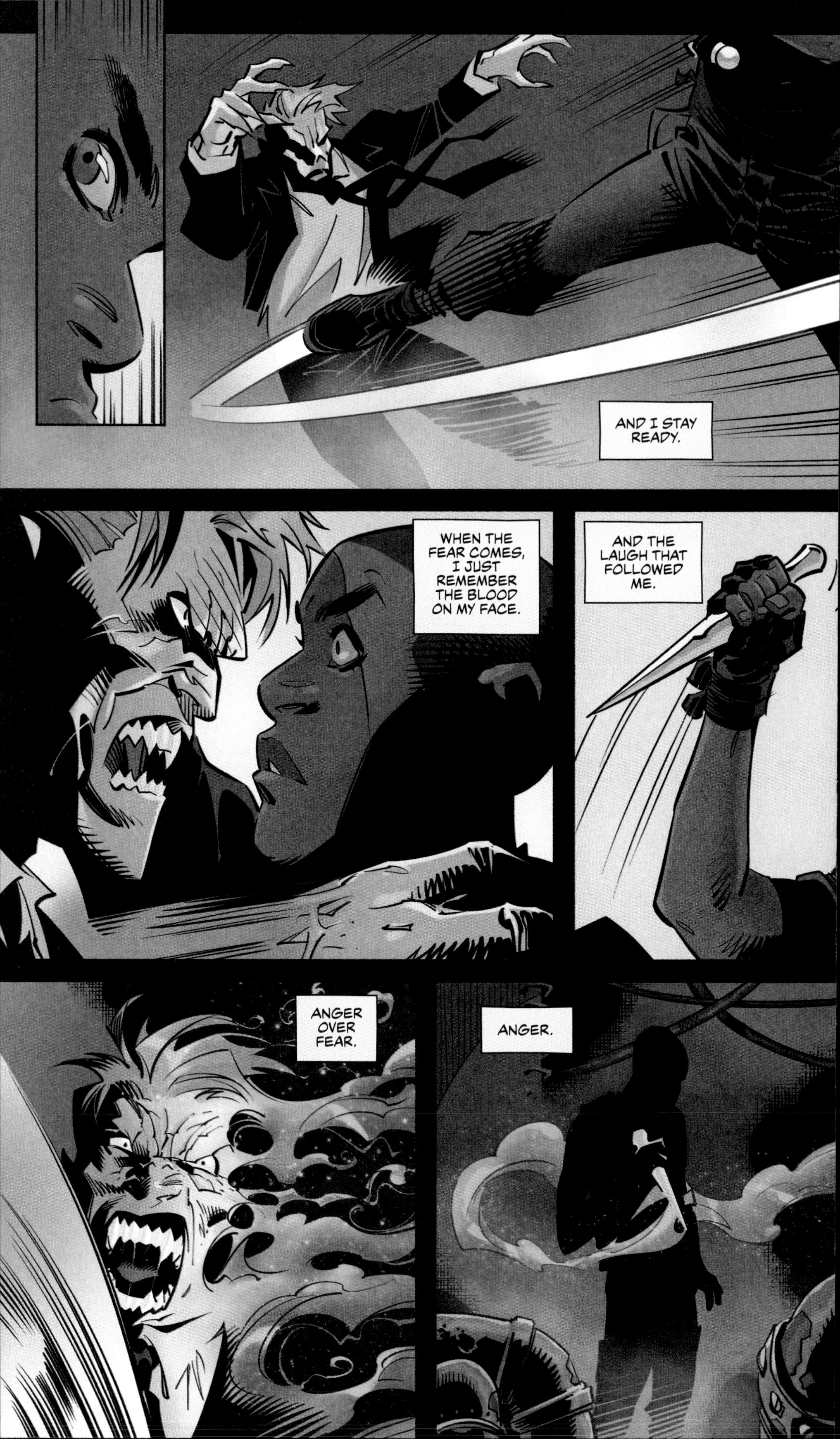
AND I STAY READY.
WHEN THE FEAR COMES, I JUST REMEMBER THE BLOOD ON MY FACE.
AND THE LAUGH THAT FOLLOWED ME.
ANGER OVER FEAR.
ANGER.

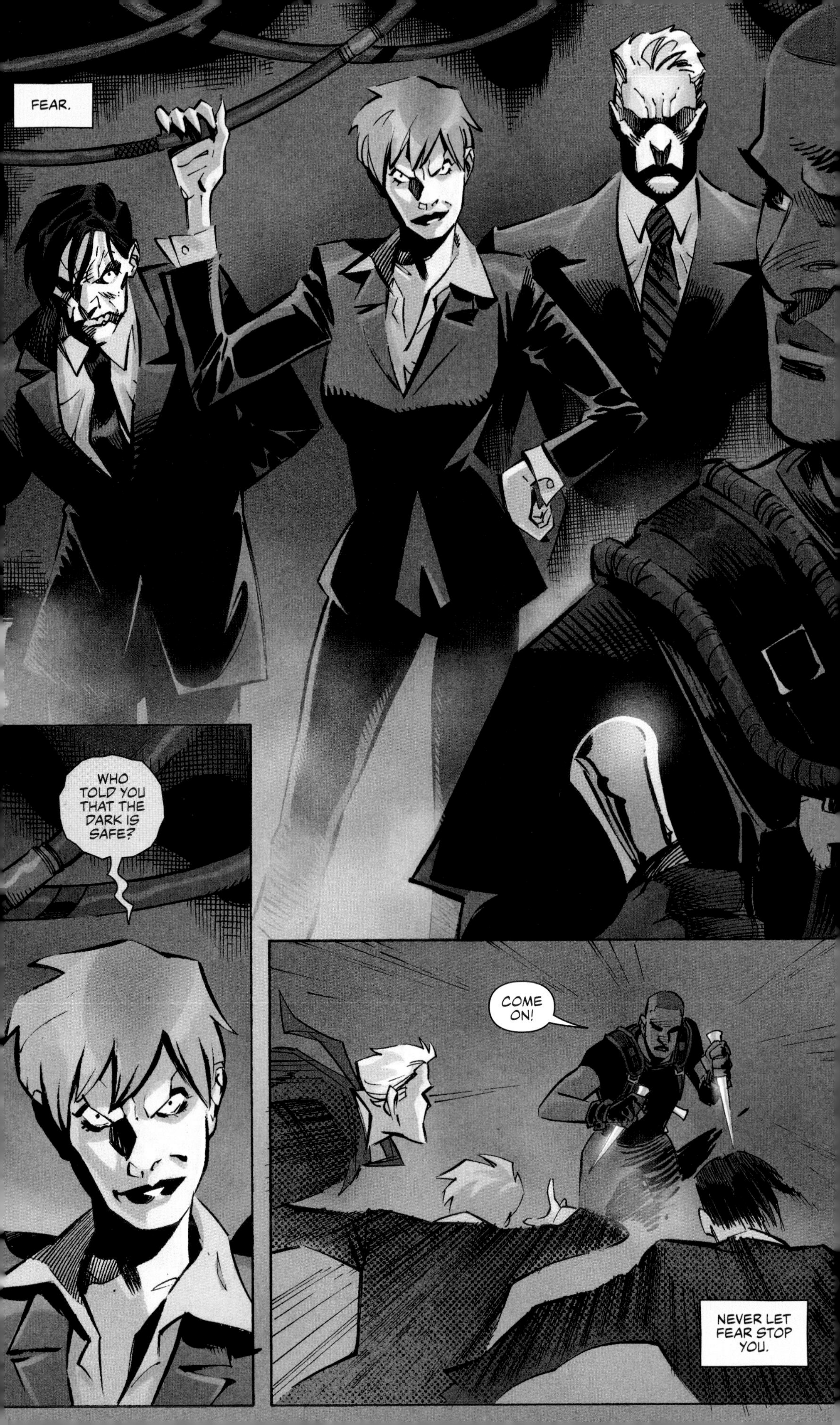
FEAR.
WHO TOLD YOU THAT THE DARK IS SAFE?
COME ON!
NEVER LET FEAR STOP YOU.

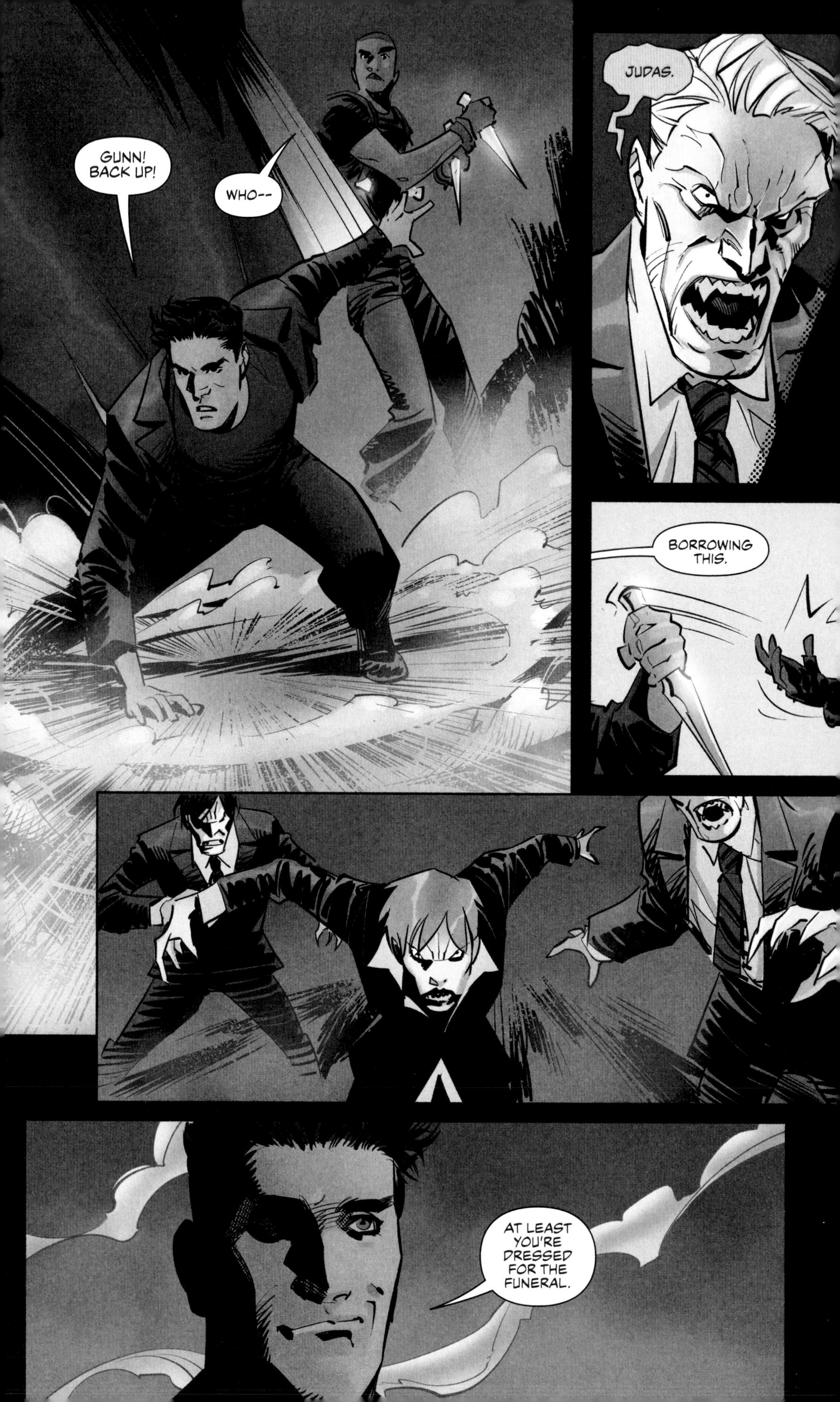
GUNN! BACK UP!
WHO--
JUDAS.
BORROWING THIS.
AT LEAST YOU'RE DRESSED FOR THE FUNERAL.

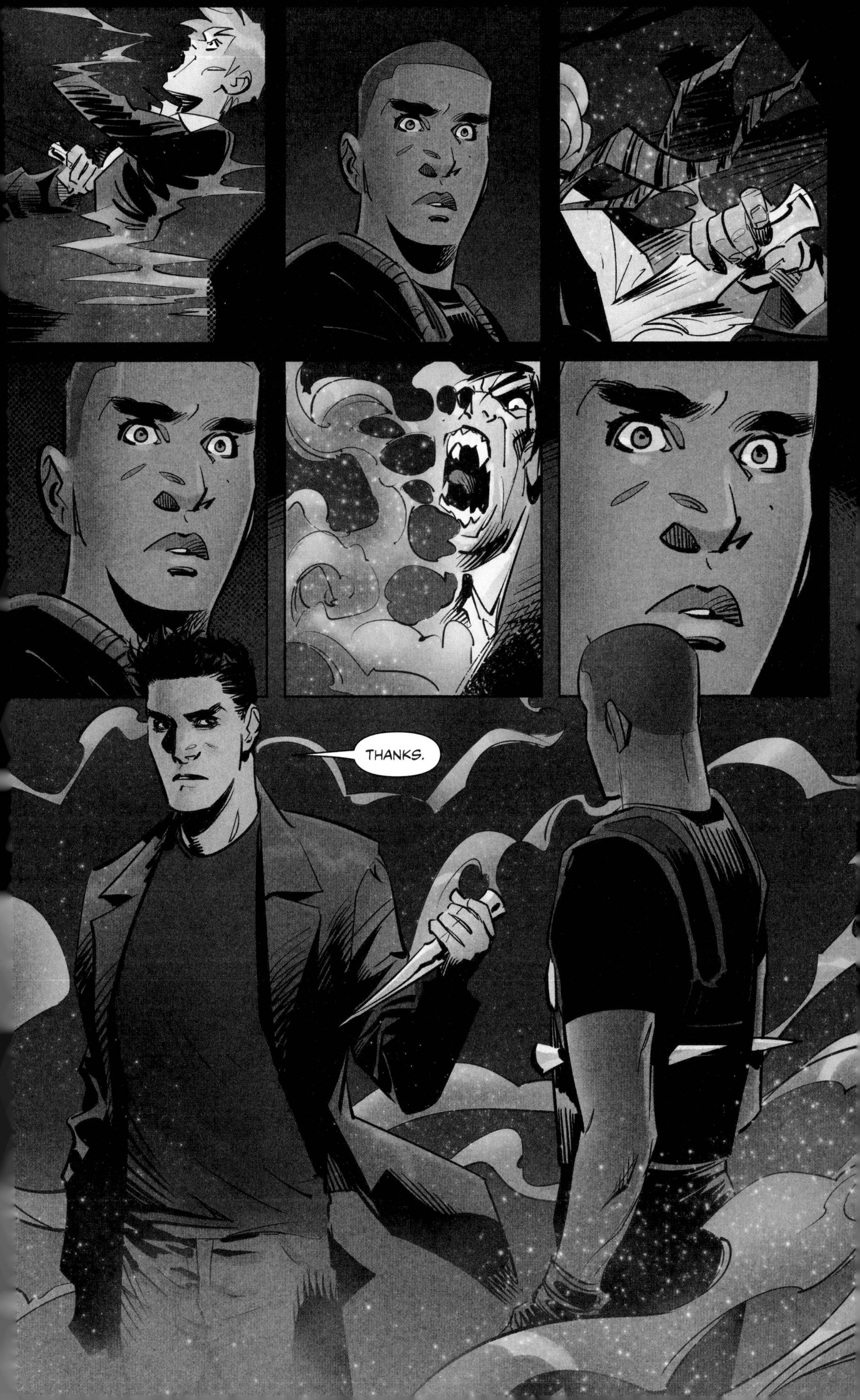
THANKS.

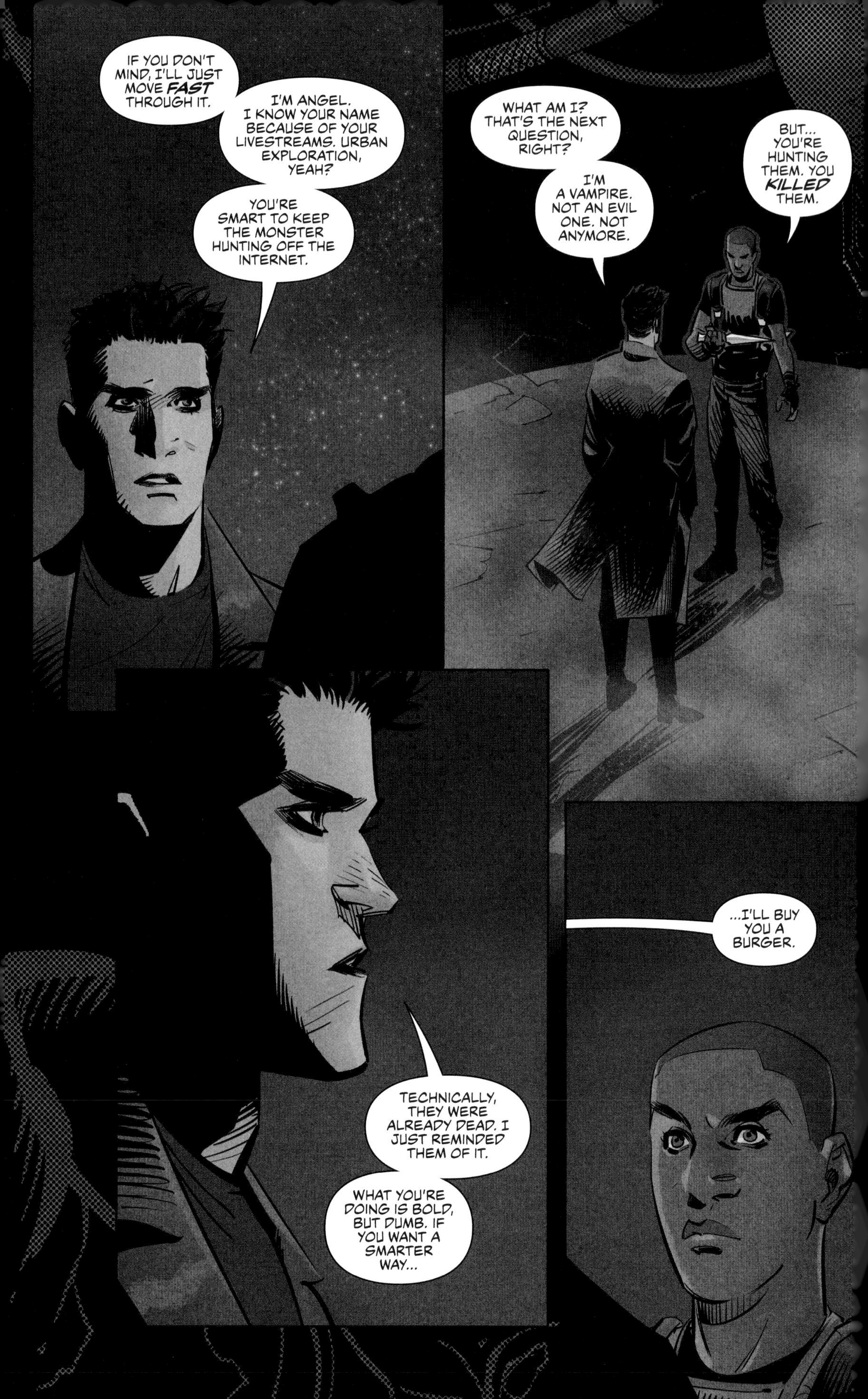
IF YOU DON'T MIND, I'LL JUST MOVE **FAST** THROUGH IT.
I'M ANGEL. I KNOW YOUR NAME BECAUSE OF YOUR LIVESTREAMS. URBAN EXPLORATION, YEAH?
YOU'RE SMART TO KEEP THE MONSTER HUNTING OFF THE INTERNET.
WHAT AM I? THAT'S THE NEXT QUESTION, RIGHT?
I'M A VAMPIRE. NOT AN EVIL ONE. NOT ANYMORE.
BUT... YOU'RE HUNTING THEM. YOU ***KILLED*** THEM.
TECHNICALLY, THEY WERE ALREADY DEAD. I JUST REMINDED THEM OF IT.
WHAT YOU'RE DOING IS BOLD, BUT DUMB. IF YOU WANT A SMARTER WAY...
...I'LL BUY YOU A BURGER.

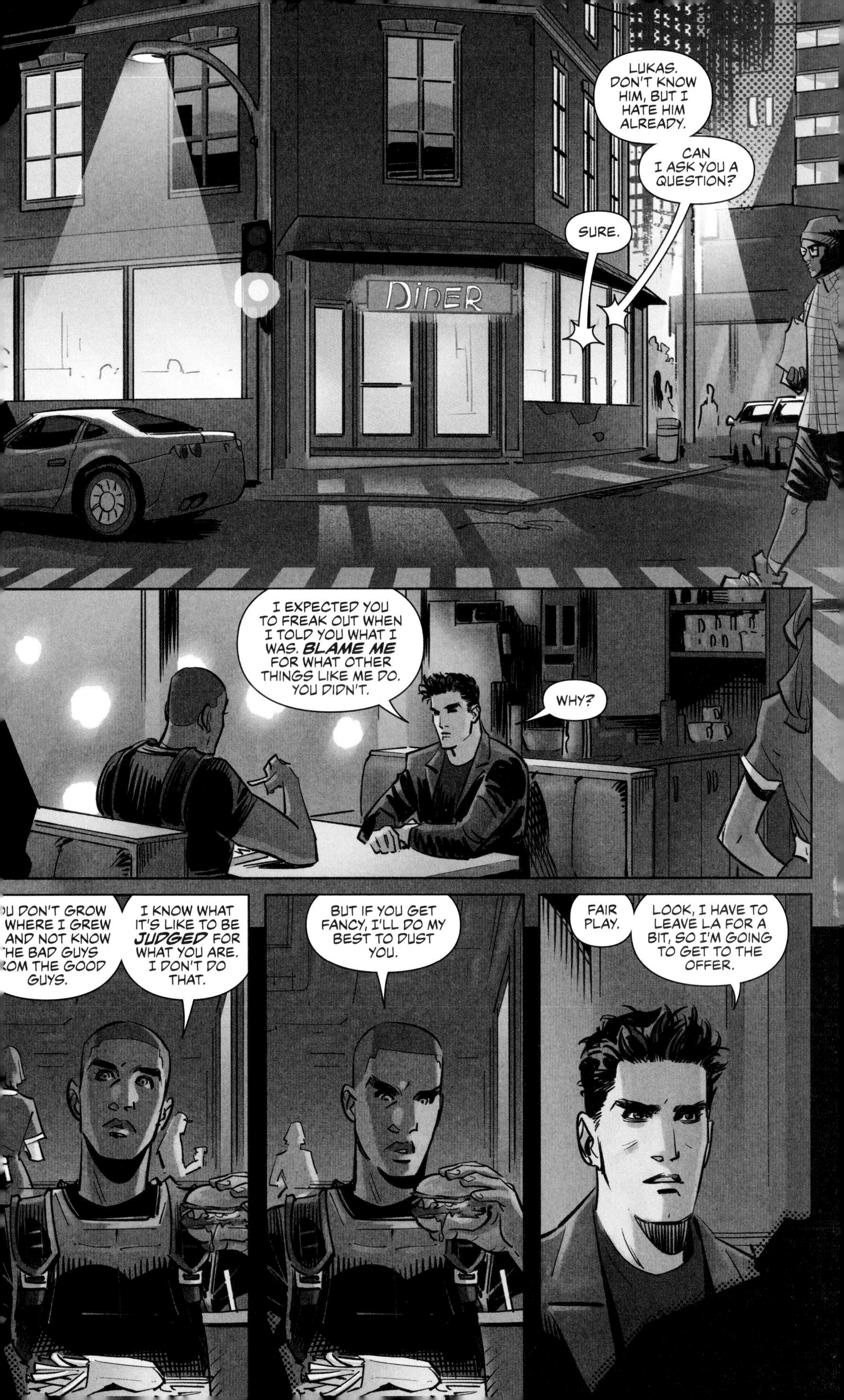
LUKAS. DON'T KNOW HIM, BUT I HATE HIM ALREADY.
CAN I ASK YOU A QUESTION?
SURE.
DINER
I EXPECTED YOU TO FREAK OUT WHEN I TOLD YOU WHAT I WAS. BLAME ME FOR WHAT OTHER THINGS LIKE ME DO. YOU DIDN'T.
WHY?
U DON'T GROW WHERE I GREW AND NOT KNOW HE BAD GUYS ROM THE GOOD GUYS.
I KNOW WHAT IT'S LIKE TO BE JUDGED FOR WHAT YOU ARE. I DON'T DO THAT.
BUT IF YOU GET FANCY, I'LL DO MY BEST TO DUST YOU.
FAIR PLAY.
LOOK, I HAVE TO LEAVE LA FOR A BIT, SO I'M GOING TO GET TO THE OFFER.

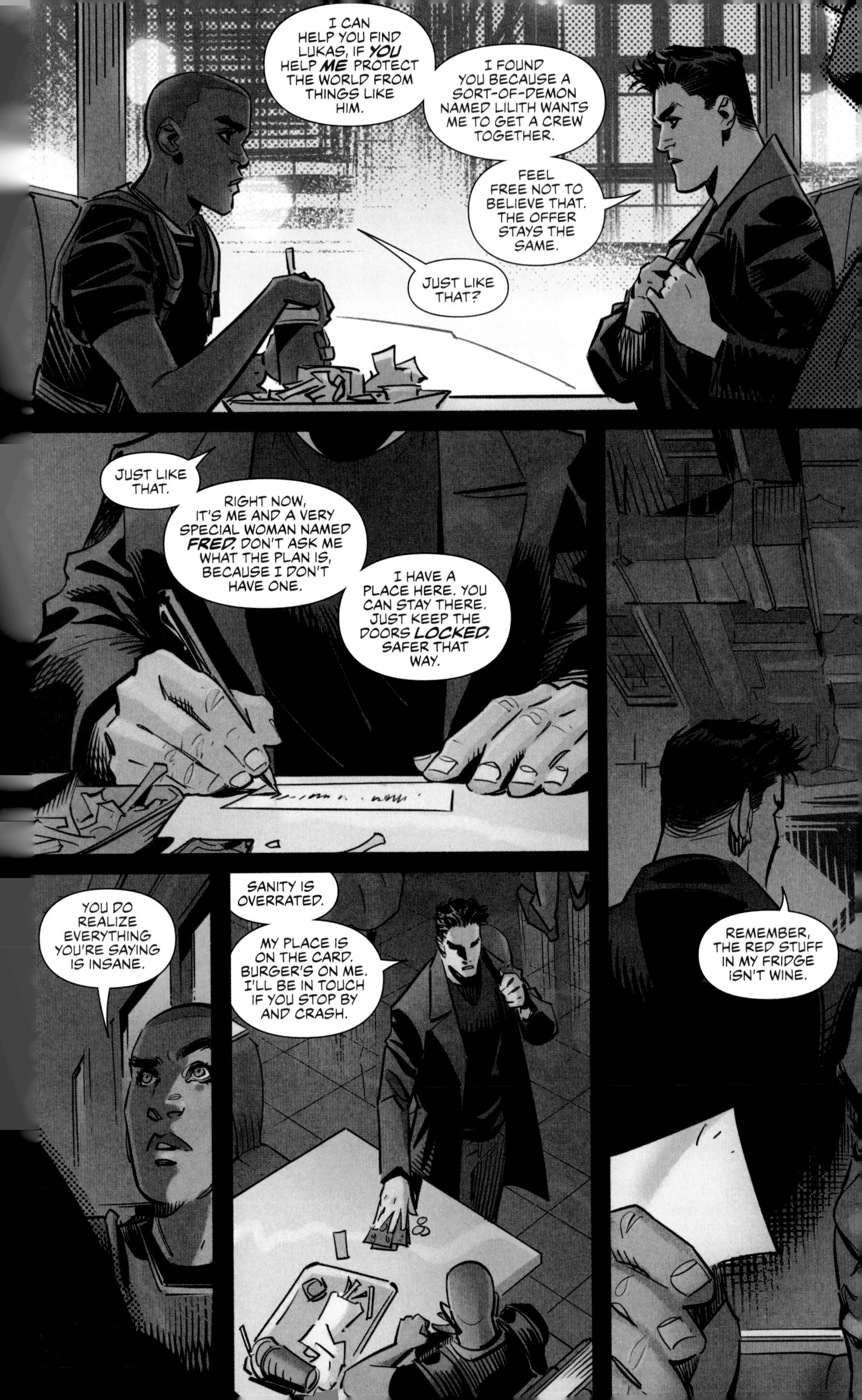
I CAN HELP YOU FIND LUKAS, IF YOU HELP ME PROTECT THE WORLD FROM THINGS LIKE HIM.
I FOUND YOU BECAUSE A SORT-OF-DEMON NAMED LILITH WANTS ME TO GET A CREW TOGETHER.
FEEL FREE NOT TO BELIEVE THAT. THE OFFER STAYS THE SAME.
JUST LIKE THAT?
JUST LIKE THAT.
RIGHT NOW, IT'S ME AND A VERY SPECIAL WOMAN NAMED FRED. DON'T ASK ME WHAT THE PLAN IS, BECAUSE I DON'T HAVE ONE.
I HAVE A PLACE HERE. YOU CAN STAY THERE. JUST KEEP THE DOORS LOCKED. SAFER THAT WAY.
YOU DO REALIZE EVERYTHING YOU'RE SAYING IS INSANE.
SANITY IS OVERRATED.
MY PLACE IS ON THE CARD. BURGER'S ON ME. I'LL BE IN TOUCH IF YOU STOP BY AND CRASH.
REMEMBER, THE RED STUFF IN MY FRIDGE ISN'T WINE.

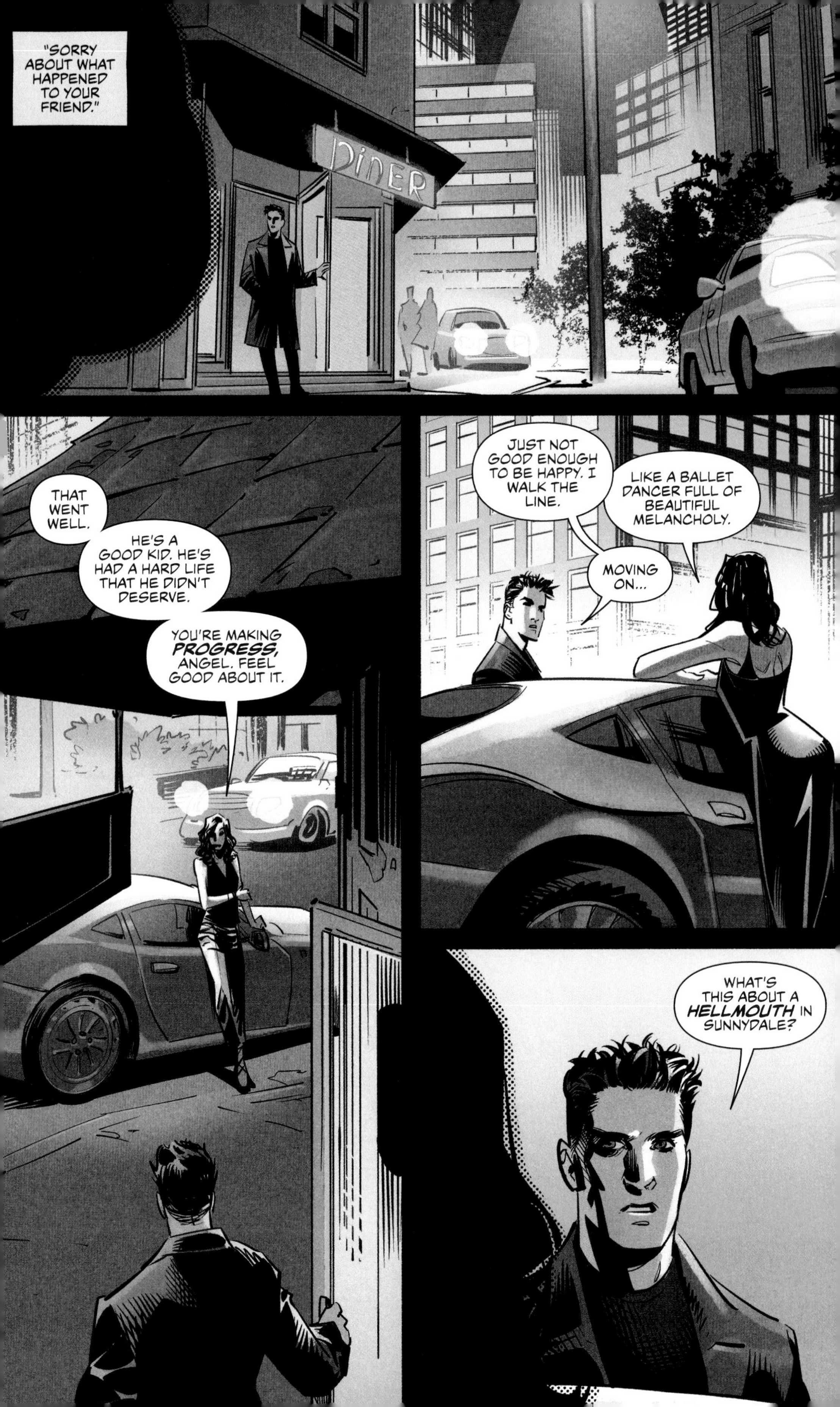
"SORRY ABOUT WHAT HAPPENED TO YOUR FRIEND."
DINER
THAT WENT WELL.
HE'S A GOOD KID. HE'S HAD A HARD LIFE THAT HE DIDN'T DESERVE.
YOU'RE MAKING **PROGRESS,** ANGEL. FEEL GOOD ABOUT IT.
JUST NOT GOOD ENOUGH TO BE HAPPY. I WALK THE LINE.
LIKE A BALLET DANCER FULL OF BEAUTIFUL MELANCHOLY.
MOVING ON...
WHAT'S THIS ABOUT A **HELLMOUTH** IN SUNNYDALE?

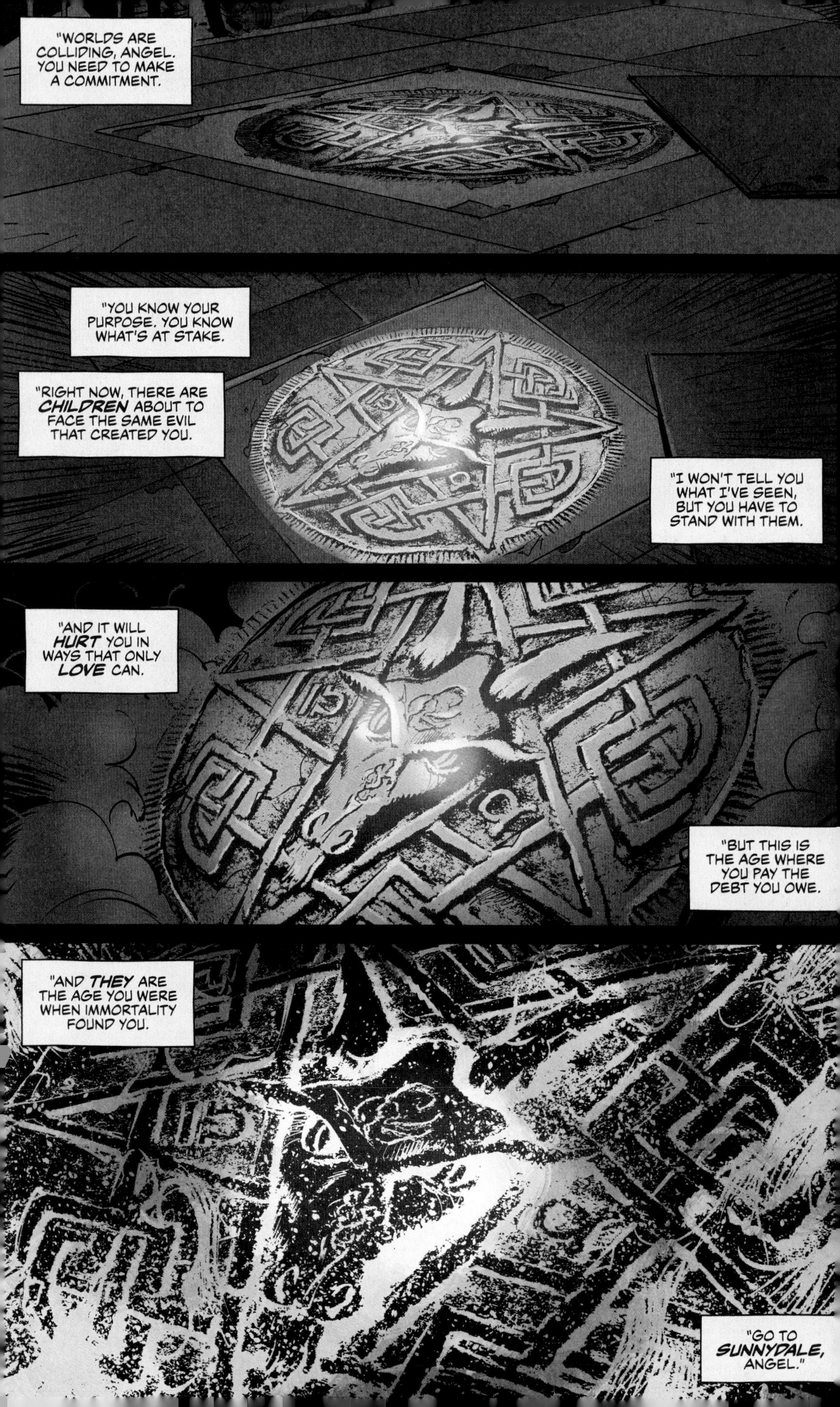
"WORLDS ARE COLLIDING, ANGEL. YOU NEED TO MAKE A COMMITMENT.
"YOU KNOW YOUR PURPOSE. YOU KNOW WHAT'S AT STAKE.
"RIGHT NOW, THERE ARE CHILDREN ABOUT TO FACE THE SAME EVIL THAT CREATED YOU.
"I WON'T TELL YOU WHAT I'VE SEEN, BUT YOU HAVE TO STAND WITH THEM.
"AND IT WILL HURT YOU IN WAYS THAT ONLY LOVE CAN.
"BUT THIS IS THE AGE WHERE YOU PAY THE DEBT YOU OWE.
"AND THEY ARE THE AGE YOU WERE WHEN IMMORTALITY FOUND YOU.
"GO TO SUNNYDALE, ANGEL."

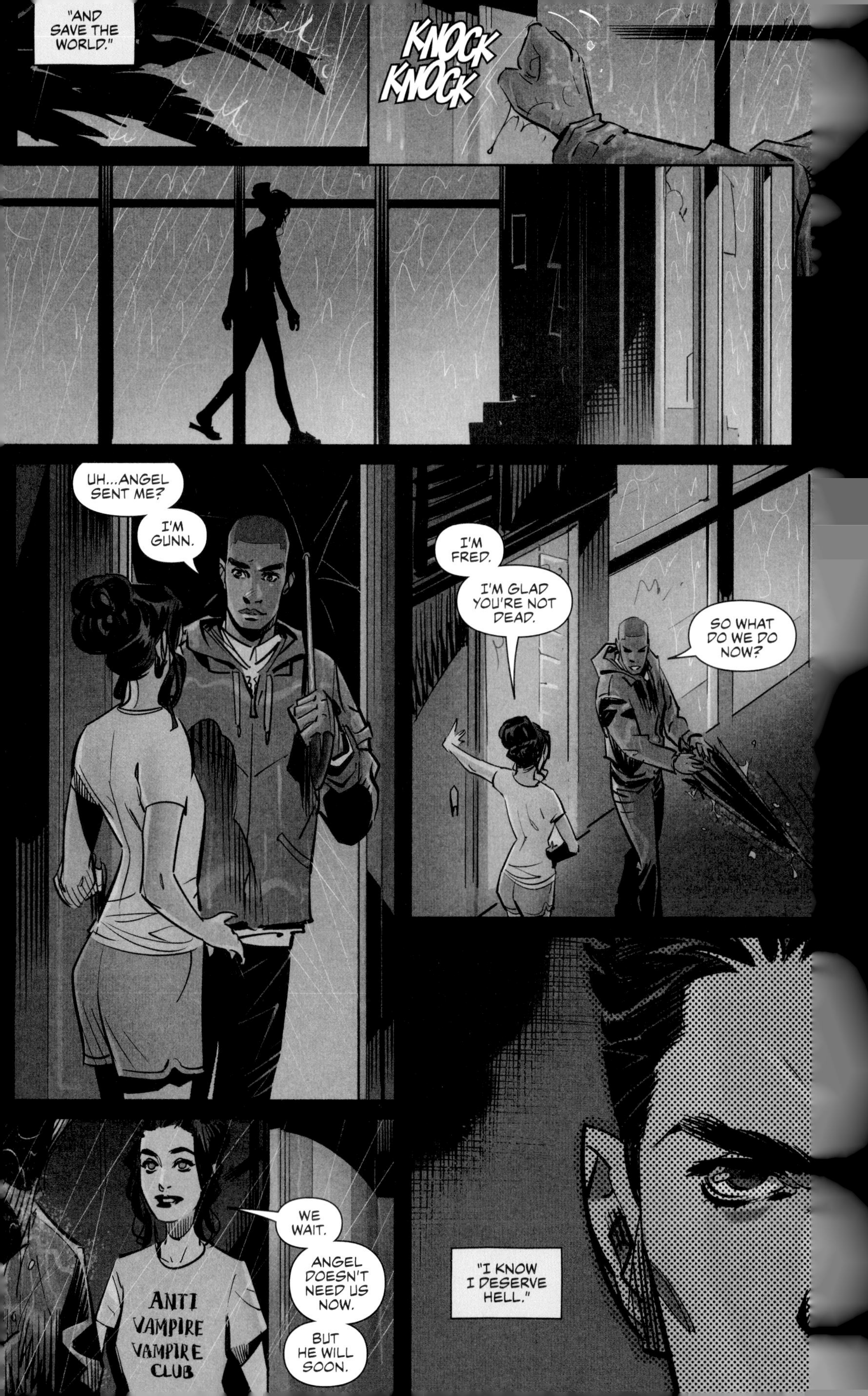
"AND SAVE THE WORLD."
KNOCK KNOCK
UH...ANGEL SENT ME?
I'M GUNN.
I'M FRED.
I'M GLAD YOU'RE NOT DEAD.
SO WHAT DO WE DO NOW?
WE WAIT.
ANGEL DOESN'T NEED US NOW.
BUT HE WILL SOON.
ANTI VAMPIRE VAMPIRE CLUB
"I KNOW I DESERVE HELL."

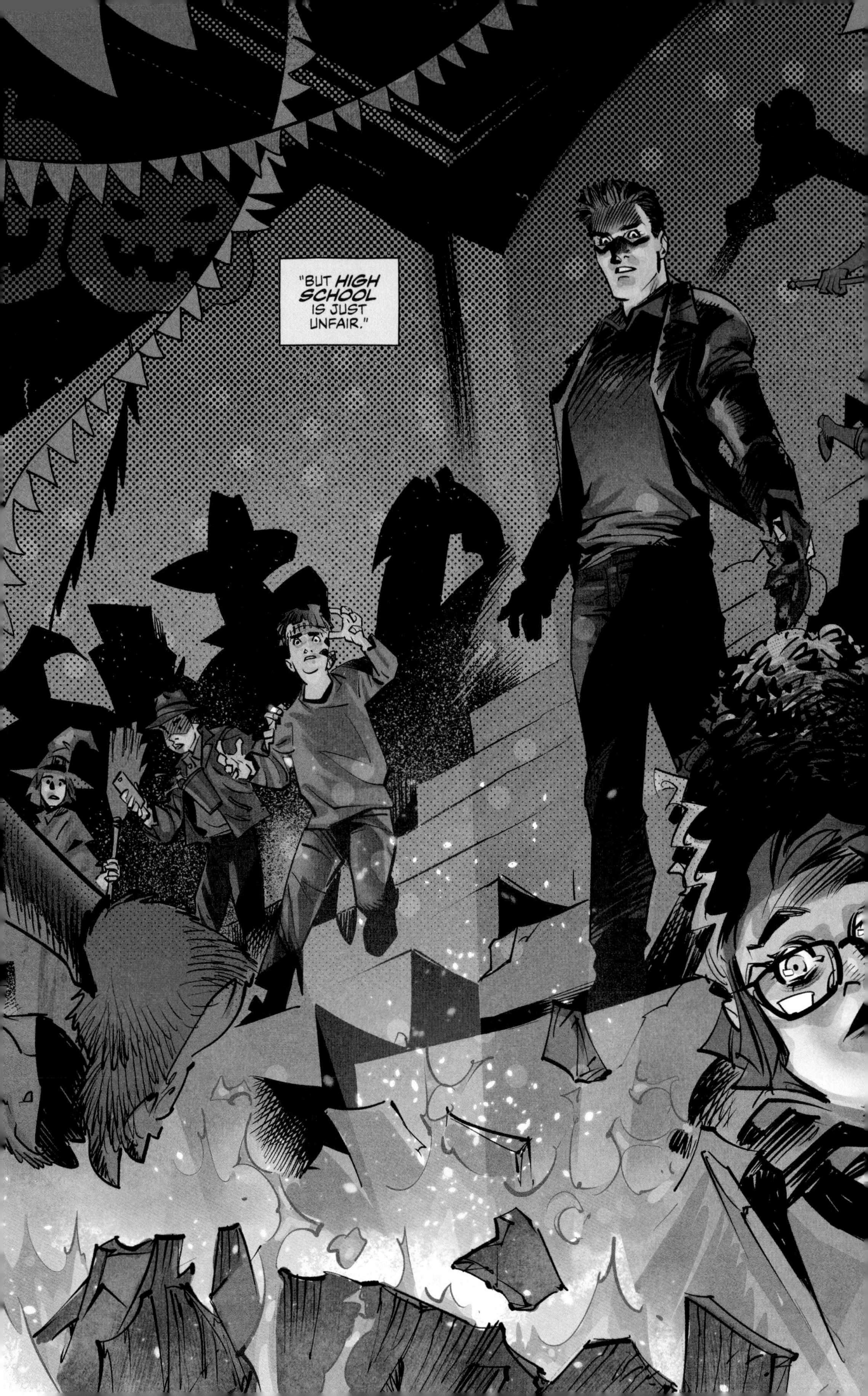
"BUT HIGH SCHOOL IS JUST UNFAIR."

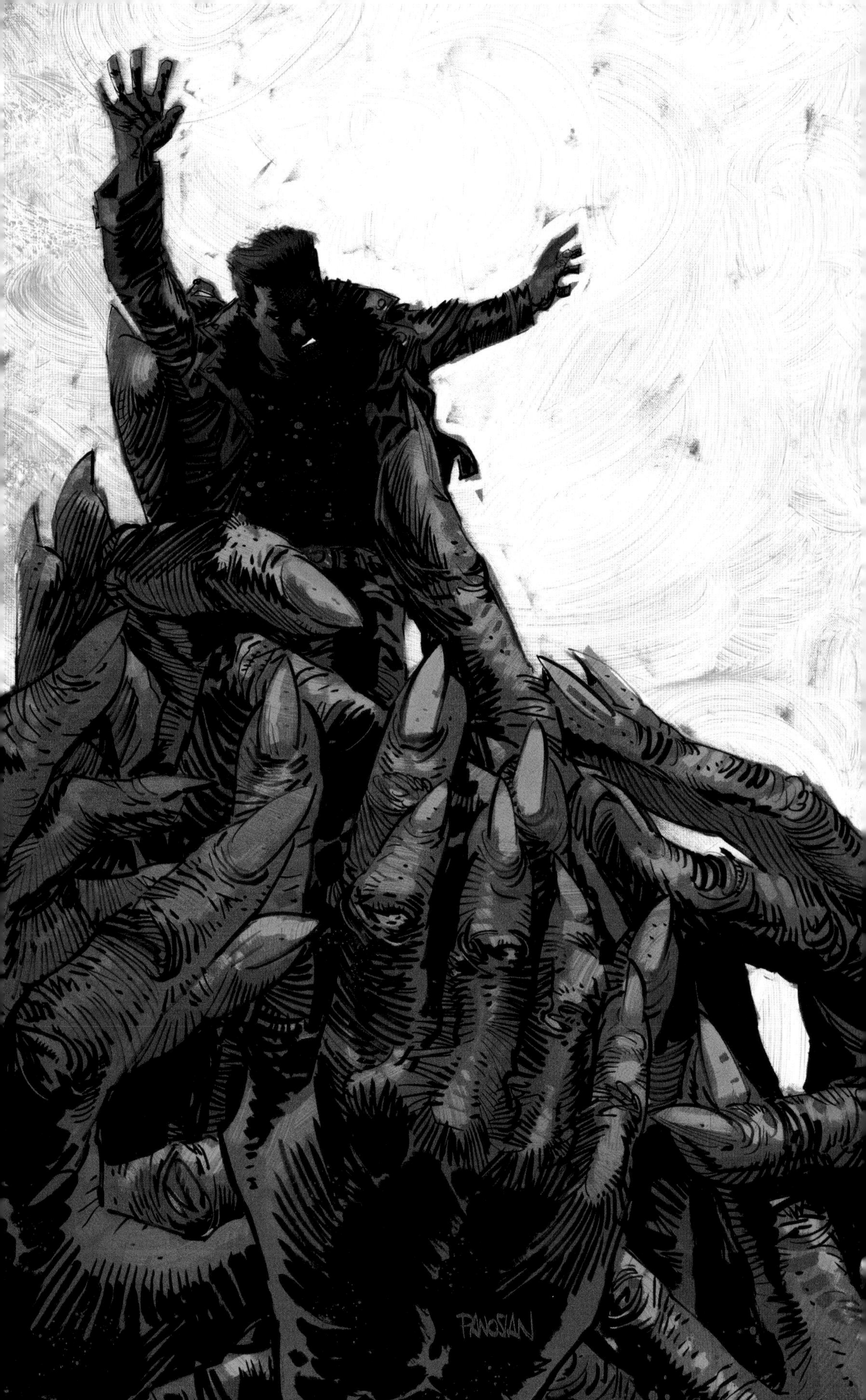
PANOSIAN

Angel #5 Main Cover by **Dan Panosian**

CHAPTER SIX

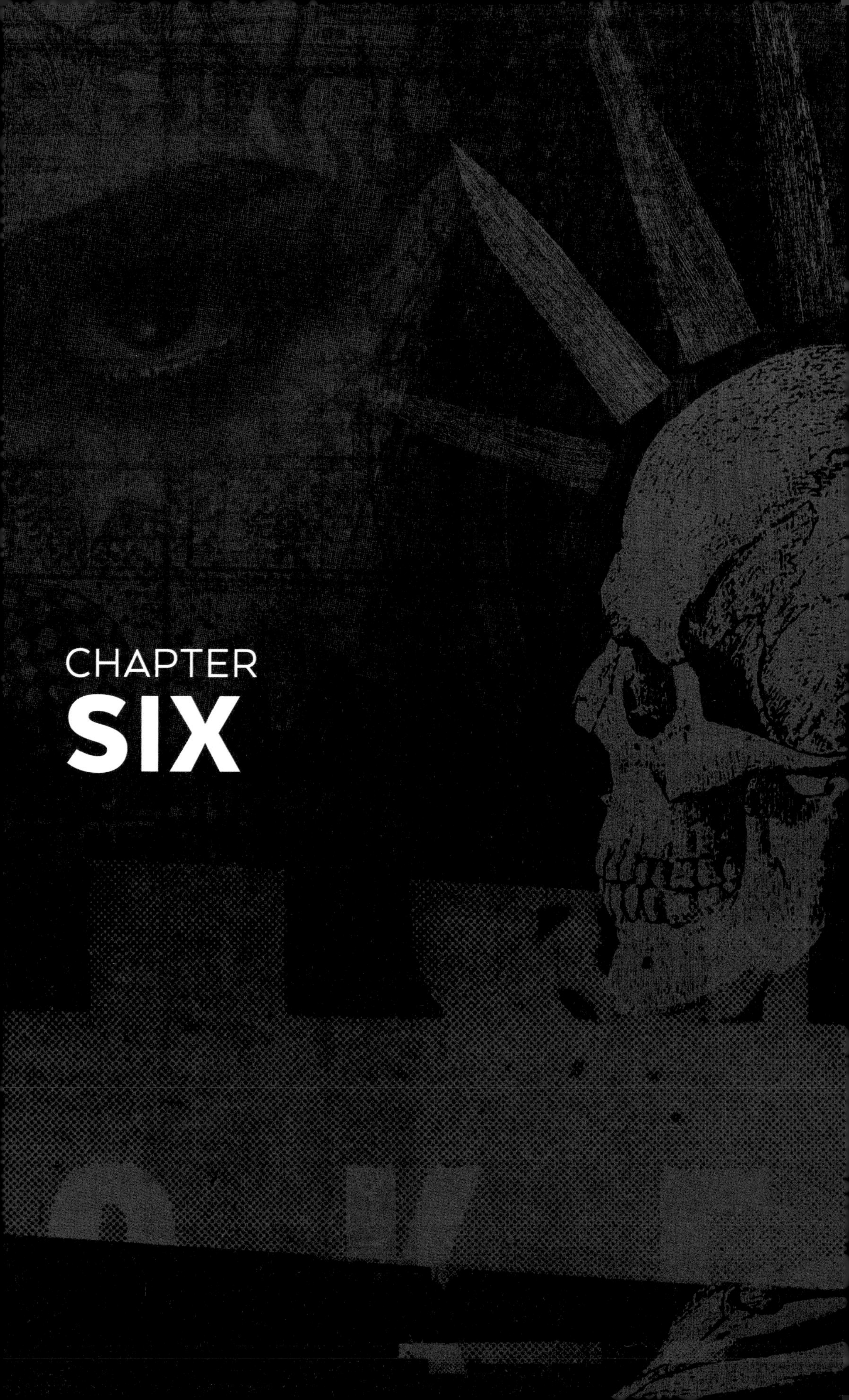

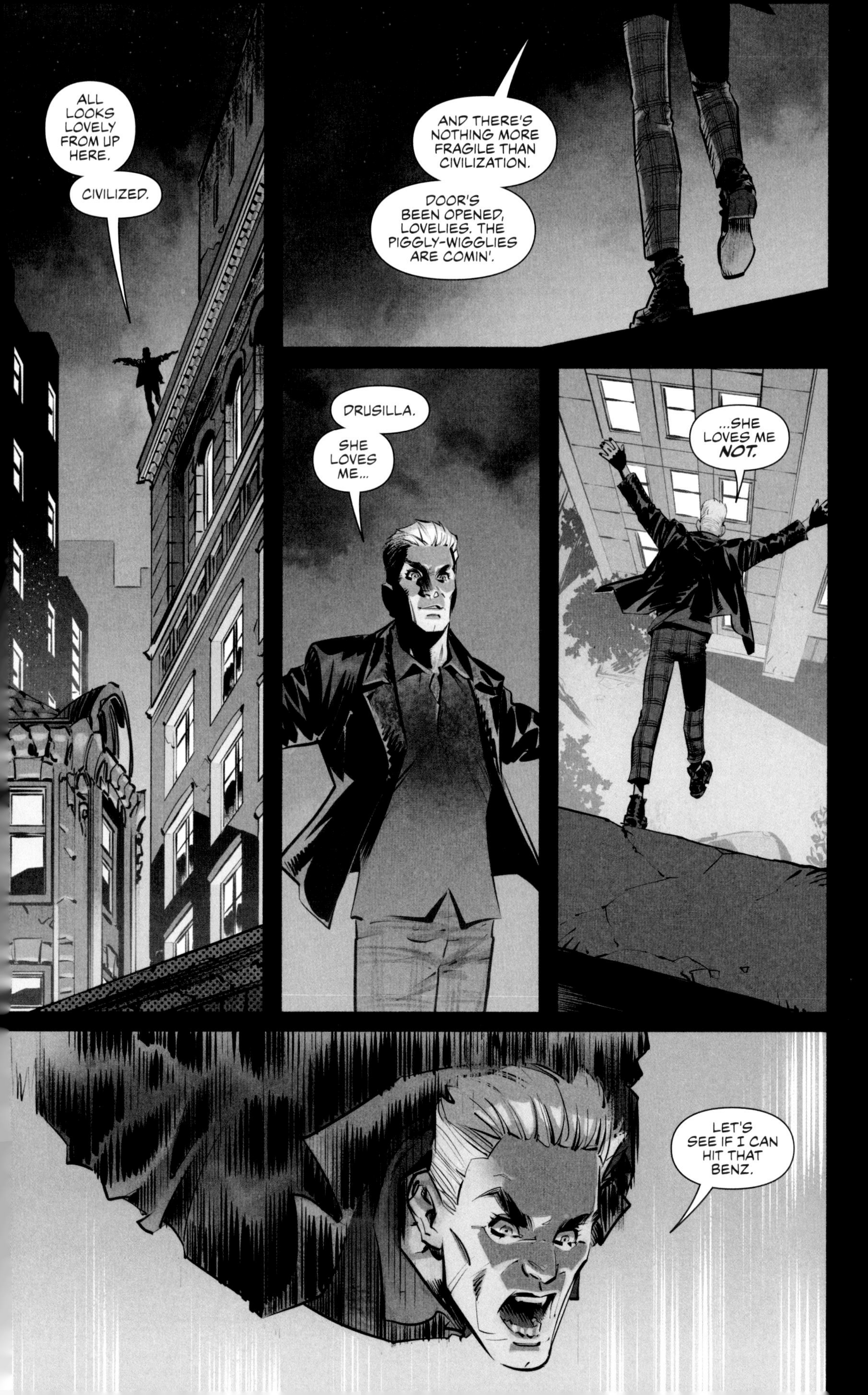

ALL LOOKS LOVELY FROM UP HERE.
CIVILIZED.
AND THERE'S NOTHING MORE FRAGILE THAN CIVILIZATION.
DOOR'S BEEN OPENED, LOVELIES. THE PIGGLY-WIGGLIES ARE COMIN'.
DRUSILLA.
SHE LOVES ME...
...SHE LOVES ME *NOT.*
LET'S SEE IF I CAN HIT THAT BENZ.

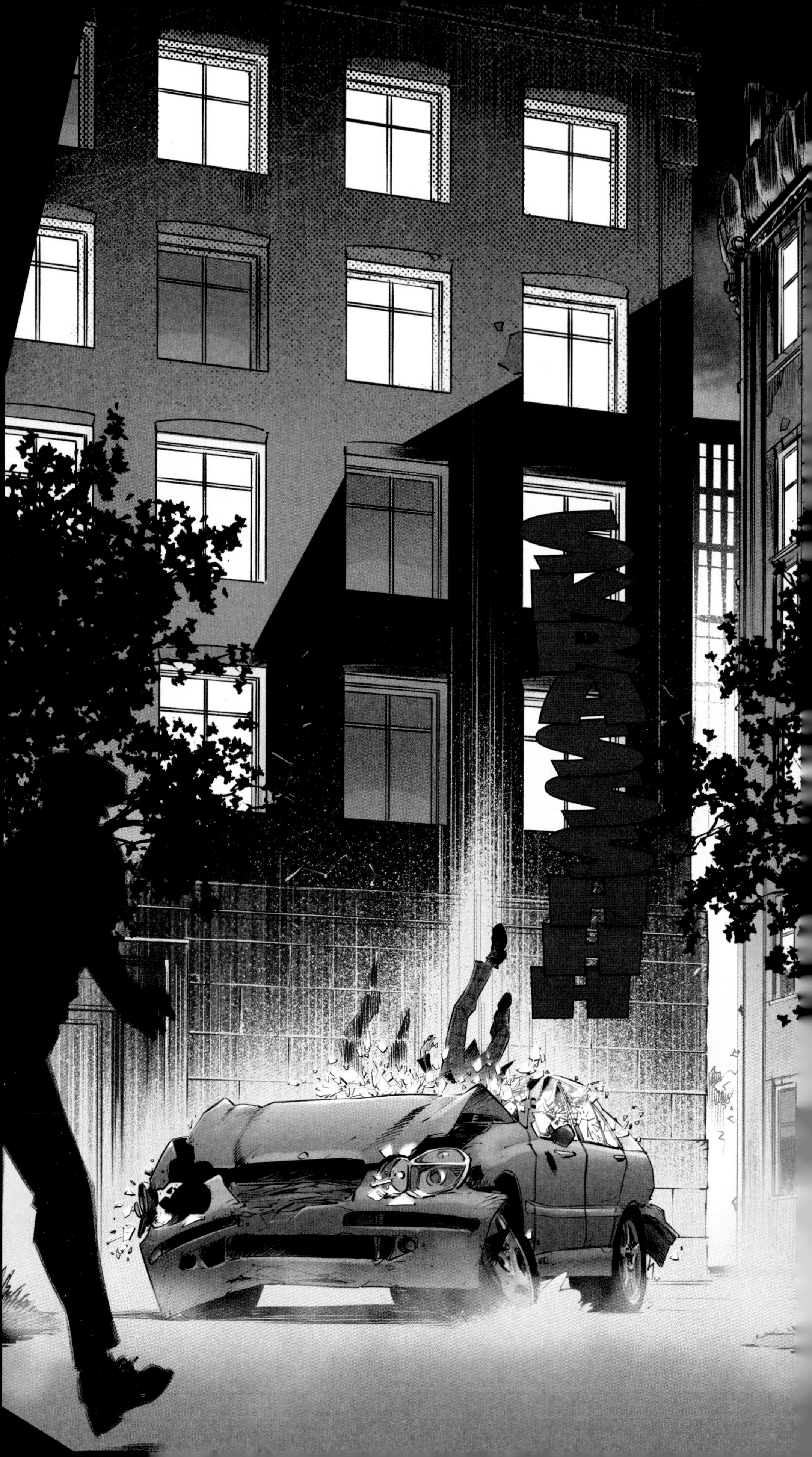
SKRASSSHHH

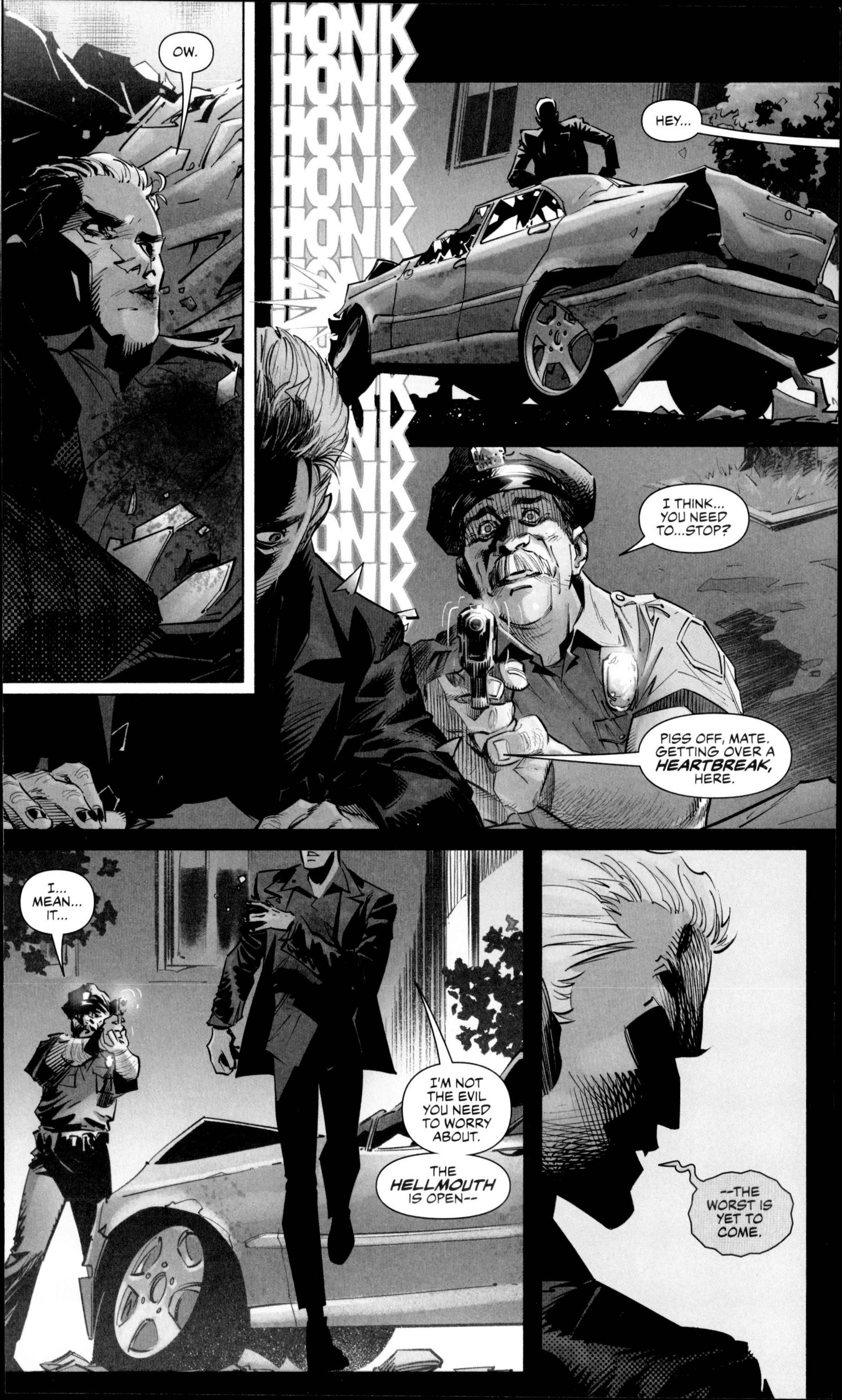
OW.
HONK HONK HONK HONK HONK
HEY...
I THINK... YOU NEED TO...STOP?
PISS OFF, MATE. GETTING OVER A HEARTBREAK, HERE.
I... MEAN... IT...
I'M NOT THE EVIL YOU NEED TO WORRY ABOUT.
THE HELLMOUTH IS OPEN--
--THE WORST IS YET TO COME.

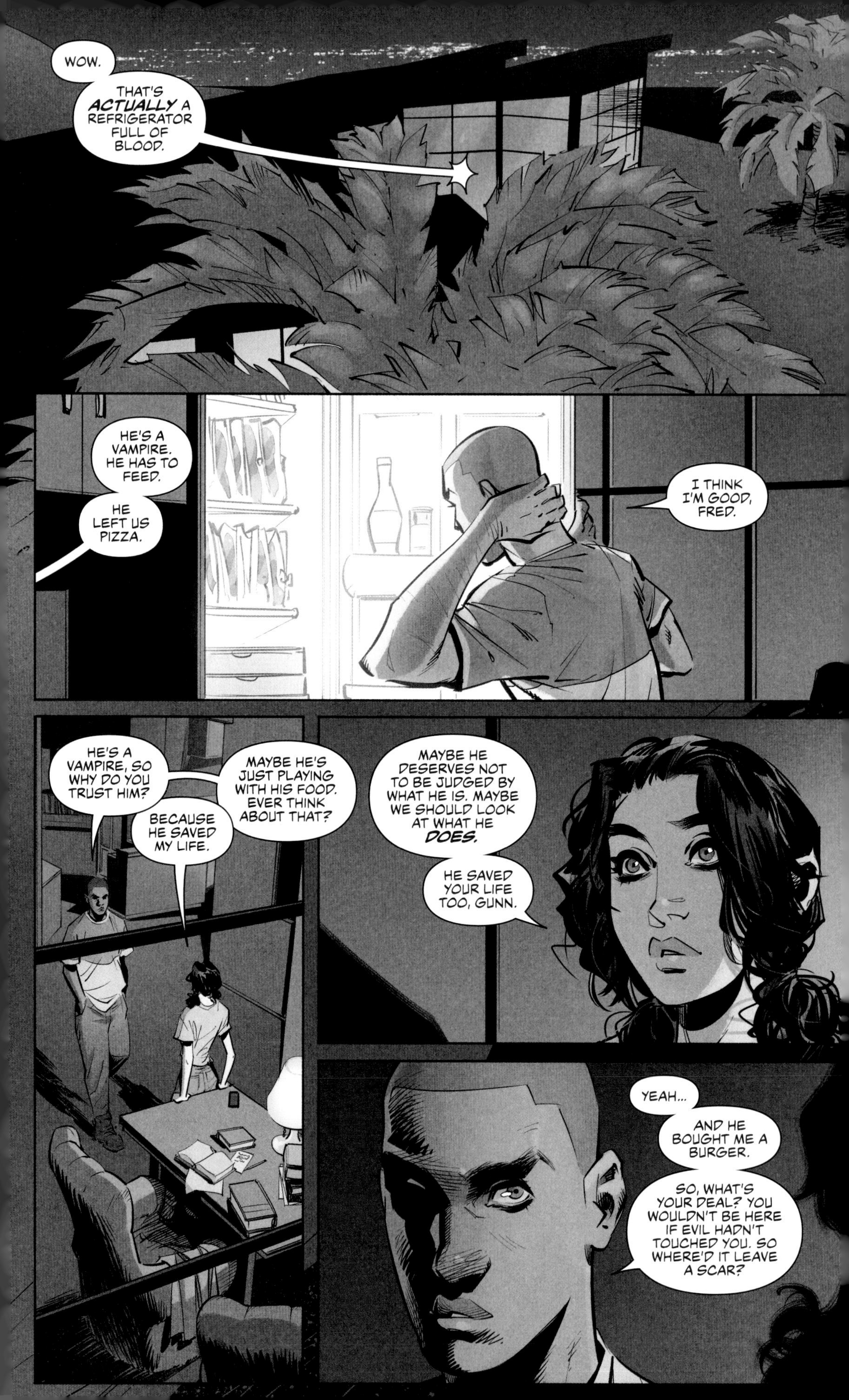
WOW.
THAT'S ACTUALLY A REFRIGERATOR FULL OF BLOOD.
HE'S A VAMPIRE. HE HAS TO FEED.
HE LEFT US PIZZA.
I THINK I'M GOOD, FRED.
HE'S A VAMPIRE, SO WHY DO YOU TRUST HIM?
BECAUSE HE SAVED MY LIFE.
MAYBE HE'S JUST PLAYING WITH HIS FOOD. EVER THINK ABOUT THAT?
MAYBE HE DESERVES NOT TO BE JUDGED BY WHAT HE IS. MAYBE WE SHOULD LOOK AT WHAT HE DOES.
HE SAVED YOUR LIFE TOO, GUNN.
YEAH...
AND HE BOUGHT ME A BURGER.
SO, WHAT'S YOUR DEAL? YOU WOULDN'T BE HERE IF EVIL HADN'T TOUCHED YOU. SO WHERE'D IT LEAVE A SCAR?

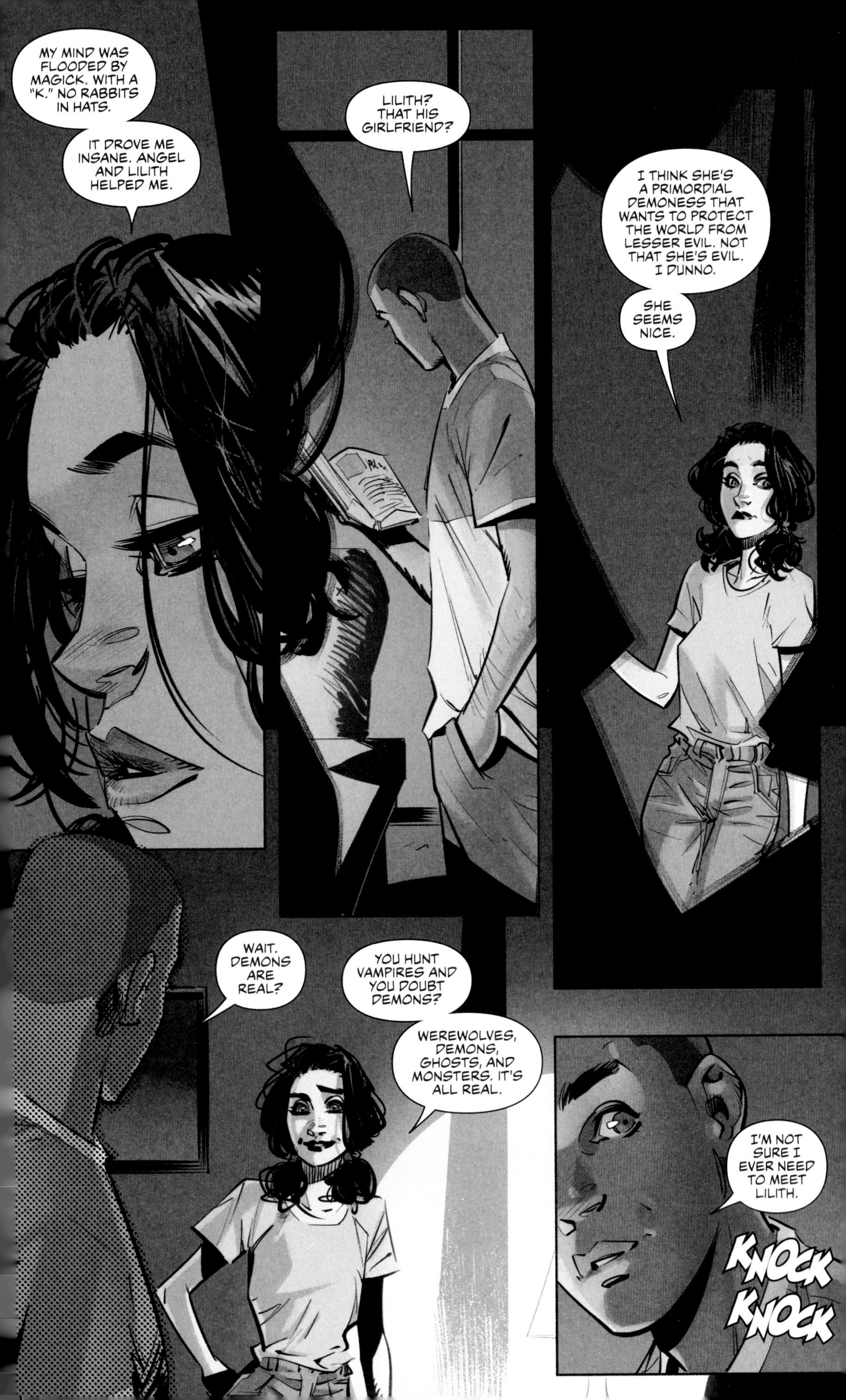
MY MIND WAS FLOODED BY MAGICK. WITH A "K." NO RABBITS IN HATS.
IT DROVE ME INSANE. ANGEL AND LILITH HELPED ME.
LILITH? THAT HIS GIRLFRIEND?
I THINK SHE'S A PRIMORDIAL DEMONESS THAT WANTS TO PROTECT THE WORLD FROM LESSER EVIL. NOT THAT SHE'S EVIL. I DUNNO.
SHE SEEMS NICE.
WAIT. DEMONS ARE REAL?
YOU HUNT VAMPIRES AND YOU DOUBT DEMONS?
WEREWOLVES, DEMONS, GHOSTS, AND MONSTERS. IT'S ALL REAL.
I'M NOT SURE I EVER NEED TO MEET LILITH.
KNOCK
KNOCK

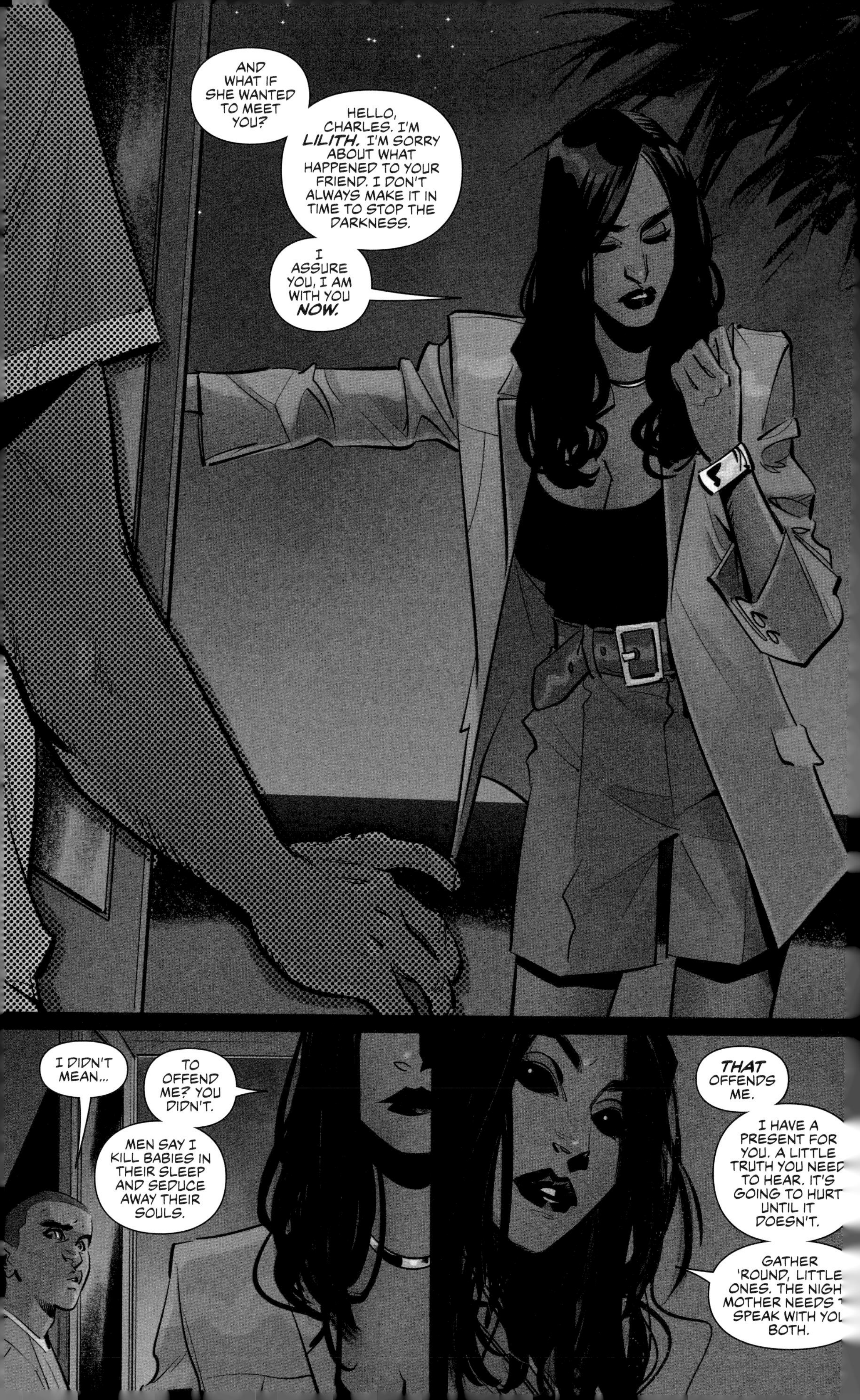
AND WHAT IF SHE WANTED TO MEET YOU?
HELLO, CHARLES. I'M LILITH. I'M SORRY ABOUT WHAT HAPPENED TO YOUR FRIEND. I DON'T ALWAYS MAKE IT IN TIME TO STOP THE DARKNESS.
I ASSURE YOU, I AM WITH YOU NOW.
I DIDN'T MEAN...
TO OFFEND ME? YOU DIDN'T.
MEN SAY I KILL BABIES IN THEIR SLEEP AND SEDUCE AWAY THEIR SOULS.
THAT OFFENDS ME.
I HAVE A PRESENT FOR YOU. A LITTLE TRUTH YOU NEED TO HEAR. IT'S GOING TO HURT UNTIL IT DOESN'T.

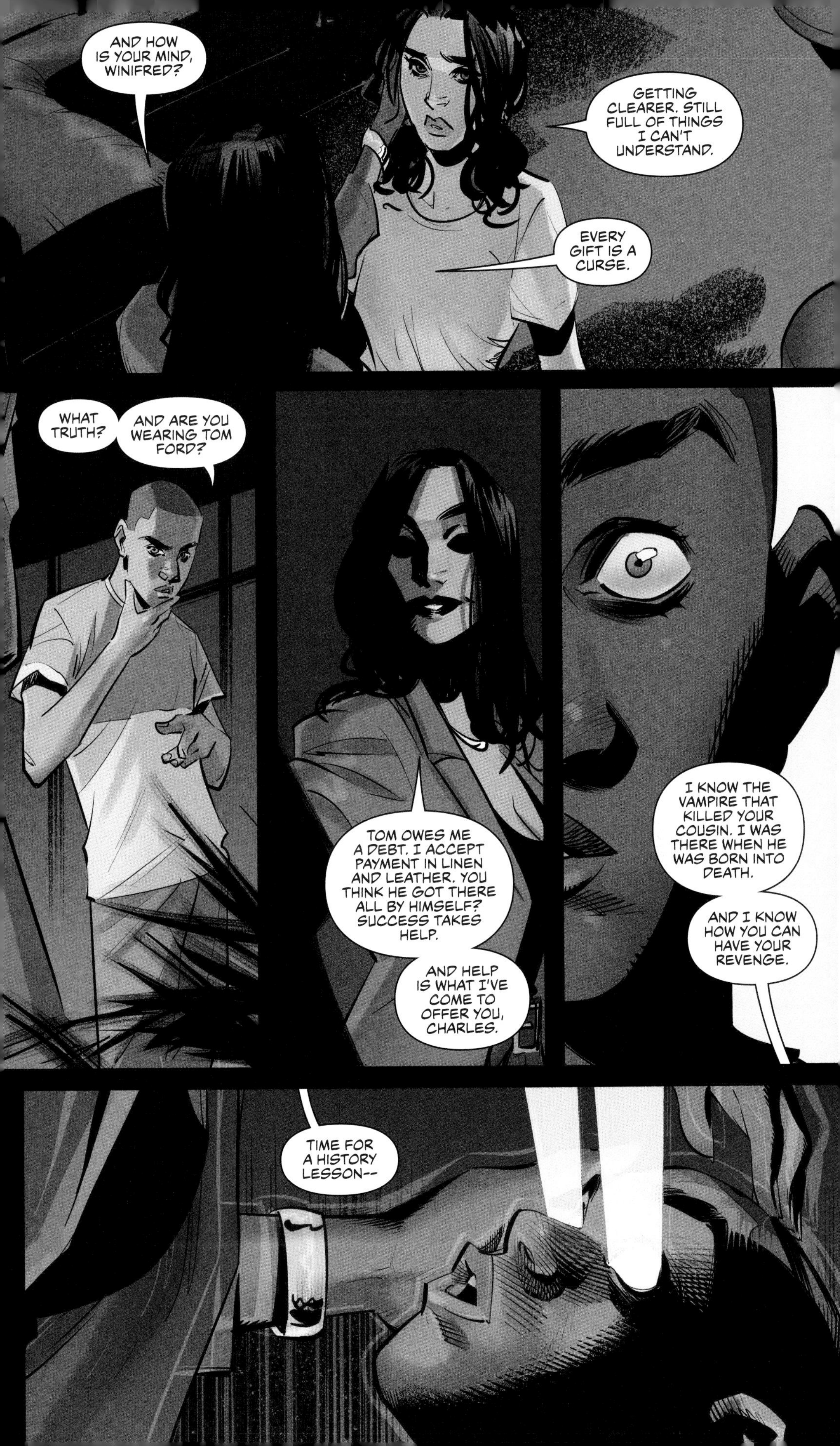
AND HOW IS YOUR MIND, WINIFRED?
GETTING CLEARER. STILL FULL OF THINGS I CAN'T UNDERSTAND.
EVERY GIFT IS A CURSE.
WHAT TRUTH?
AND ARE YOU WEARING TOM FORD?
TOM OWES ME A DEBT. I ACCEPT PAYMENT IN LINEN AND LEATHER. YOU THINK HE GOT THERE ALL BY HIMSELF? SUCCESS TAKES HELP.
AND HELP IS WHAT I'VE COME TO OFFER YOU, CHARLES.
I KNOW THE VAMPIRE THAT KILLED YOUR COUSIN. I WAS THERE WHEN HE WAS BORN INTO DEATH.
AND I KNOW HOW YOU CAN HAVE YOUR REVENGE.
TIME FOR A HISTORY LESSON--

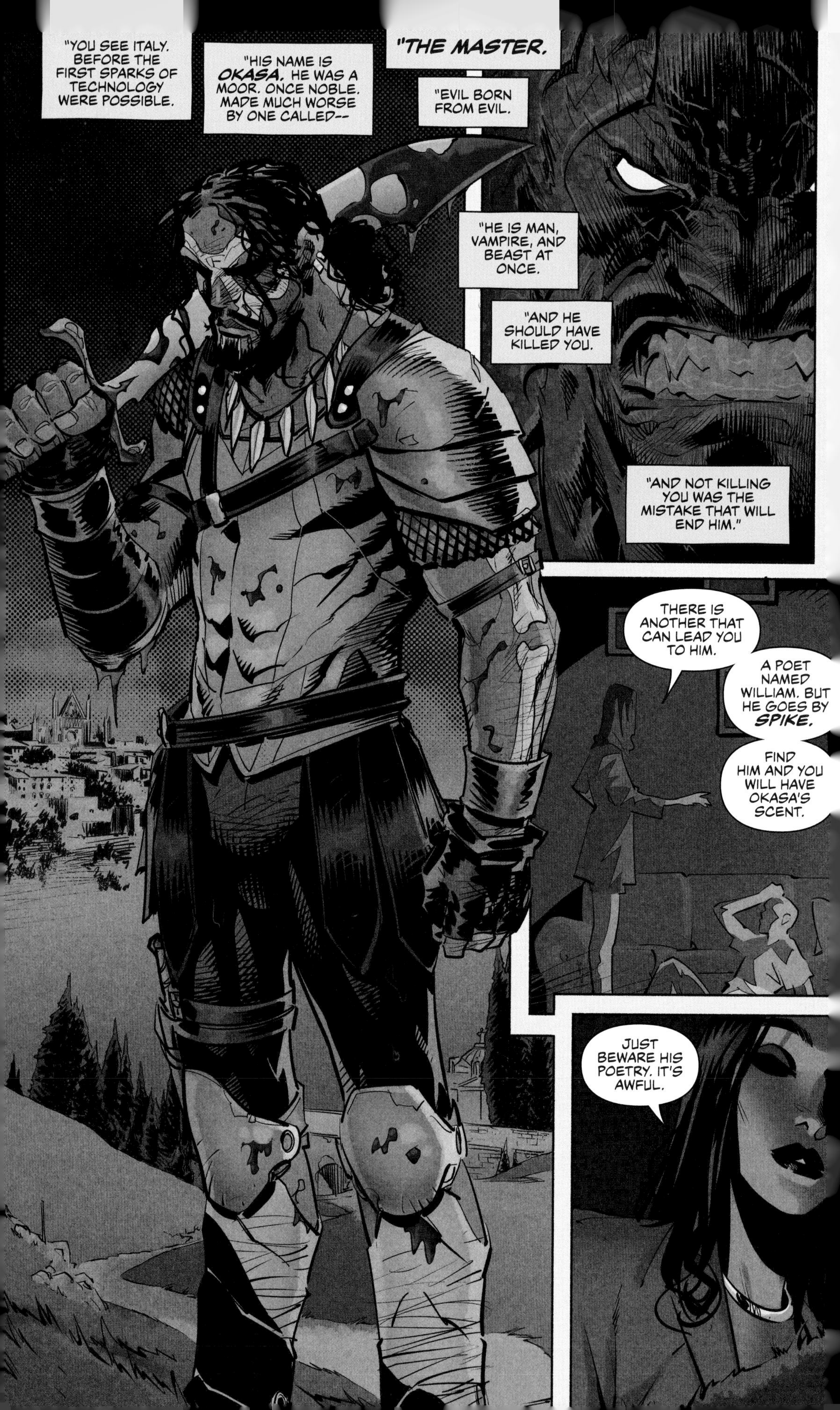
"YOU SEE ITALY. BEFORE THE FIRST SPARKS OF TECHNOLOGY WERE POSSIBLE.
"HIS NAME IS OKASA. HE WAS A MOOR. ONCE NOBLE. MADE MUCH WORSE BY ONE CALLED--
"THE MASTER.
"EVIL BORN FROM EVIL.
"HE IS MAN, VAMPIRE, AND BEAST AT ONCE.
"AND HE SHOULD HAVE KILLED YOU.
"AND NOT KILLING YOU WAS THE MISTAKE THAT WILL END HIM."
THERE IS ANOTHER THAT CAN LEAD YOU TO HIM.
A POET NAMED WILLIAM. BUT HE GOES BY SPIKE.
FIND HIM AND YOU WILL HAVE OKASA'S SCENT.
JUST BEWARE HIS POETRY. IT'S AWFUL.

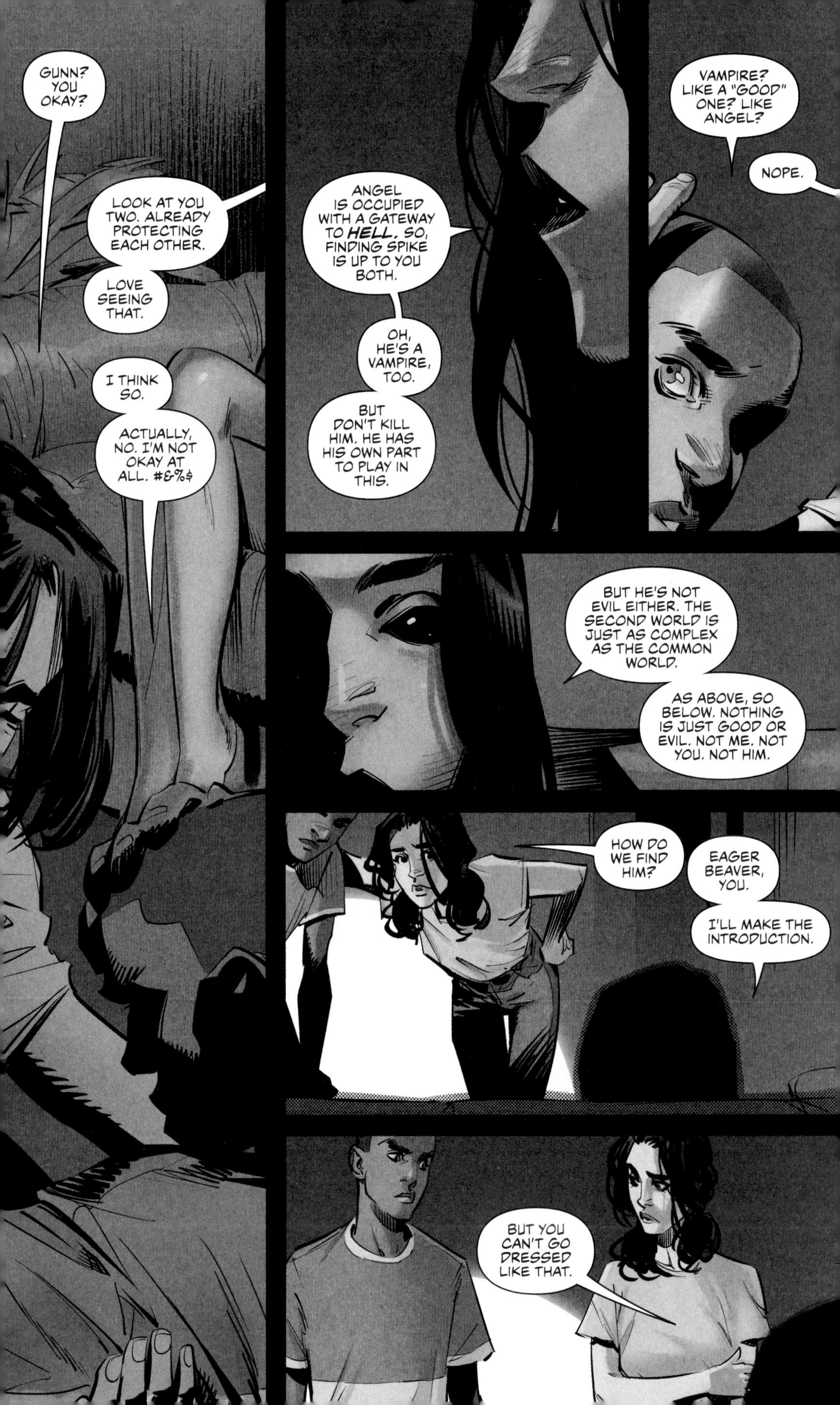
GUNN? YOU OKAY?
LOOK AT YOU TWO. ALREADY PROTECTING EACH OTHER.
LOVE SEEING THAT.
I THINK SO.
ACTUALLY, NO. I'M NOT OKAY AT ALL. #&%$
ANGEL IS OCCUPIED WITH A GATEWAY TO HELL. SO, FINDING SPIKE IS UP TO YOU BOTH.
OH, HE'S A VAMPIRE, TOO.
BUT DON'T KILL HIM. HE HAS HIS OWN PART TO PLAY IN THIS.
VAMPIRE? LIKE A "GOOD" ONE? LIKE ANGEL?
NOPE.
BUT HE'S NOT EVIL EITHER. THE SECOND WORLD IS JUST AS COMPLEX AS THE COMMON WORLD.
AS ABOVE, SO BELOW. NOTHING IS JUST GOOD OR EVIL. NOT ME. NOT YOU. NOT HIM.
HOW DO WE FIND HIM?
EAGER BEAVER, YOU.
I'LL MAKE THE INTRODUCTION.
BUT YOU CAN'T GO DRESSED LIKE THAT.

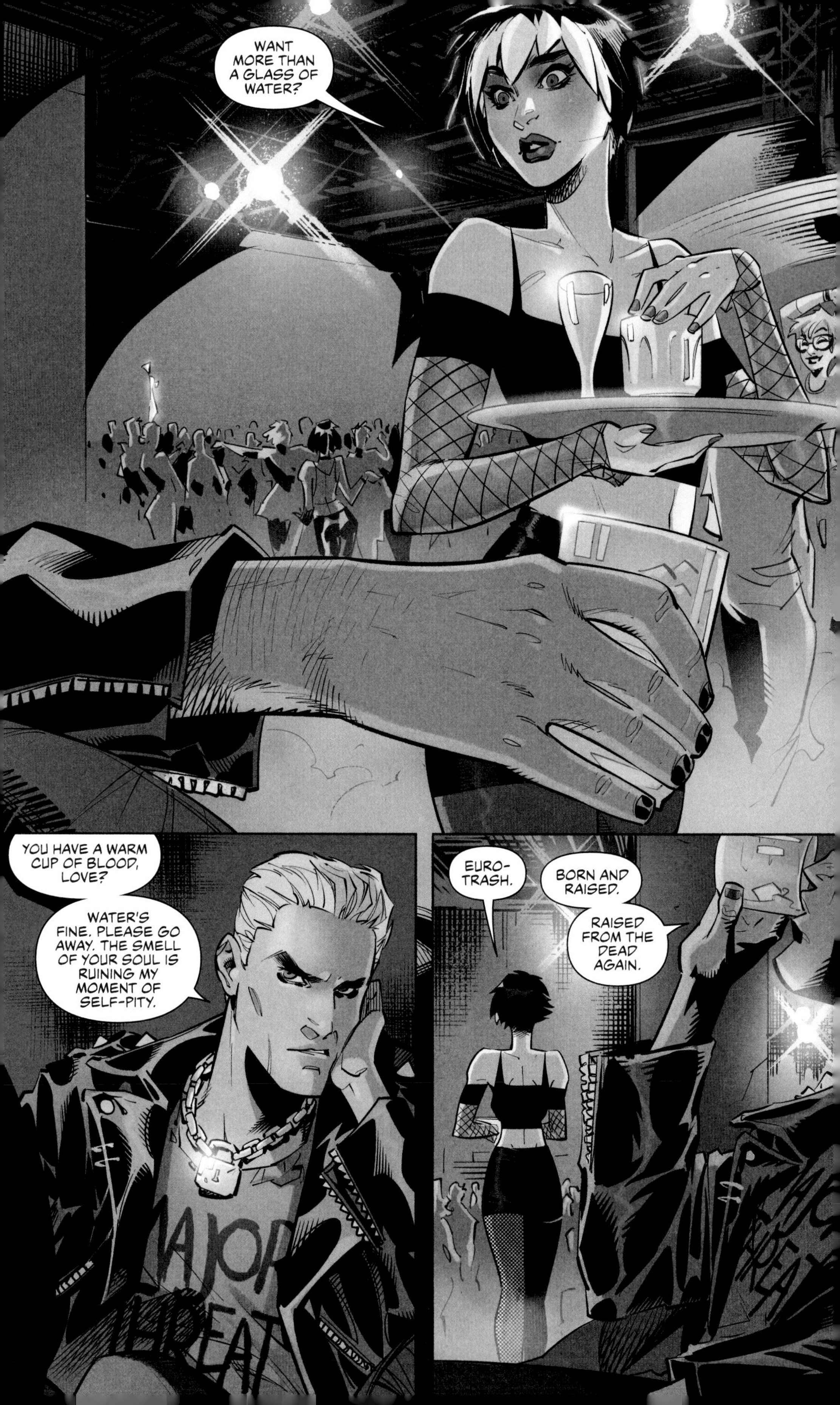
WANT MORE THAN A GLASS OF WATER?
YOU HAVE A WARM CUP OF BLOOD, LOVE?
WATER'S FINE. PLEASE GO AWAY. THE SMELL OF YOUR SOUL IS RUINING MY MOMENT OF SELF-PITY.
EURO-TRASH.
BORN AND RAISED.
RAISED FROM THE DEAD AGAIN.

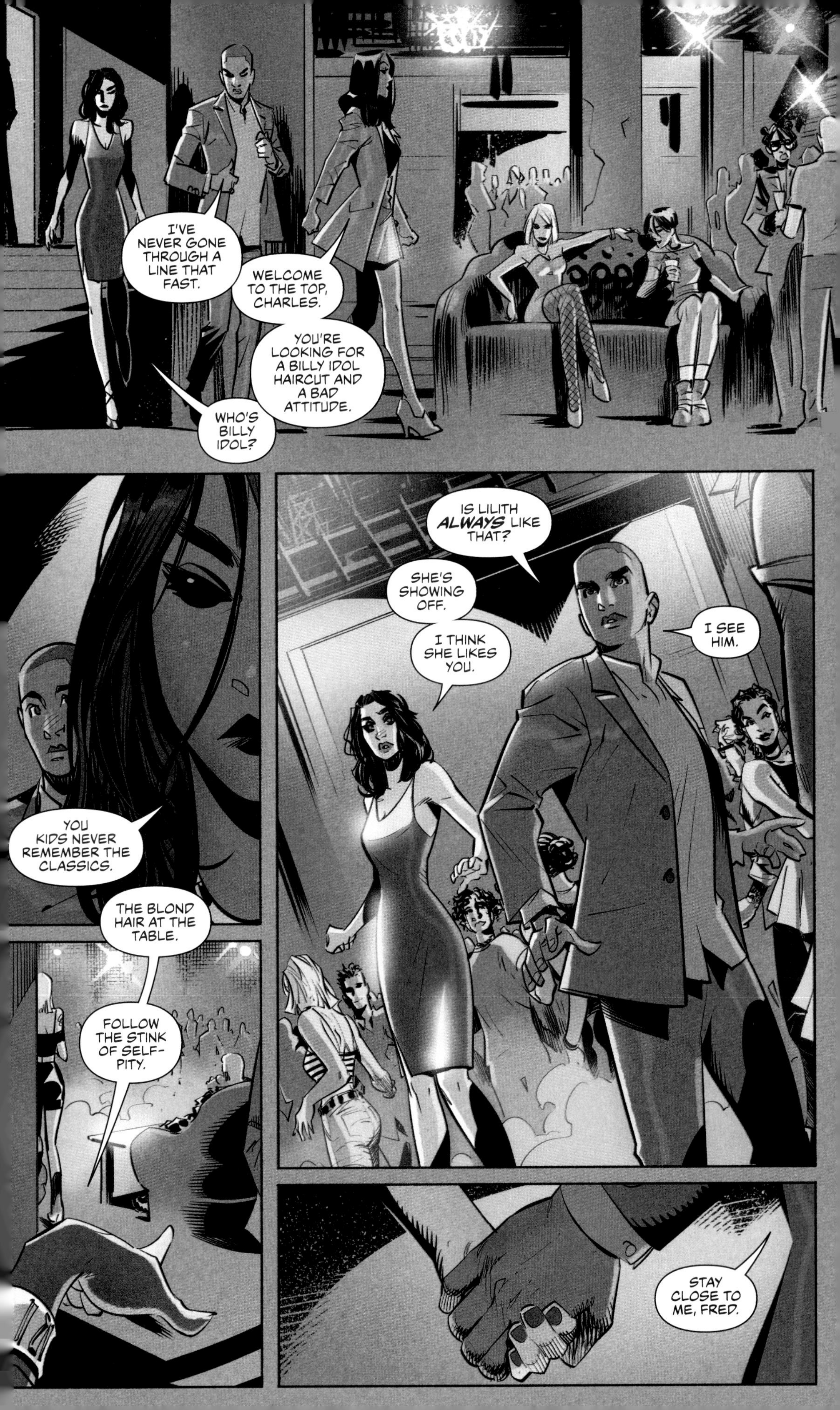

I'VE NEVER GONE THROUGH A LINE THAT FAST.
WELCOME TO THE TOP, CHARLES.
YOU'RE LOOKING FOR A BILLY IDOL HAIRCUT AND A BAD ATTITUDE.
WHO'S BILLY IDOL?
YOU KIDS NEVER REMEMBER THE CLASSICS.
THE BLOND HAIR AT THE TABLE.
FOLLOW THE STINK OF SELF-PITY.
IS LILITH *ALWAYS* LIKE THAT?
SHE'S SHOWING OFF.
I THINK SHE LIKES YOU.
I SEE HIM.
STAY CLOSE TO ME, FRED.

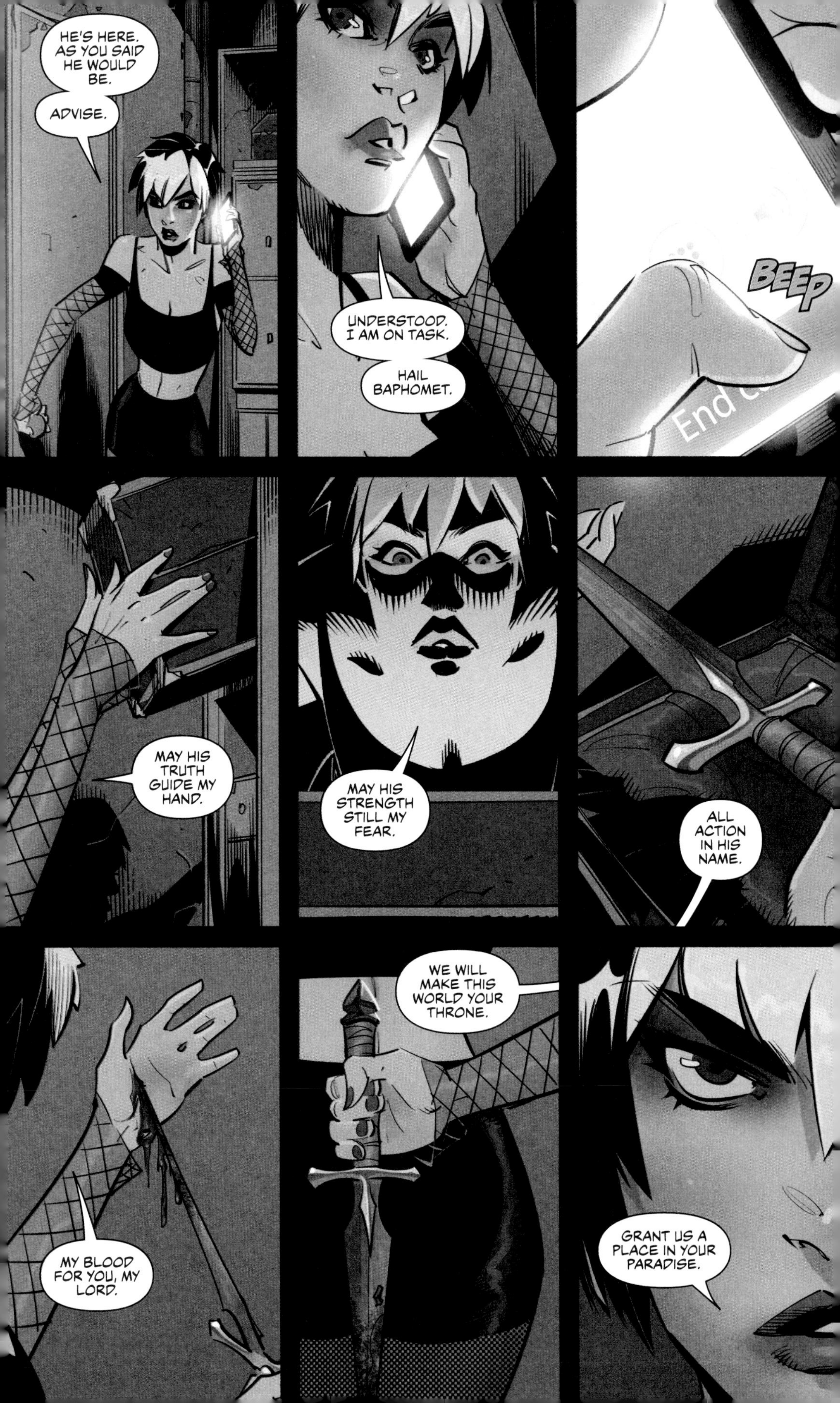
HE'S HERE. AS YOU SAID HE WOULD BE.
ADVISE.
UNDERSTOOD. I AM ON TASK.
HAIL BAPHOMET.
BEEP
End
MAY HIS TRUTH GUIDE MY HAND.
MAY HIS STRENGTH STILL MY FEAR.
ALL ACTION IN HIS NAME.
MY BLOOD FOR YOU, MY LORD.
WE WILL MAKE THIS WORLD YOUR THRONE.
GRANT US A PLACE IN YOUR PARADISE.

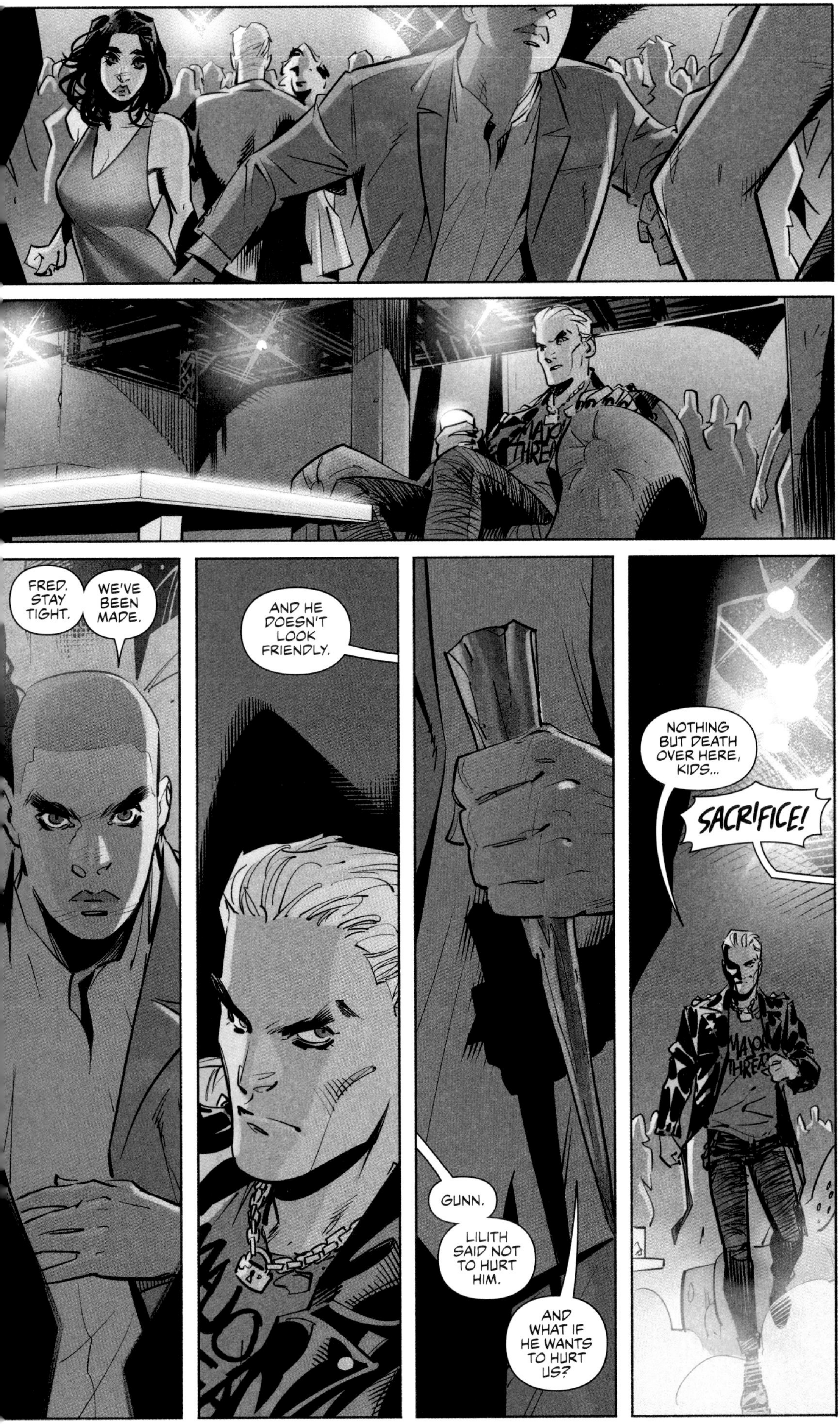
FRED. STAY TIGHT.
WE'VE BEEN MADE.
AND HE DOESN'T LOOK FRIENDLY.
GUNN.
LILITH SAID NOT TO HURT HIM.
AND WHAT IF HE WANTS TO HURT US?
NOTHING BUT DEATH OVER HERE, KIDS...
SACRIFICE!

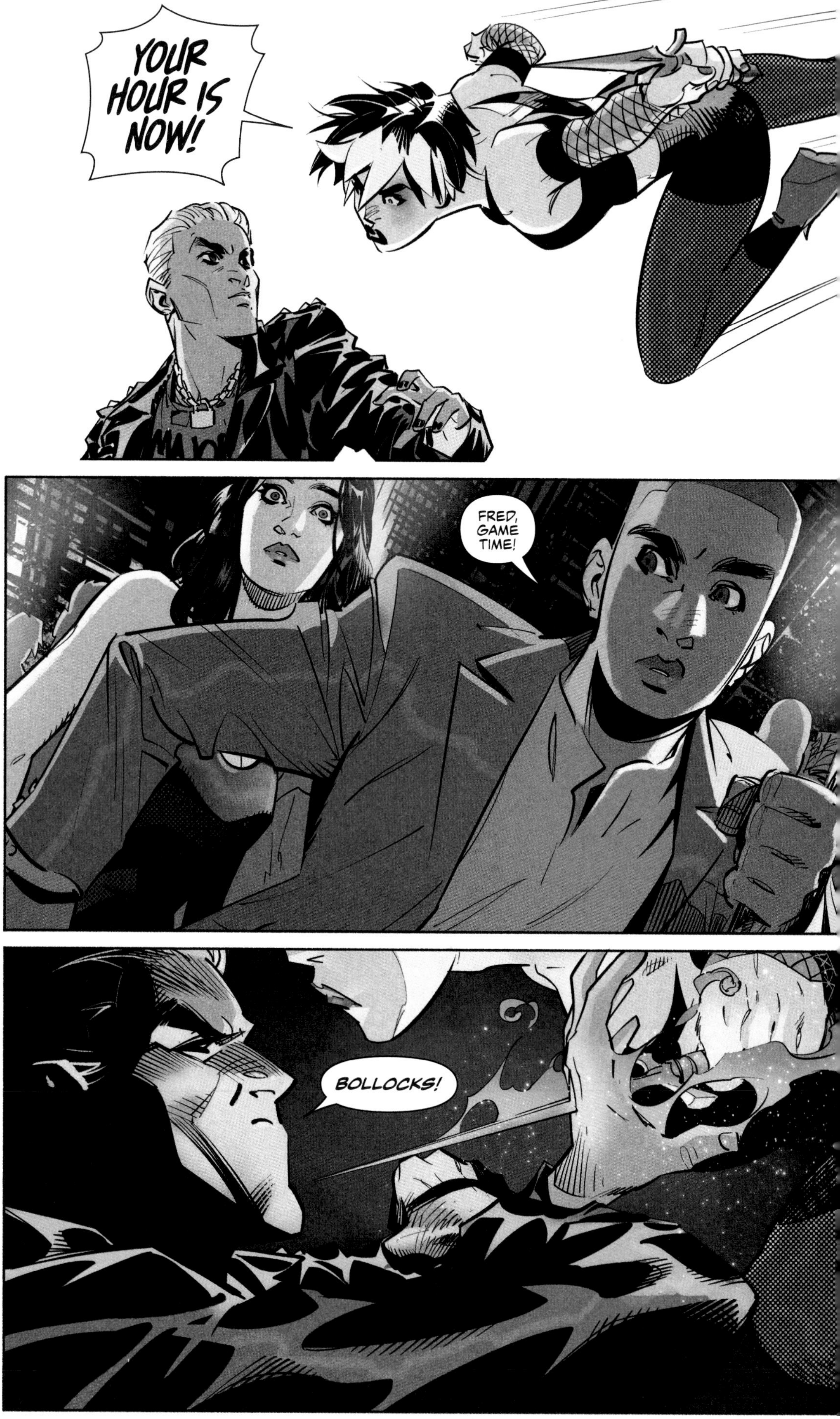
YOUR HOUR IS NOW!
FRED, GAME TIME!
BOLLOCKS!

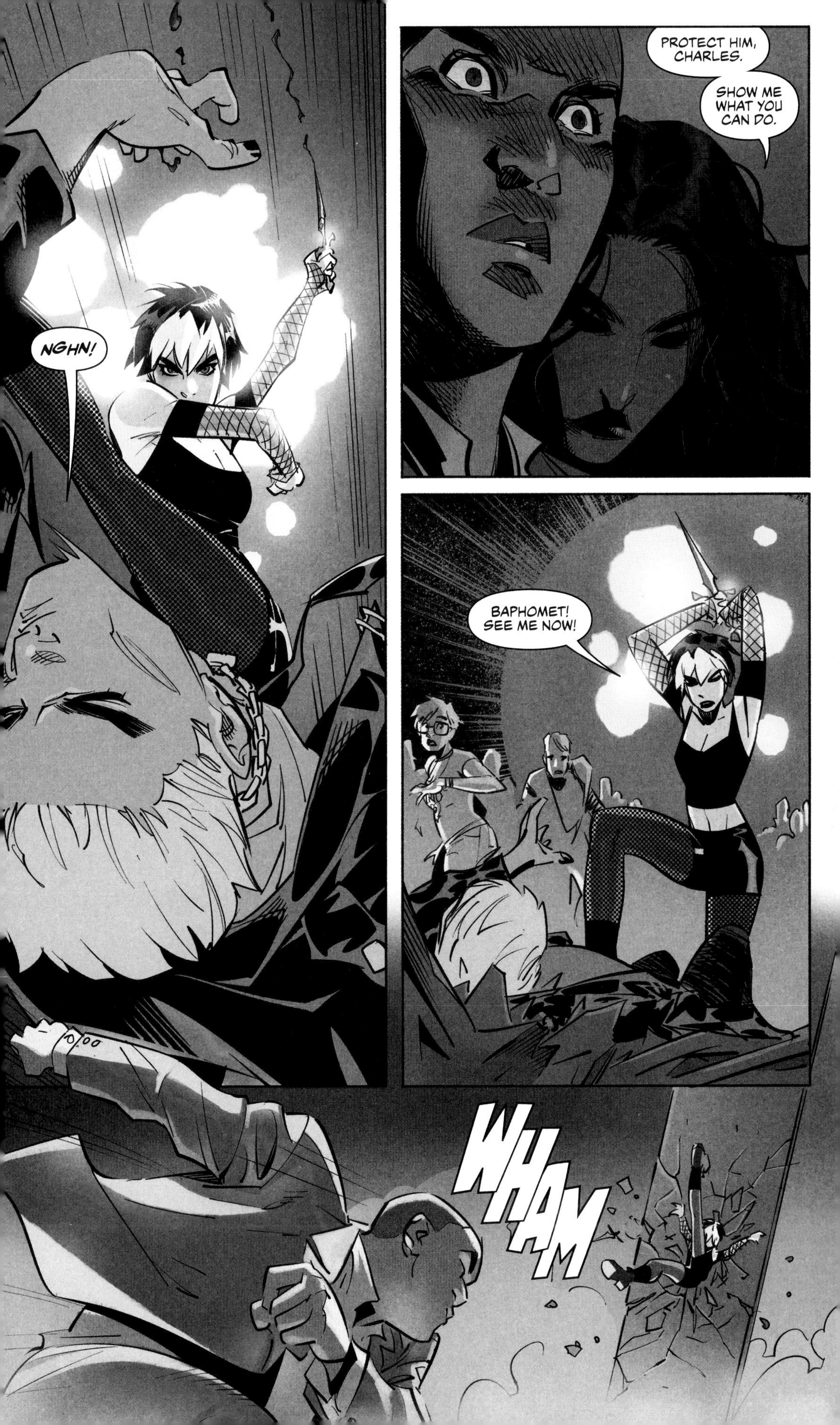
NGHN!
PROTECT HIM, CHARLES.
SHOW ME WHAT YOU CAN DO.
BAPHOMET! SEE ME NOW!
WHAM

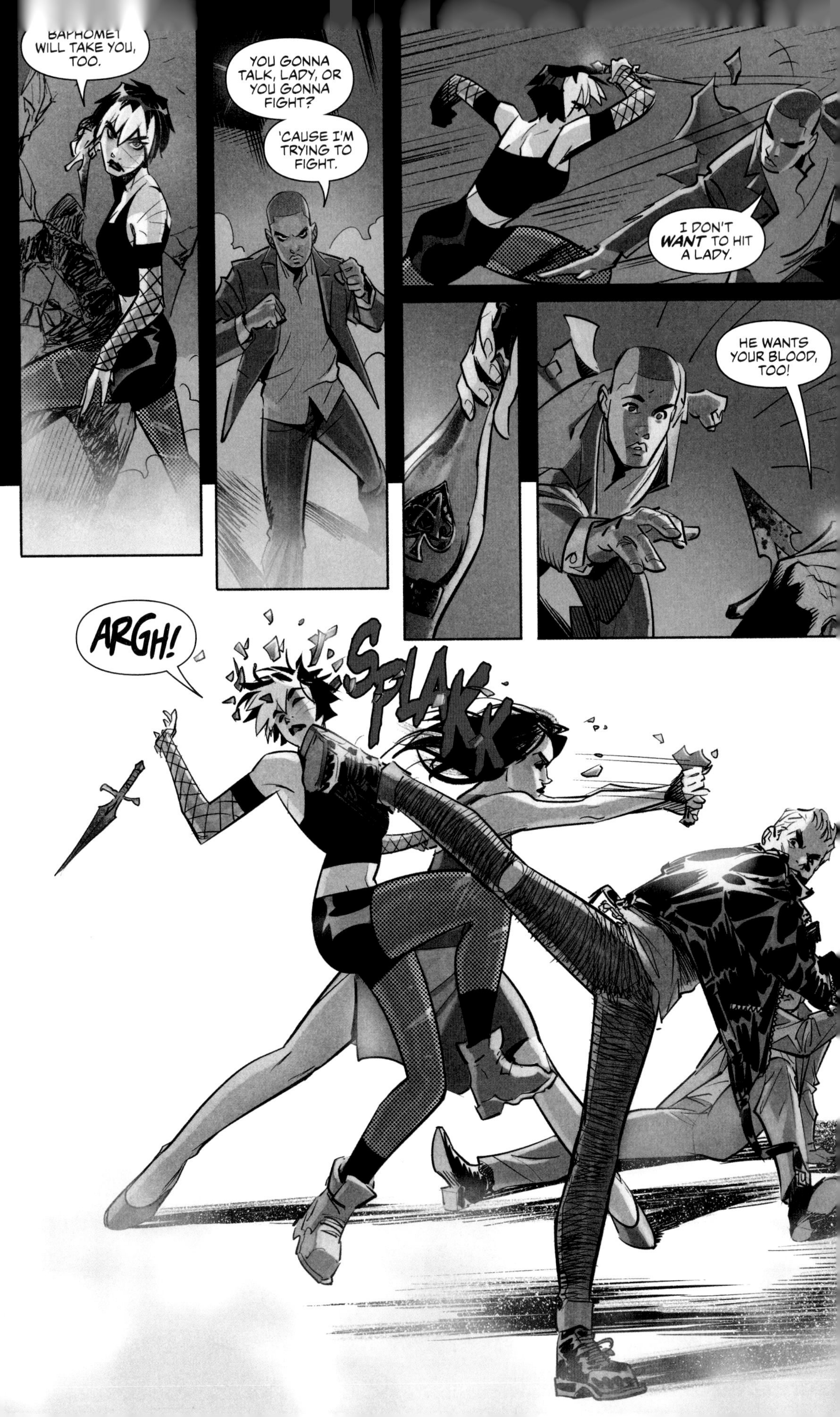
BAPHOMET WILL TAKE YOU, TOO.
YOU GONNA TALK, LADY, OR YOU GONNA FIGHT?
'CAUSE I'M TRYING TO FIGHT.
I DON'T WANT TO HIT A LADY.
HE WANTS YOUR BLOOD, TOO!
ARGH!
SPLAKK

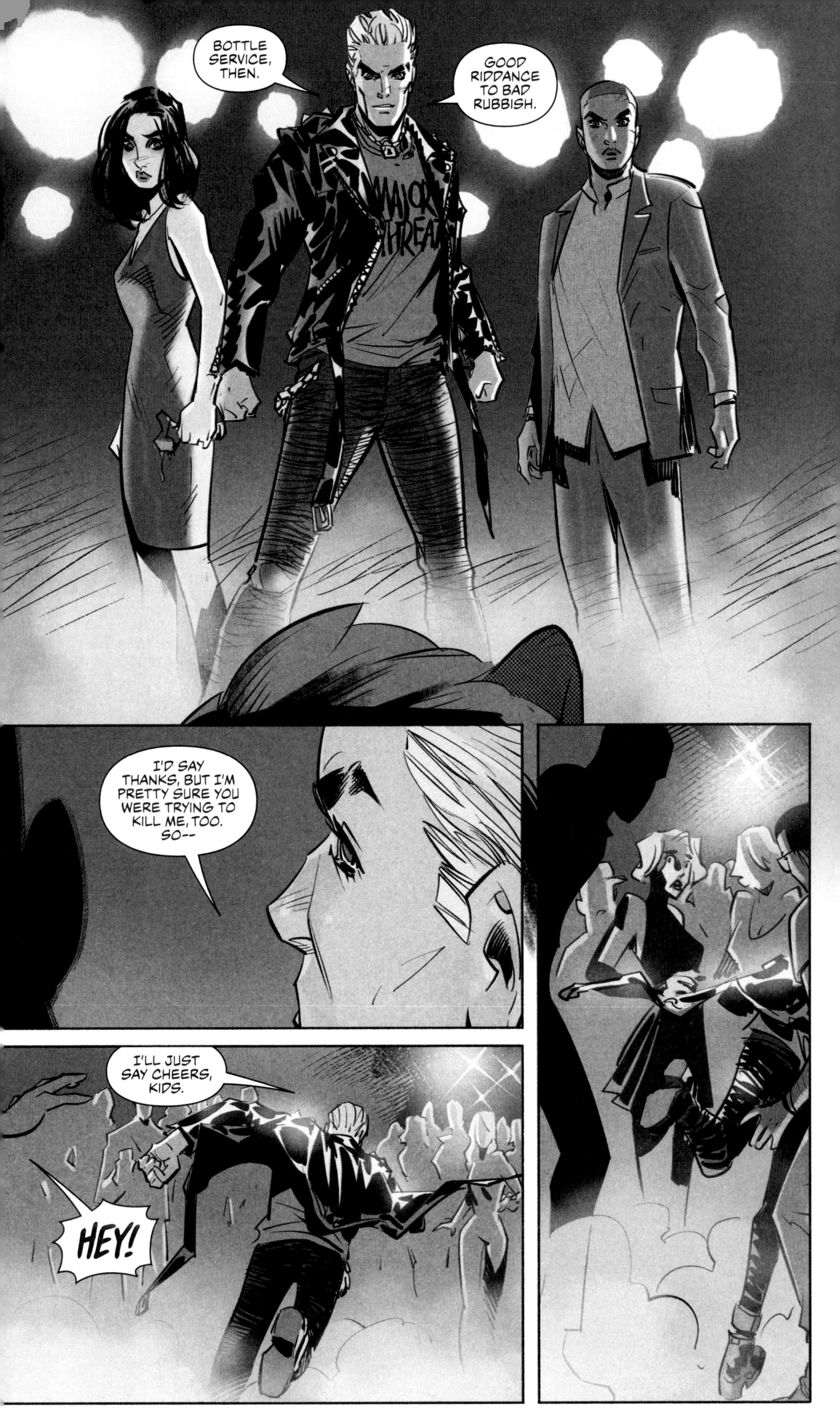
BOTTLE SERVICE, THEN.
GOOD RIDDANCE TO BAD RUBBISH.
MAJOR THREAT
I'D SAY THANKS, BUT I'M PRETTY SURE YOU WERE TRYING TO KILL ME, TOO. SO--
I'LL JUST SAY CHEERS, KIDS.
HEY!

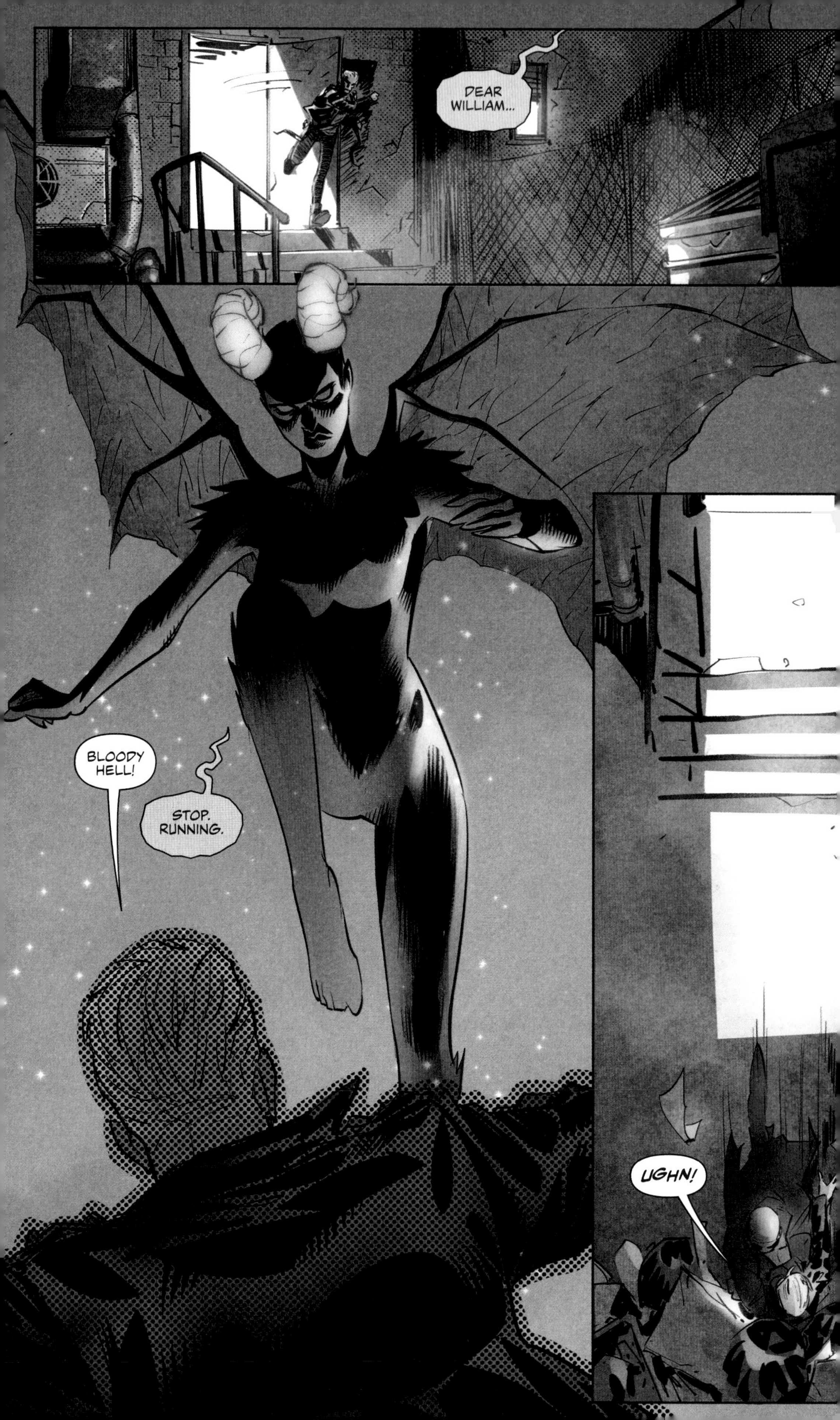
DEAR WILLIAM...
BLOODY HELL!
STOP. RUNNING.
UGHN!

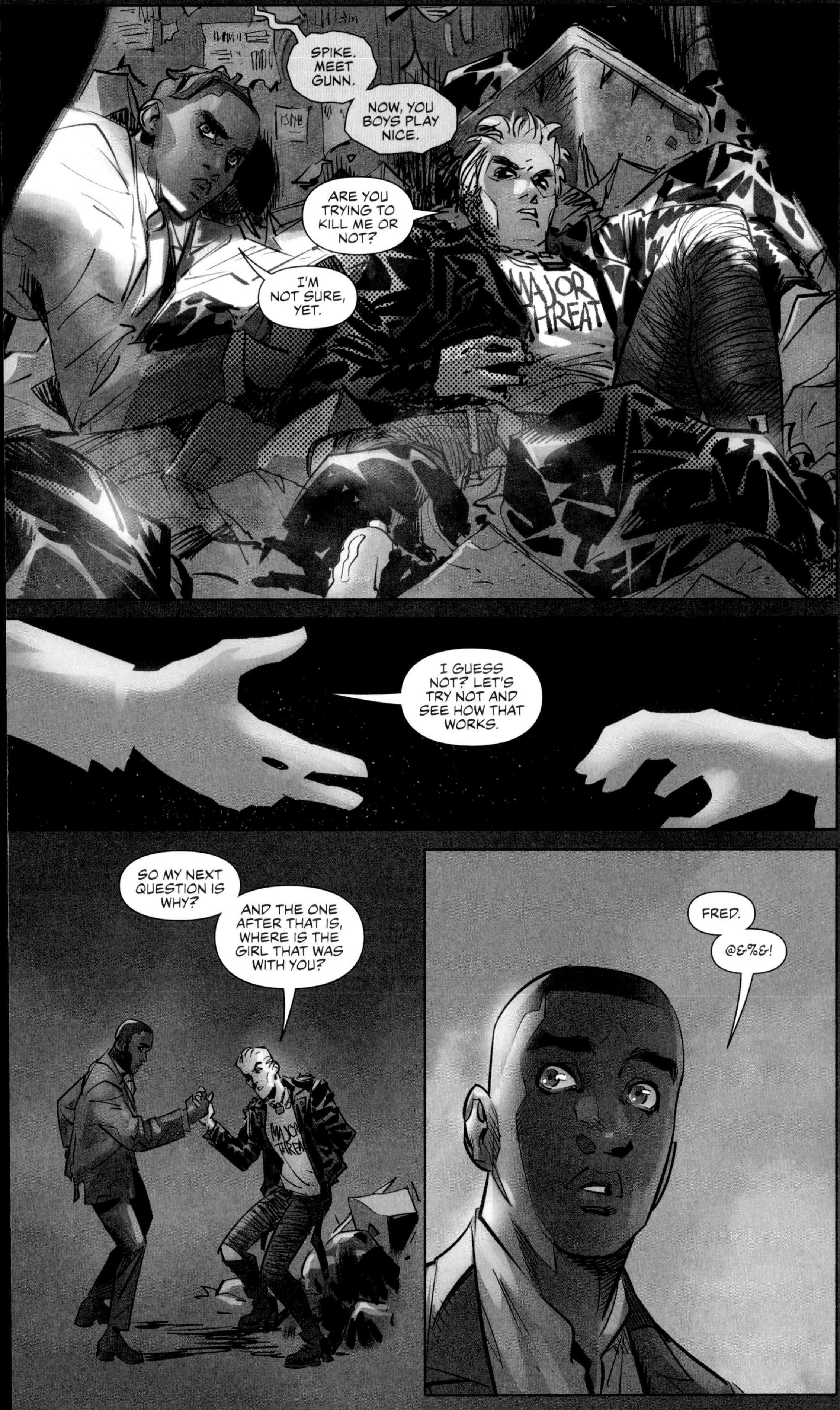
SPIKE. MEET GUNN.
NOW, YOU BOYS PLAY NICE.
ARE YOU TRYING TO KILL ME OR NOT?
I'M NOT SURE, YET.
I GUESS NOT? LET'S TRY NOT AND SEE HOW THAT WORKS.
SO MY NEXT QUESTION IS WHY?
AND THE ONE AFTER THAT IS, WHERE IS THE GIRL THAT WAS WITH YOU?
FRED.
@&%&!
MAJOR THREAT

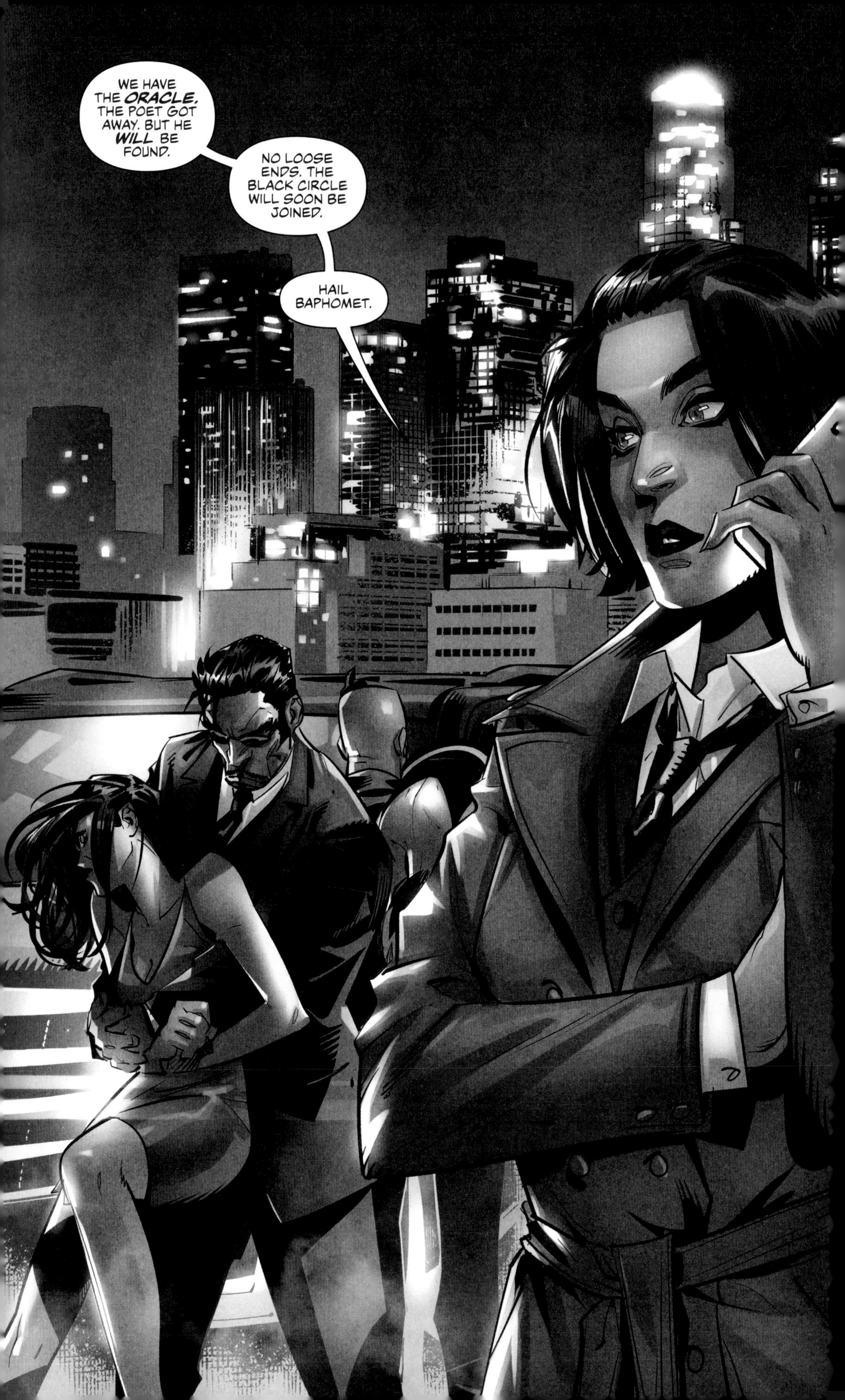
WE HAVE THE ORACLE. THE POET GOT AWAY. BUT HE WILL BE FOUND.
NO LOOSE ENDS. THE BLACK CIRCLE WILL SOON BE JOINED.
HAIL BAPHOMET.

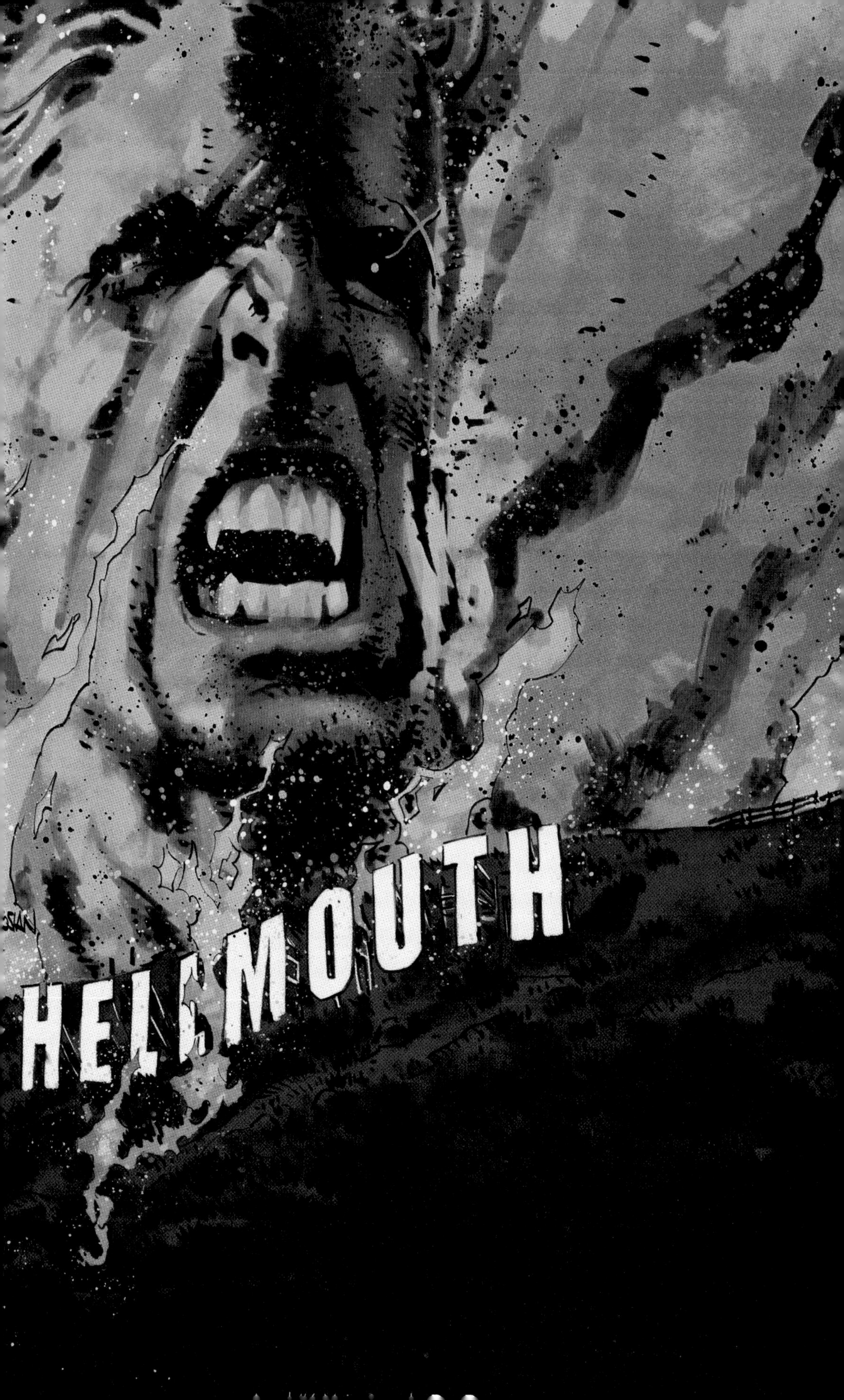
HELLMOUTH

CHAPTER
SEVEN

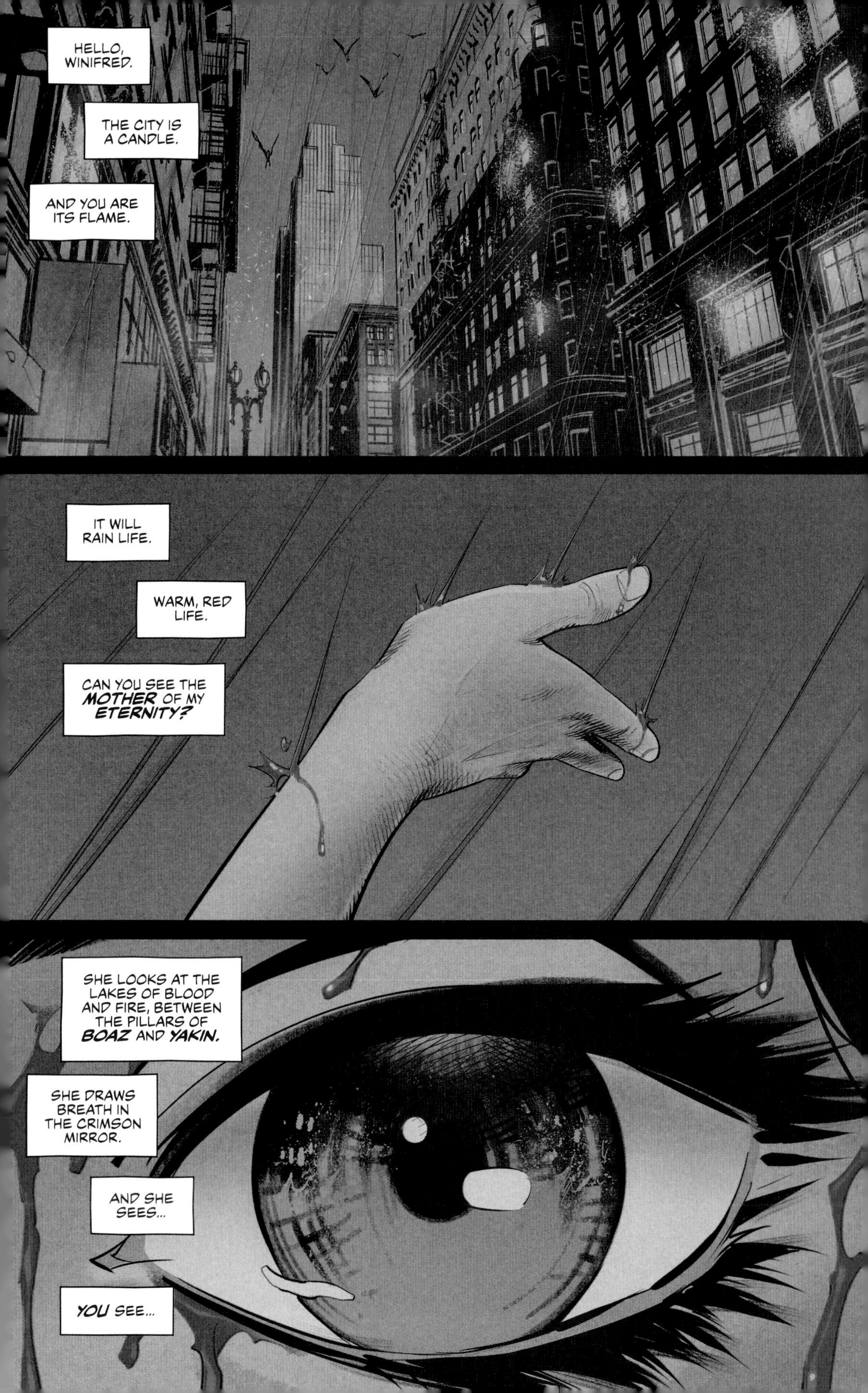
HELLO, WINIFRED.
THE CITY IS A CANDLE.
AND YOU ARE ITS FLAME.
IT WILL RAIN LIFE.
WARM, RED LIFE.
CAN YOU SEE THE ***MOTHER*** OF MY ***ETERNITY?***
SHE LOOKS AT THE LAKES OF BLOOD AND FIRE, BETWEEN THE PILLARS OF ***BOAZ*** AND ***YAKIN.***
SHE DRAWS BREATH IN THE CRIMSON MIRROR.
AND SHE SEES...
YOU SEE...

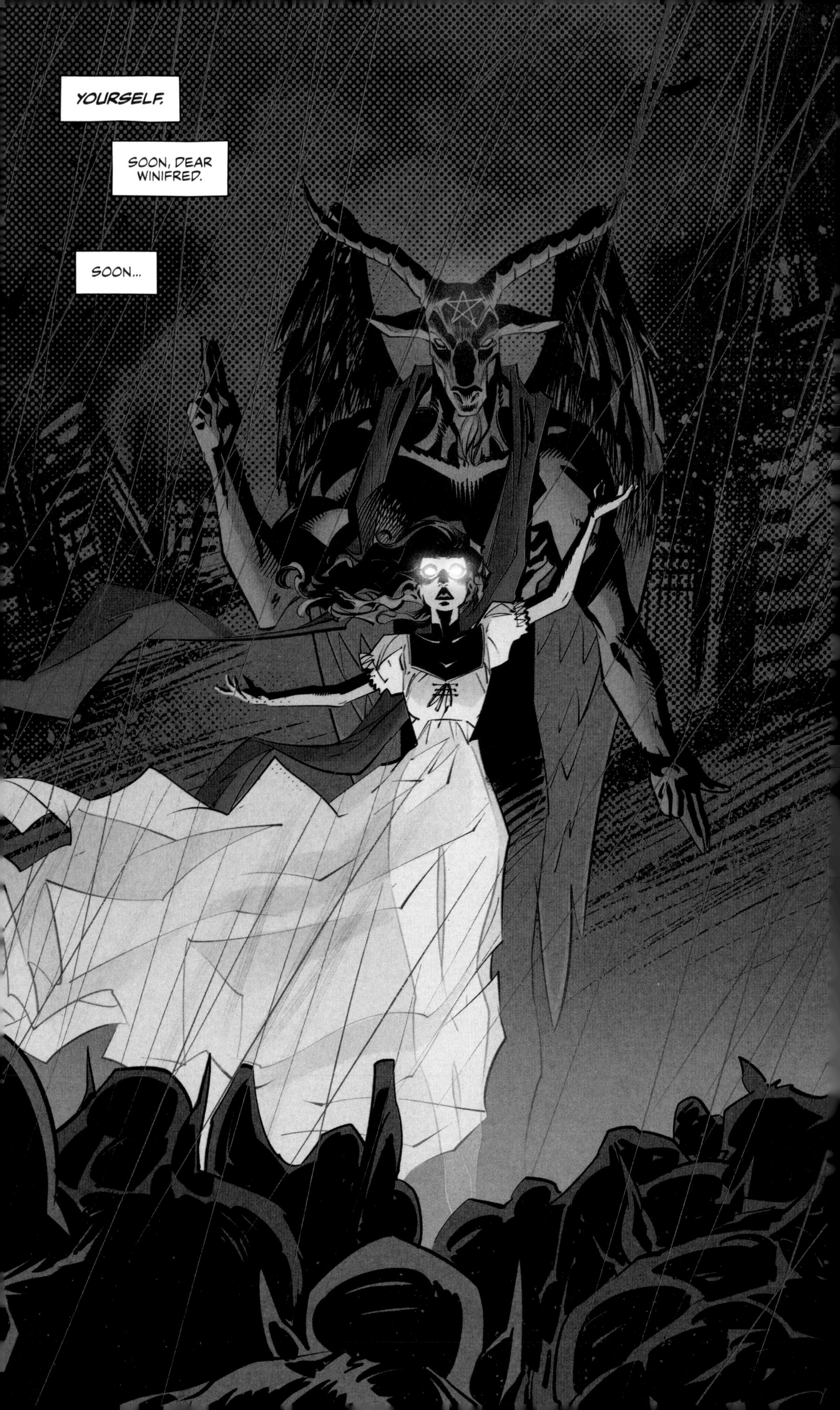
YOURSELF.
SOON, DEAR WINIFRED.
SOON...

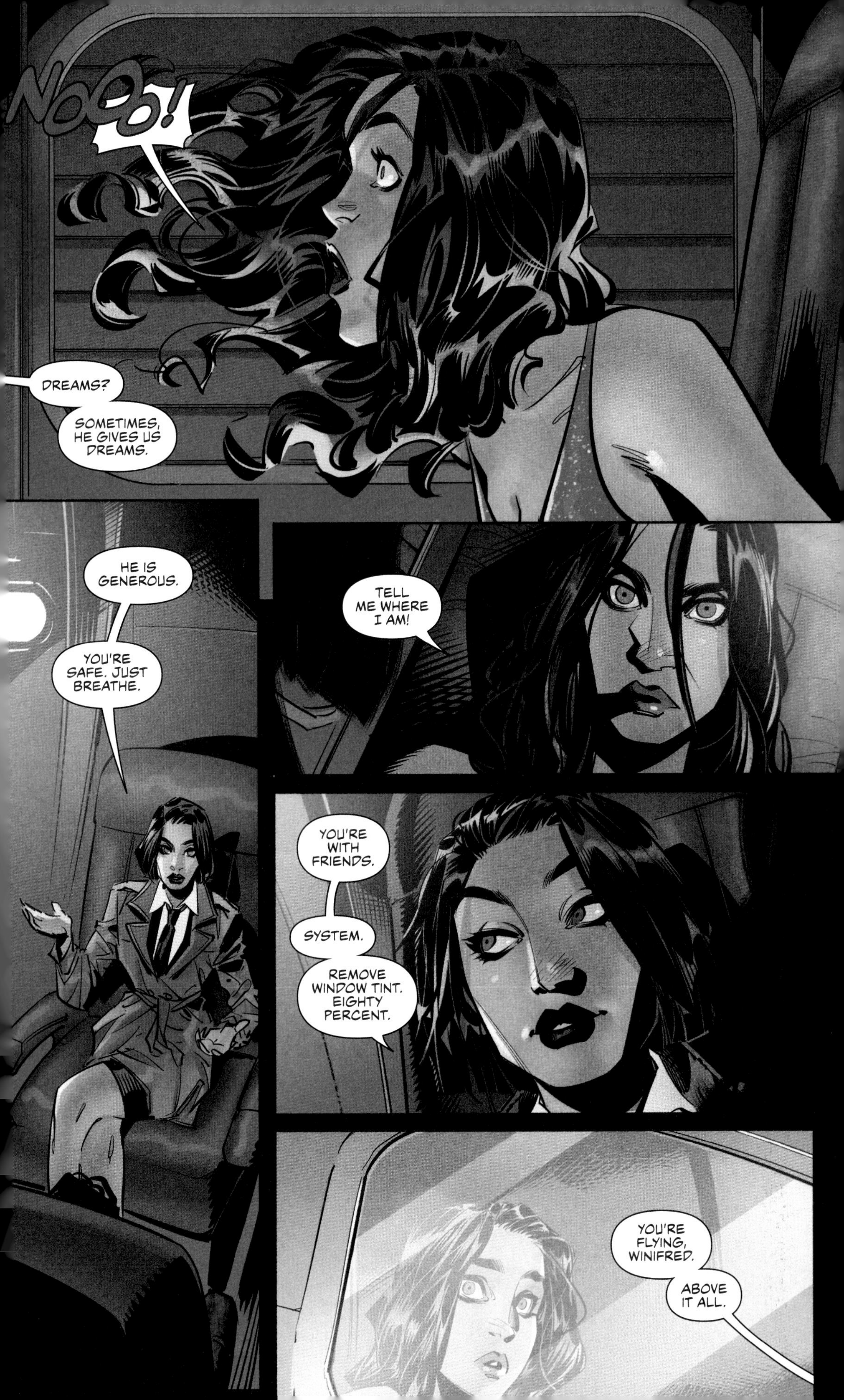
NOOOO!
DREAMS?
SOMETIMES, HE GIVES US DREAMS.
HE IS GENEROUS.
YOU'RE SAFE. JUST BREATHE.
TELL ME WHERE I AM!
YOU'RE WITH FRIENDS.
SYSTEM.
REMOVE WINDOW TINT. EIGHTY PERCENT.
YOU'RE FLYING, WINIFRED.
ABOVE IT ALL.

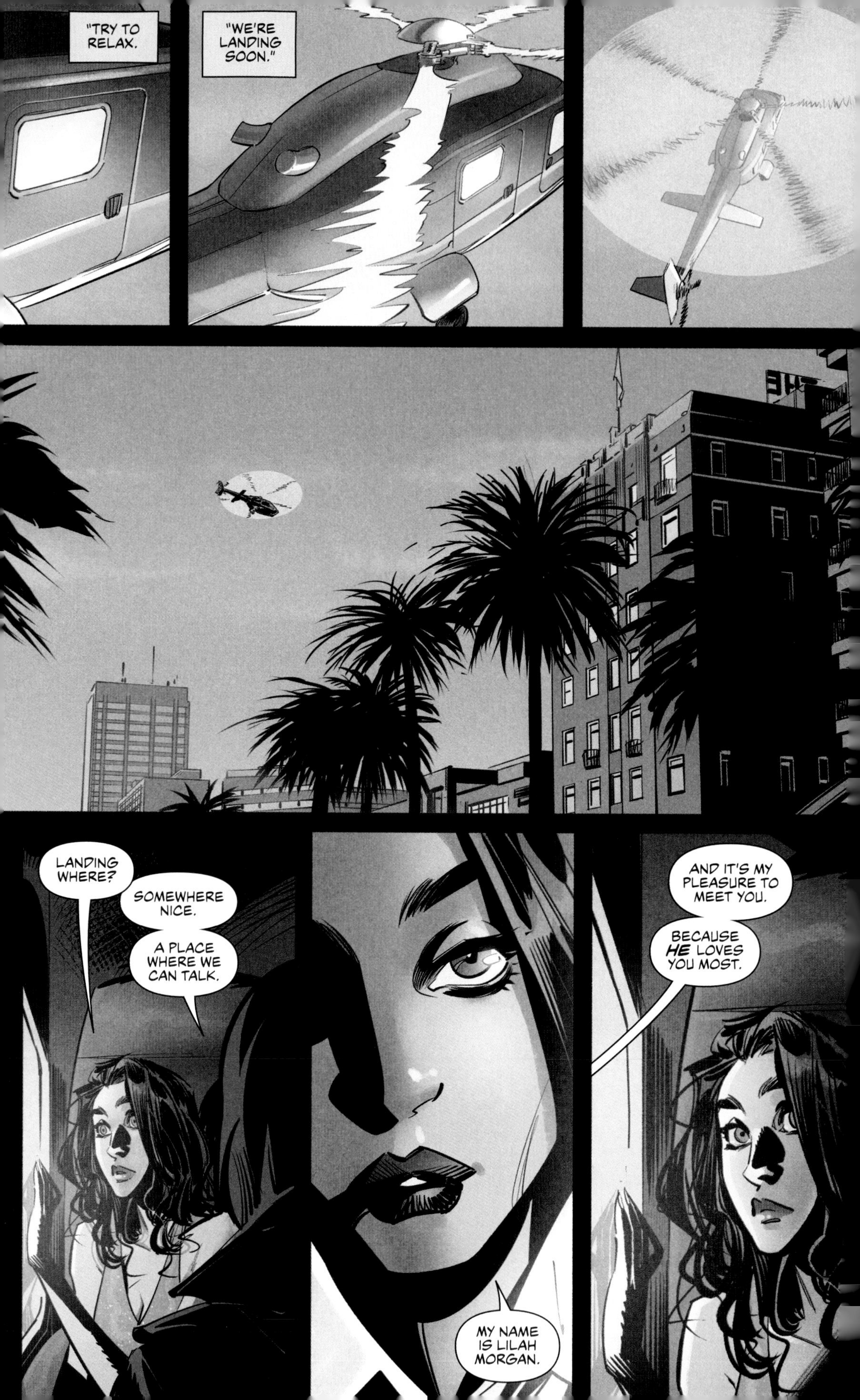
"TRY TO RELAX.
"WE'RE LANDING SOON."
LANDING WHERE?
SOMEWHERE NICE.
A PLACE WHERE WE CAN TALK.
MY NAME IS LILAH MORGAN.
AND IT'S MY PLEASURE TO MEET YOU.
BECAUSE HE LOVES YOU MOST.

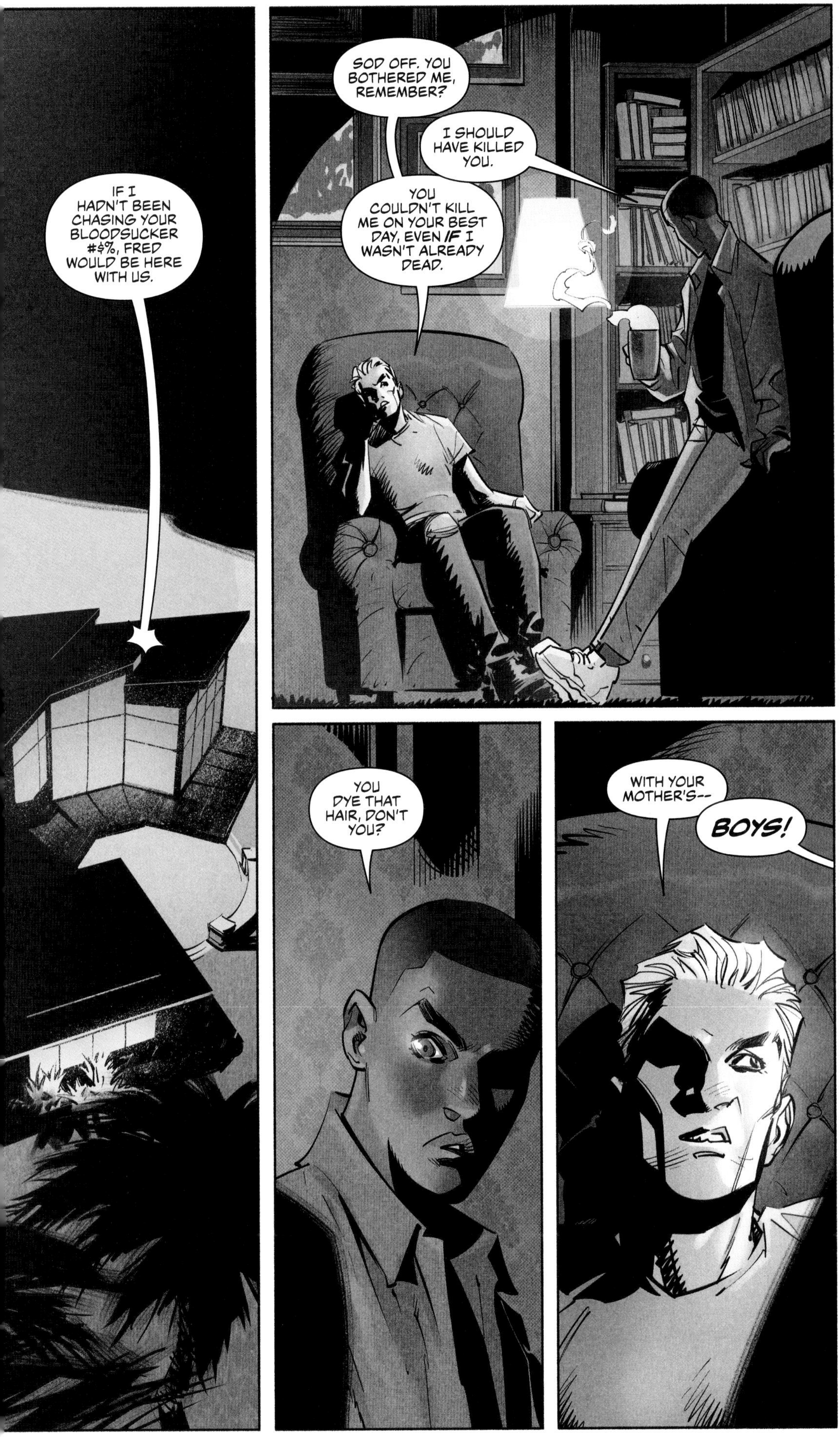
IF I HADN'T BEEN CHASING YOUR BLOODSUCKER #$%, FRED WOULD BE HERE WITH US.
SOD OFF. YOU BOTHERED ME, REMEMBER?
I SHOULD HAVE KILLED YOU.
YOU COULDN'T KILL ME ON YOUR BEST DAY, EVEN IF I WASN'T ALREADY DEAD.
YOU DYE THAT HAIR, DON'T YOU?
WITH YOUR MOTHER'S--
BOYS!

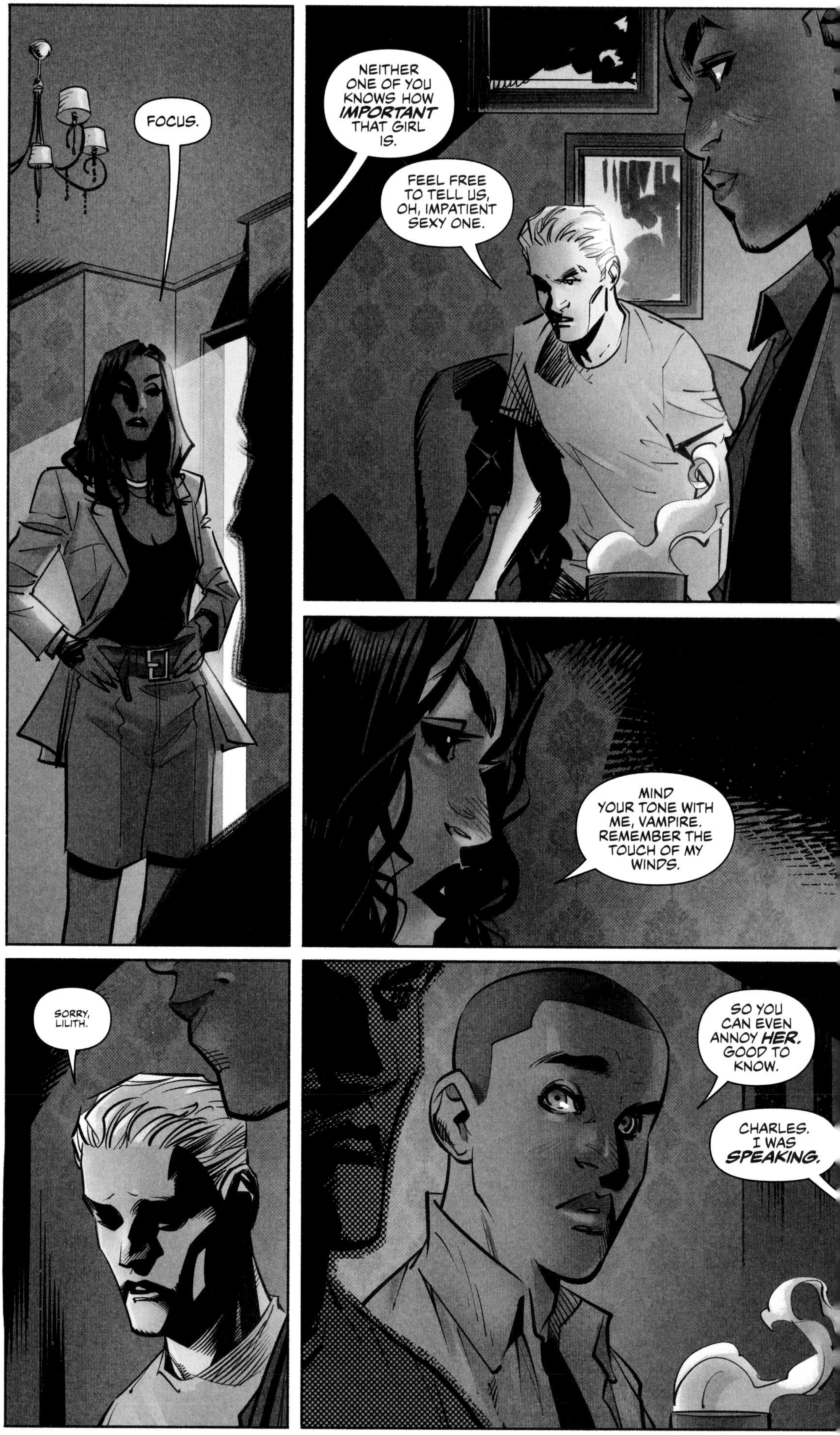
FOCUS.
NEITHER ONE OF YOU KNOWS HOW IMPORTANT THAT GIRL IS.
FEEL FREE TO TELL US, OH, IMPATIENT SEXY ONE.
MIND YOUR TONE WITH ME, VAMPIRE. REMEMBER THE TOUCH OF MY WINDS.
SORRY, LILITH.
SO YOU CAN EVEN ANNOY HER. GOOD TO KNOW.
CHARLES. I WAS SPEAKING.

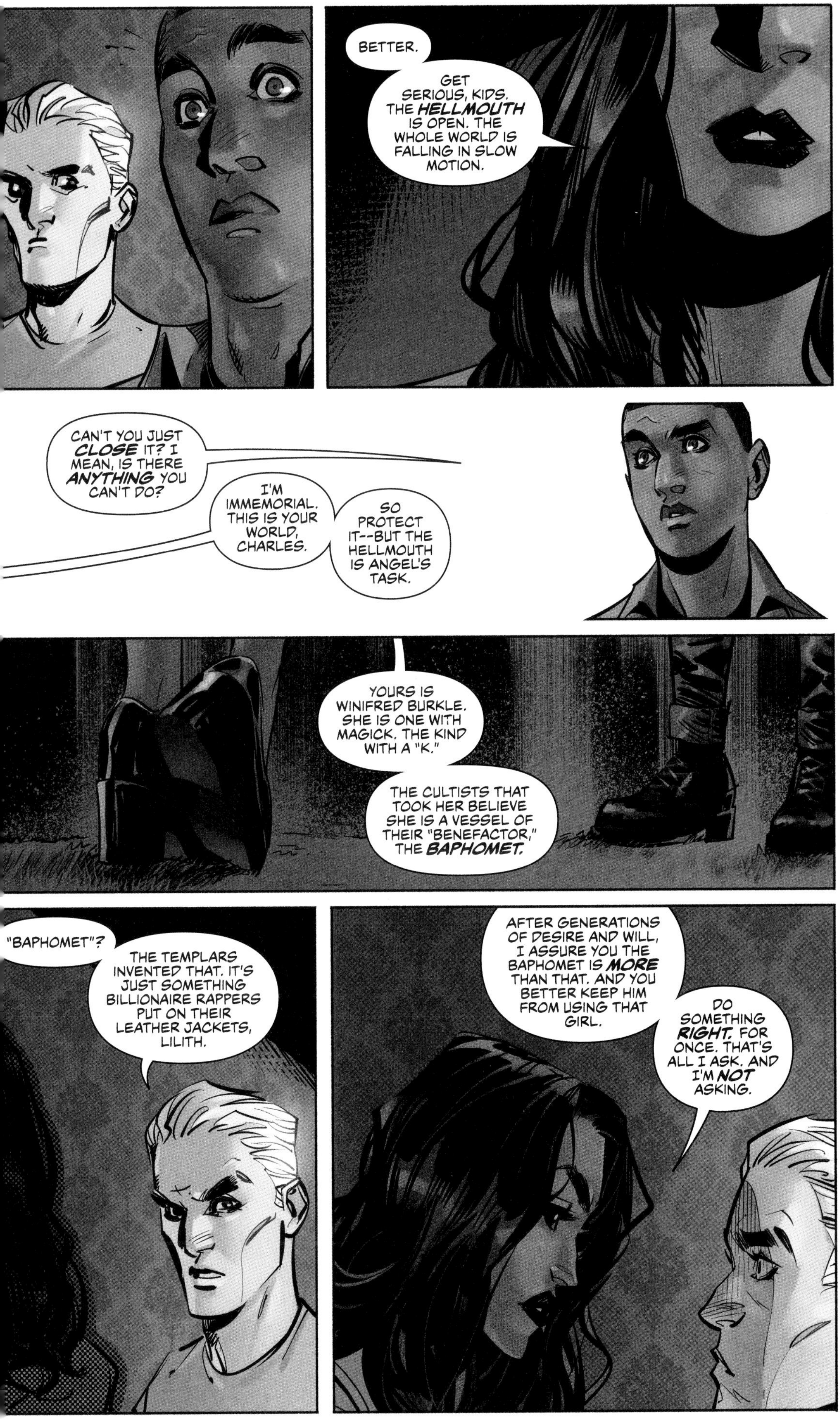

BETTER.
GET SERIOUS, KIDS. THE HELLMOUTH IS OPEN. THE WHOLE WORLD IS FALLING IN SLOW MOTION.
CAN'T YOU JUST CLOSE IT? I MEAN, IS THERE ANYTHING YOU CAN'T DO?
I'M IMMEMORIAL. THIS IS YOUR WORLD, CHARLES.
SO PROTECT IT--BUT THE HELLMOUTH IS ANGEL'S TASK.
YOURS IS WINIFRED BURKLE. SHE IS ONE WITH MAGICK. THE KIND WITH A "K."
THE CULTISTS THAT TOOK HER BELIEVE SHE IS A VESSEL OF THEIR "BENEFACTOR," THE BAPHOMET.
"BAPHOMET"?
THE TEMPLARS INVENTED THAT. IT'S JUST SOMETHING BILLIONAIRE RAPPERS PUT ON THEIR LEATHER JACKETS, LILITH.
AFTER GENERATIONS OF DESIRE AND WILL, I ASSURE YOU THE BAPHOMET IS MORE THAN THAT. AND YOU BETTER KEEP HIM FROM USING THAT GIRL.
DO SOMETHING RIGHT, FOR ONCE. THAT'S ALL I ASK. AND I'M NOT ASKING.

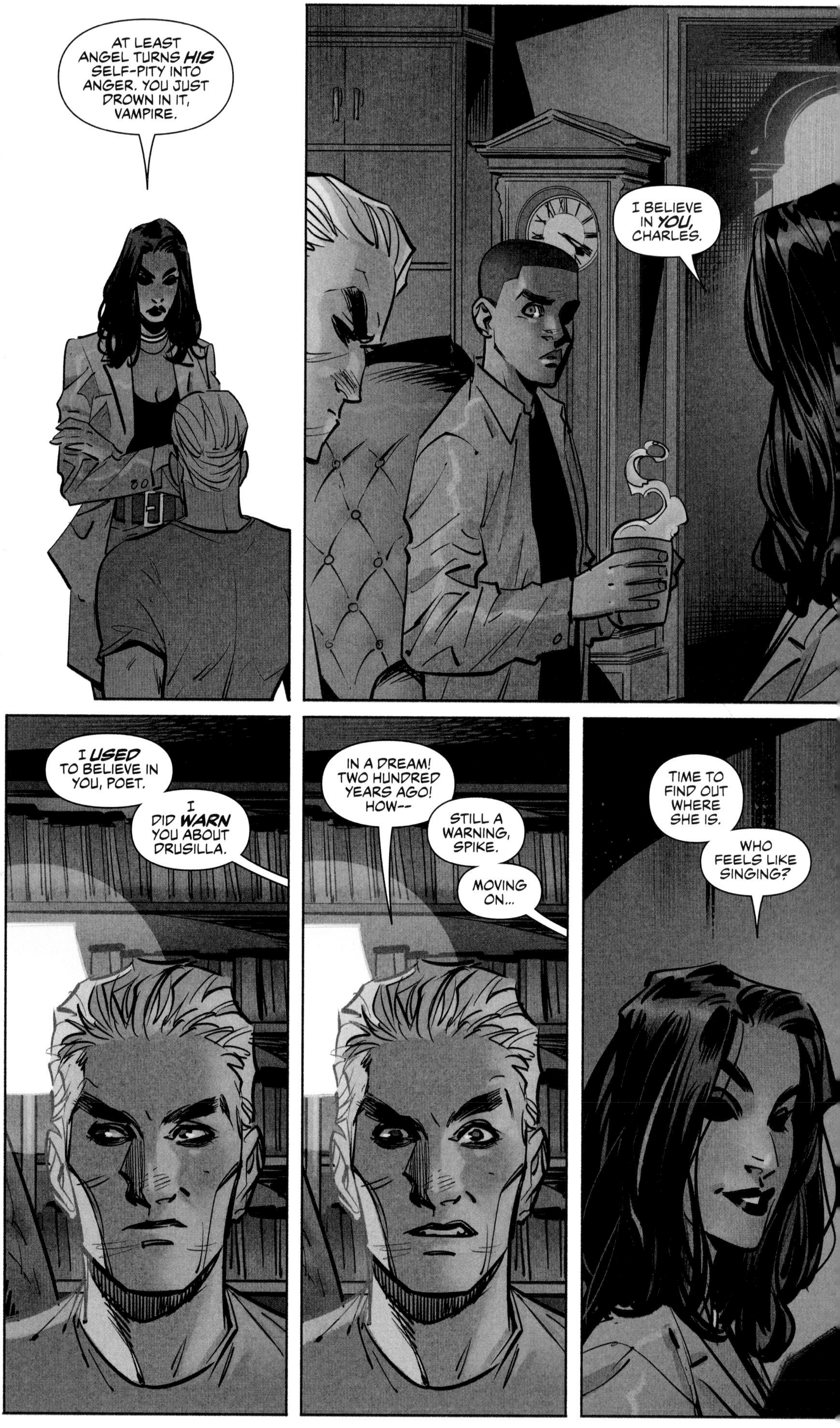
AT LEAST ANGEL TURNS HIS SELF-PITY INTO ANGER. YOU JUST DROWN IN IT, VAMPIRE.
I BELIEVE IN YOU, CHARLES.
I USED TO BELIEVE IN YOU, POET.
I DID WARN YOU ABOUT DRUSILLA.
IN A DREAM! TWO HUNDRED YEARS AGO! HOW--
STILL A WARNING, SPIKE.
MOVING ON...
TIME TO FIND OUT WHERE SHE IS.
WHO FEELS LIKE SINGING?

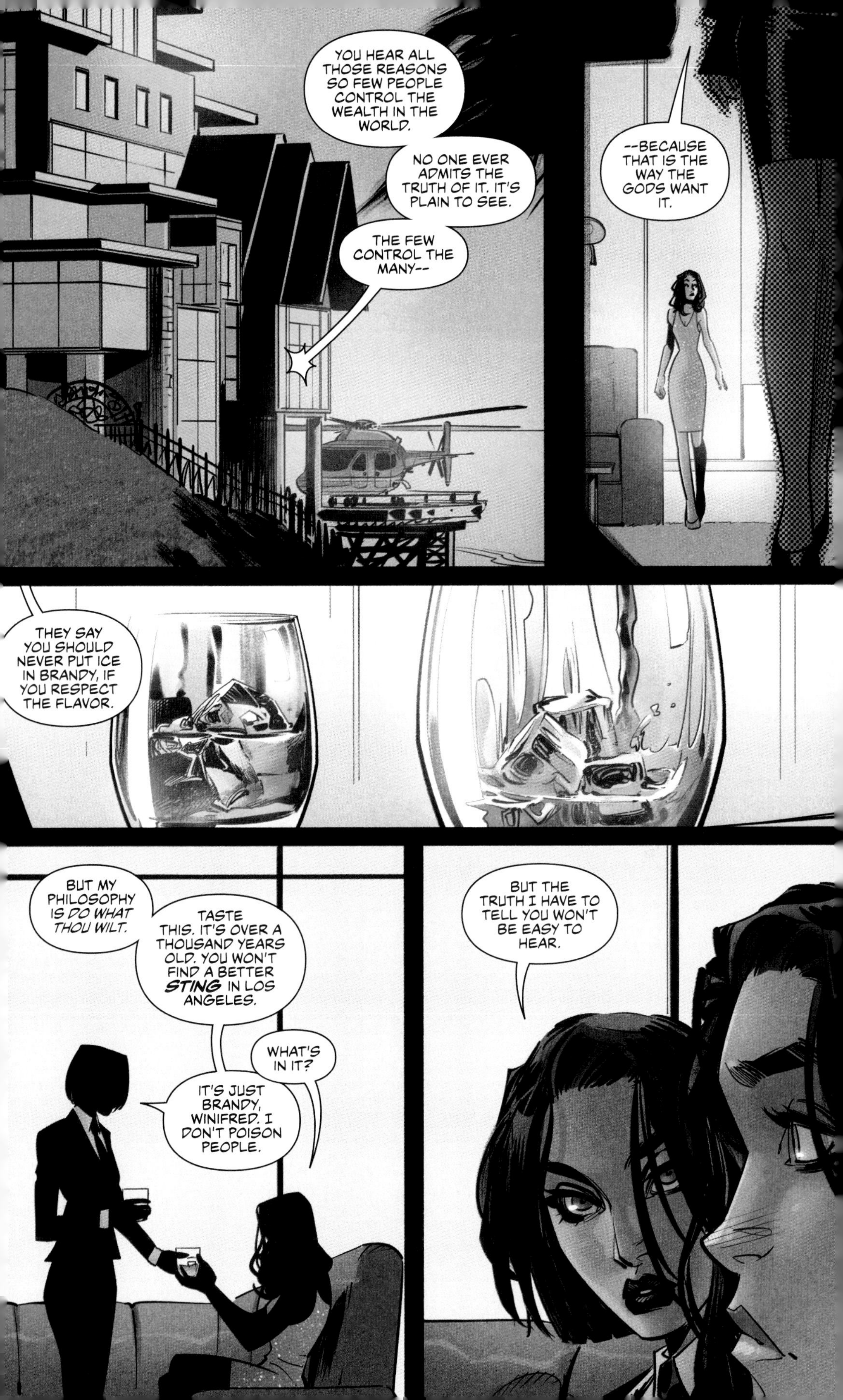

YOU HEAR ALL THOSE REASONS SO FEW PEOPLE CONTROL THE WEALTH IN THE WORLD.
NO ONE EVER ADMITS THE TRUTH OF IT. IT'S PLAIN TO SEE.
THE FEW CONTROL THE MANY--
--BECAUSE THAT IS THE WAY THE GODS WANT IT.
THEY SAY YOU SHOULD NEVER PUT ICE IN BRANDY, IF YOU RESPECT THE FLAVOR.
BUT MY PHILOSOPHY IS *DO WHAT THOU WILT.*
TASTE THIS. IT'S OVER A THOUSAND YEARS OLD. YOU WON'T FIND A BETTER ***STING*** IN LOS ANGELES.
WHAT'S IN IT?
IT'S JUST BRANDY, WINIFRED. I DON'T POISON PEOPLE.
BUT THE TRUTH I HAVE TO TELL YOU WON'T BE EASY TO HEAR.

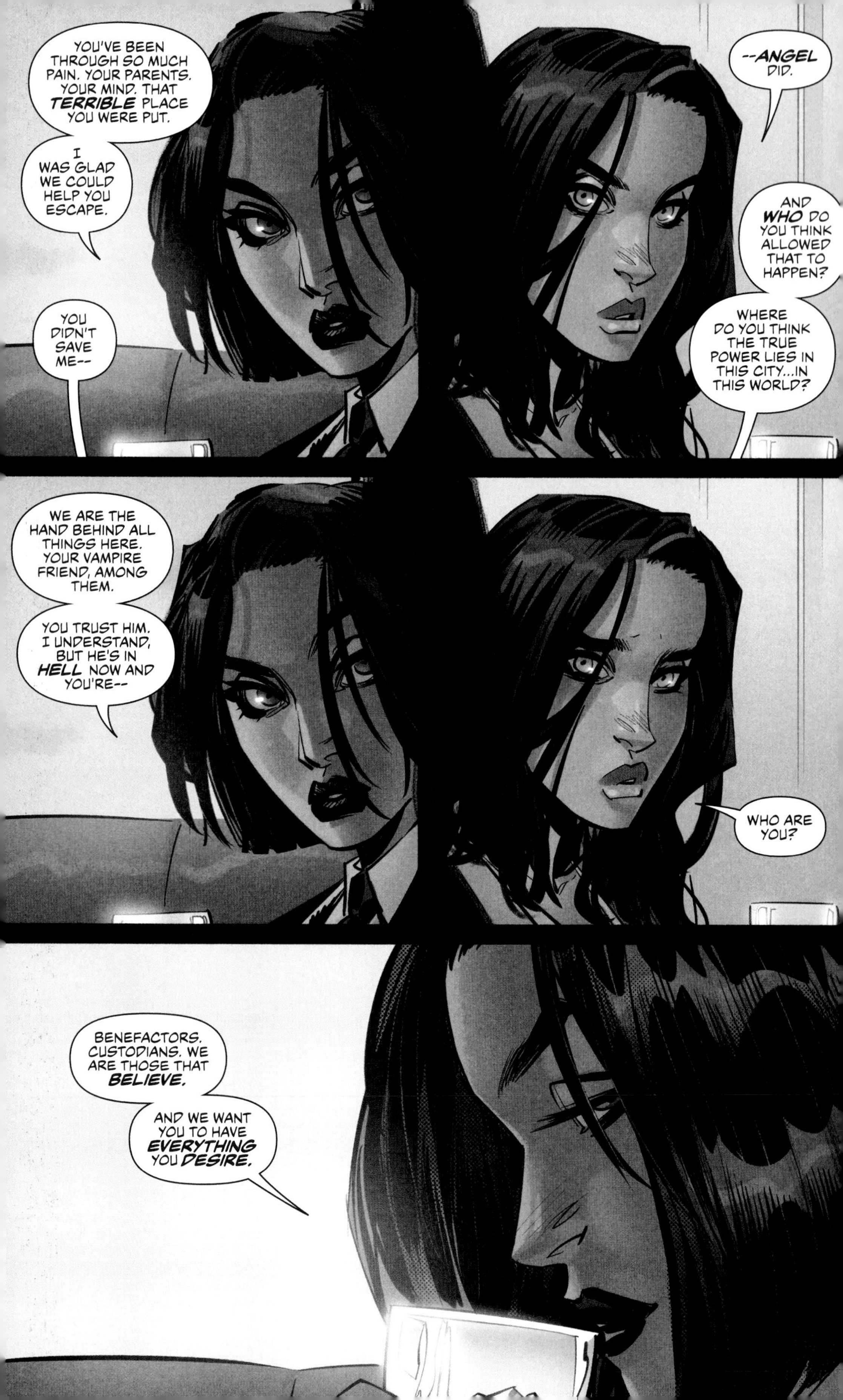

YOU'VE BEEN THROUGH SO MUCH PAIN. YOUR PARENTS. YOUR MIND. THAT TERRIBLE PLACE YOU WERE PUT.
I WAS GLAD WE COULD HELP YOU ESCAPE.
YOU DIDN'T SAVE ME--
--ANGEL DID.
AND WHO DO YOU THINK ALLOWED THAT TO HAPPEN?
WHERE DO YOU THINK THE TRUE POWER LIES IN THIS CITY...IN THIS WORLD?
WE ARE THE HAND BEHIND ALL THINGS HERE. YOUR VAMPIRE FRIEND, AMONG THEM.
YOU TRUST HIM. I UNDERSTAND, BUT HE'S IN HELL NOW AND YOU'RE--
WHO ARE YOU?
BENEFACTORS. CUSTODIANS. WE ARE THOSE THAT BELIEVE.
AND WE WANT YOU TO HAVE EVERYTHING YOU DESIRE.

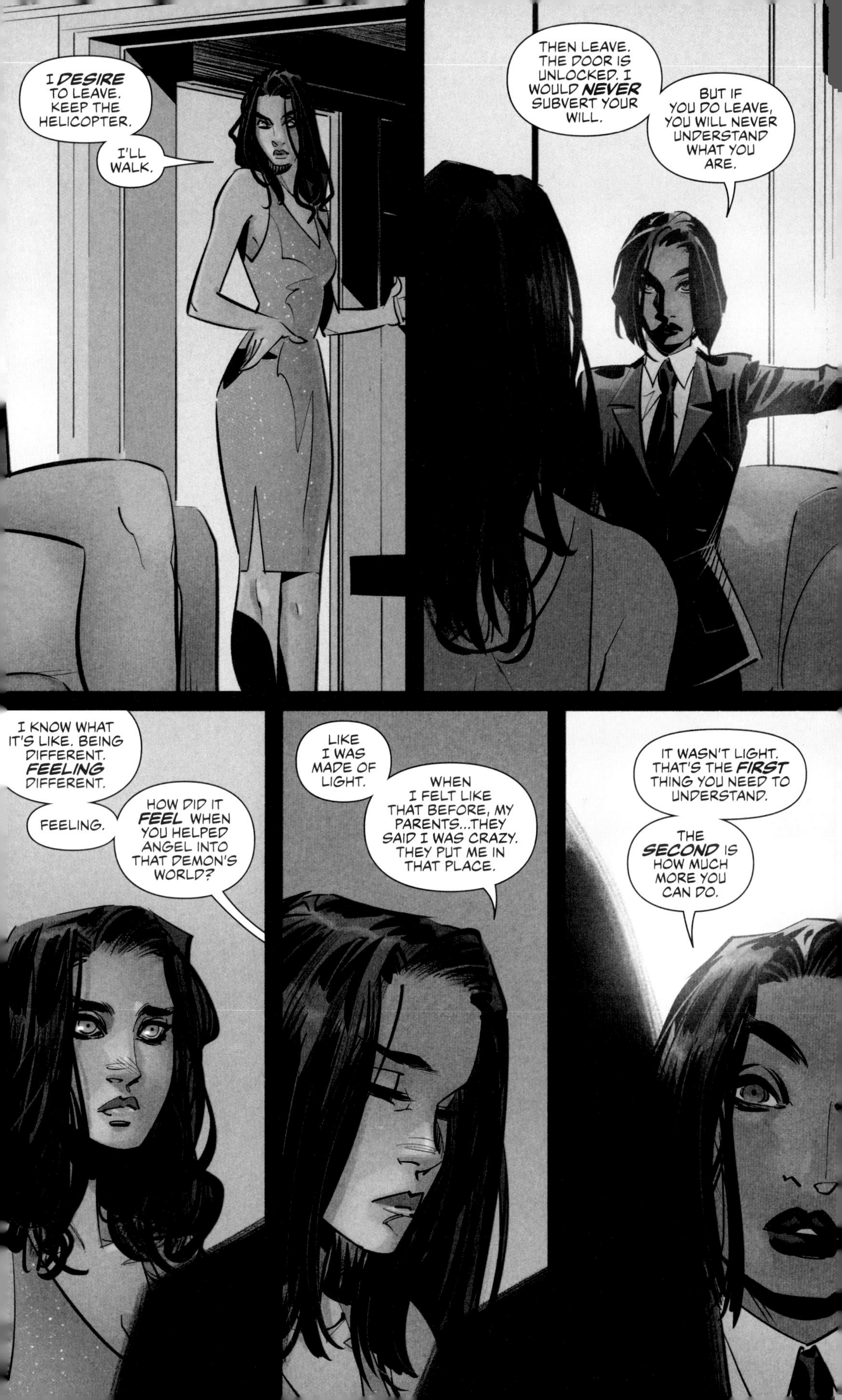
I DESIRE TO LEAVE. KEEP THE HELICOPTER.
I'LL WALK.
THEN LEAVE. THE DOOR IS UNLOCKED. I WOULD NEVER SUBVERT YOUR WILL.
BUT IF YOU DO LEAVE, YOU WILL NEVER UNDERSTAND WHAT YOU ARE.
I KNOW WHAT IT'S LIKE. BEING DIFFERENT. FEELING DIFFERENT.
FEELING.
HOW DID IT FEEL WHEN YOU HELPED ANGEL INTO THAT DEMON'S WORLD?
LIKE I WAS MADE OF LIGHT.
WHEN I FELT LIKE THAT BEFORE, MY PARENTS...THEY SAID I WAS CRAZY. THEY PUT ME IN THAT PLACE.
IT WASN'T LIGHT. THAT'S THE FIRST THING YOU NEED TO UNDERSTAND.
THE SECOND IS HOW MUCH MORE YOU CAN DO.

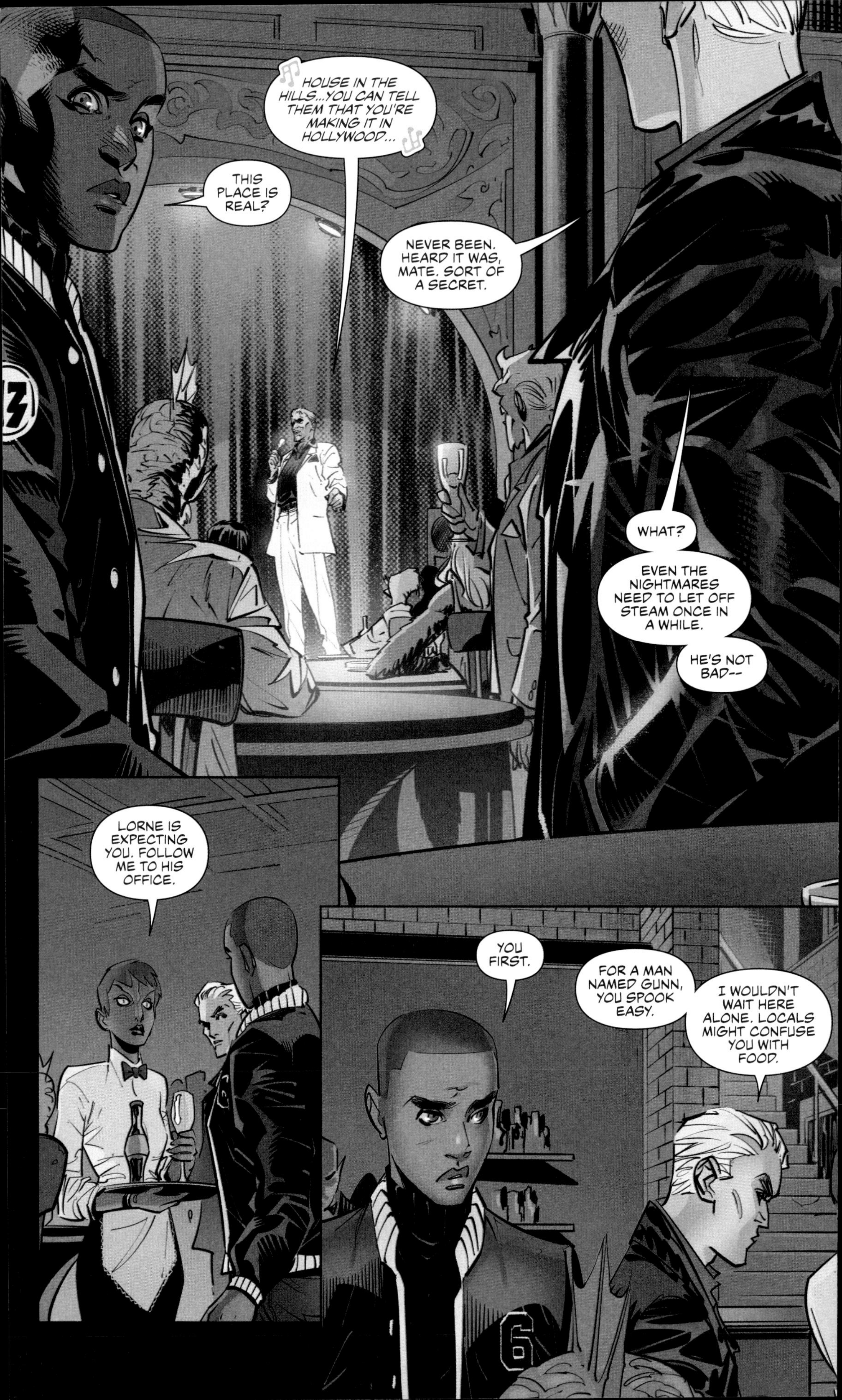
HOUSE IN THE HILLS...YOU CAN TELL THEM THAT YOU'RE MAKING IT IN HOLLYWOOD...
THIS PLACE IS REAL?
NEVER BEEN. HEARD IT WAS, MATE. SORT OF A SECRET.
WHAT?
EVEN THE NIGHTMARES NEED TO LET OFF STEAM ONCE IN A WHILE.
HE'S NOT BAD--
LORNE IS EXPECTING YOU. FOLLOW ME TO HIS OFFICE.
YOU FIRST.
FOR A MAN NAMED GUNN, YOU SPOOK EASY.
I WOULDN'T WAIT HERE ALONE. LOCALS MIGHT CONFUSE YOU WITH FOOD.

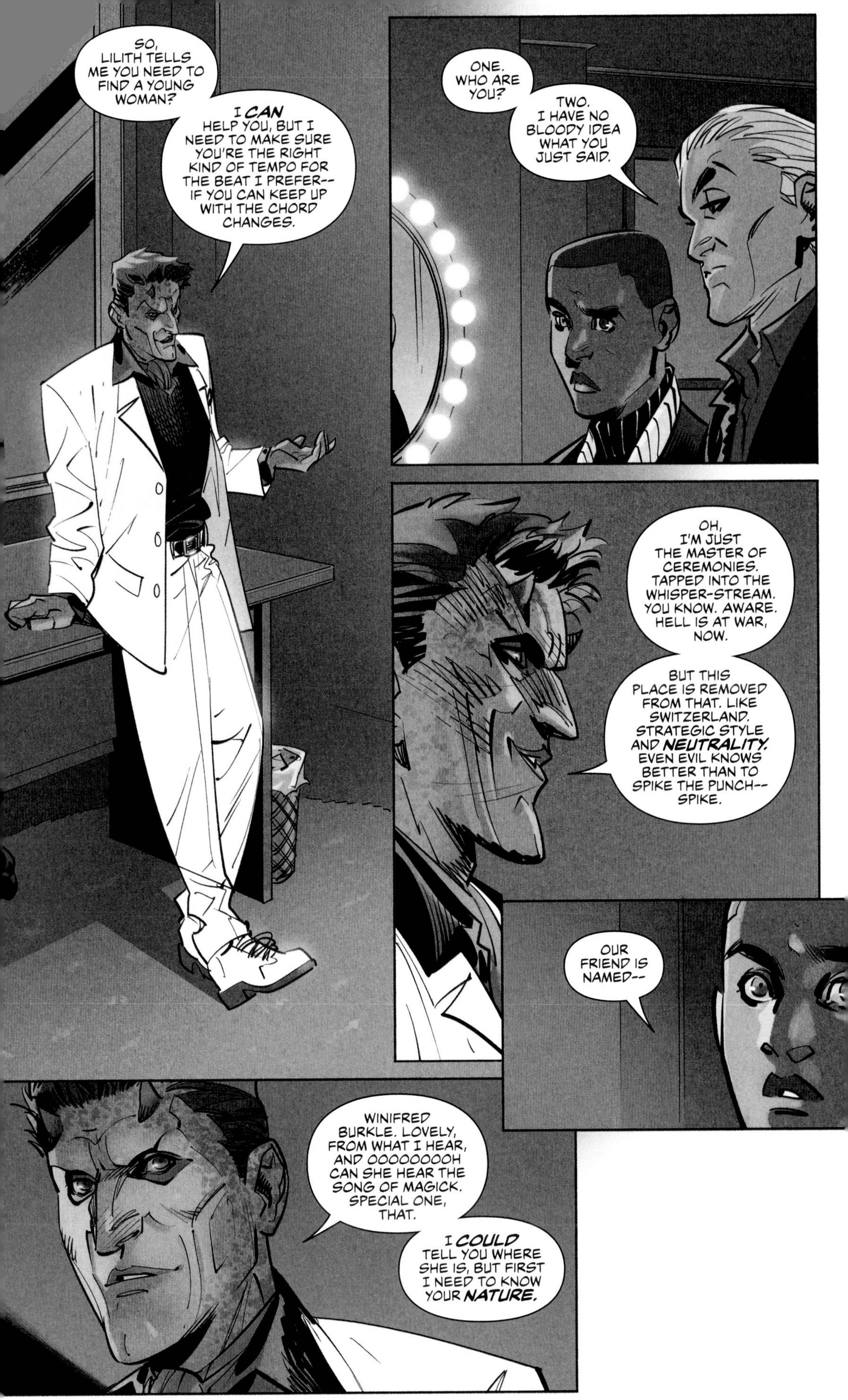
SO, LILITH TELLS ME YOU NEED TO FIND A YOUNG WOMAN?
I CAN HELP YOU, BUT I NEED TO MAKE SURE YOU'RE THE RIGHT KIND OF TEMPO FOR THE BEAT I PREFER-- IF YOU CAN KEEP UP WITH THE CHORD CHANGES.
ONE. WHO ARE YOU?
TWO. I HAVE NO BLOODY IDEA WHAT YOU JUST SAID.
OH, I'M JUST THE MASTER OF CEREMONIES. TAPPED INTO THE WHISPER-STREAM. YOU KNOW. AWARE. HELL IS AT WAR, NOW.
BUT THIS PLACE IS REMOVED FROM THAT. LIKE SWITZERLAND. STRATEGIC STYLE AND NEUTRALITY. EVEN EVIL KNOWS BETTER THAN TO SPIKE THE PUNCH-- SPIKE.
OUR FRIEND IS NAMED--
WINIFRED BURKLE. LOVELY, FROM WHAT I HEAR, AND OOOOOOOOH CAN SHE HEAR THE SONG OF MAGICK. SPECIAL ONE, THAT.
I COULD TELL YOU WHERE SHE IS, BUT FIRST I NEED TO KNOW YOUR NATURE.

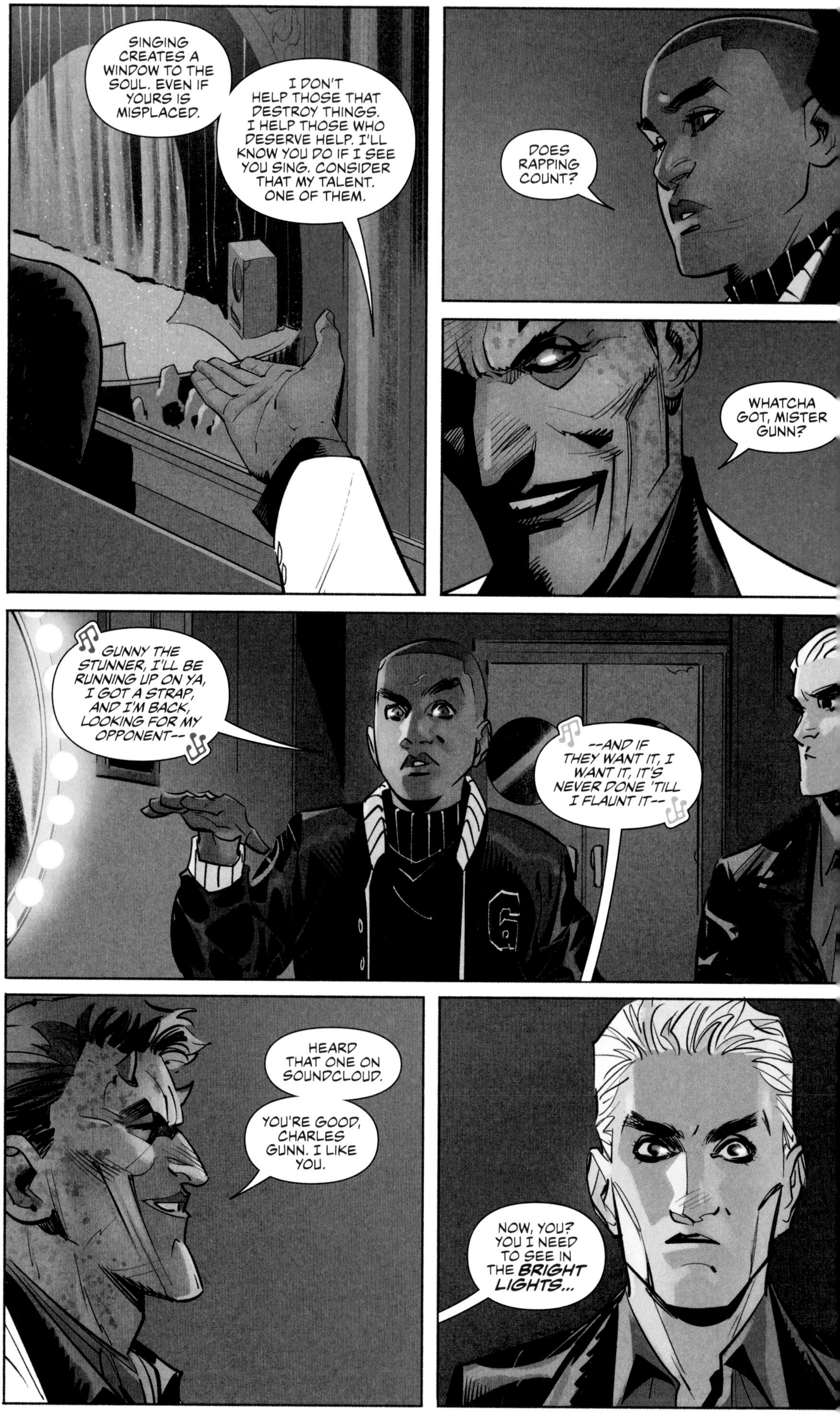
SINGING CREATES A WINDOW TO THE SOUL. EVEN IF YOURS IS MISPLACED.
I DON'T HELP THOSE THAT DESTROY THINGS. I HELP THOSE WHO DESERVE HELP. I'LL KNOW YOU DO IF I SEE YOU SING. CONSIDER THAT MY TALENT. ONE OF THEM.
DOES RAPPING COUNT?
WHATCHA GOT, MISTER GUNN?
GUNNY THE STUNNER, I'LL BE RUNNING UP ON YA, I GOT A STRAP, AND I'M BACK, LOOKING FOR MY OPPONENT--
--AND IF THEY WANT IT, I WANT IT, IT'S NEVER DONE 'TILL I FLAUNT IT--
HEARD THAT ONE ON SOUNDCLOUD.
YOU'RE GOOD, CHARLES GUNN. I LIKE YOU.
NOW, YOU? YOU I NEED TO SEE IN THE BRIGHT LIGHTS...

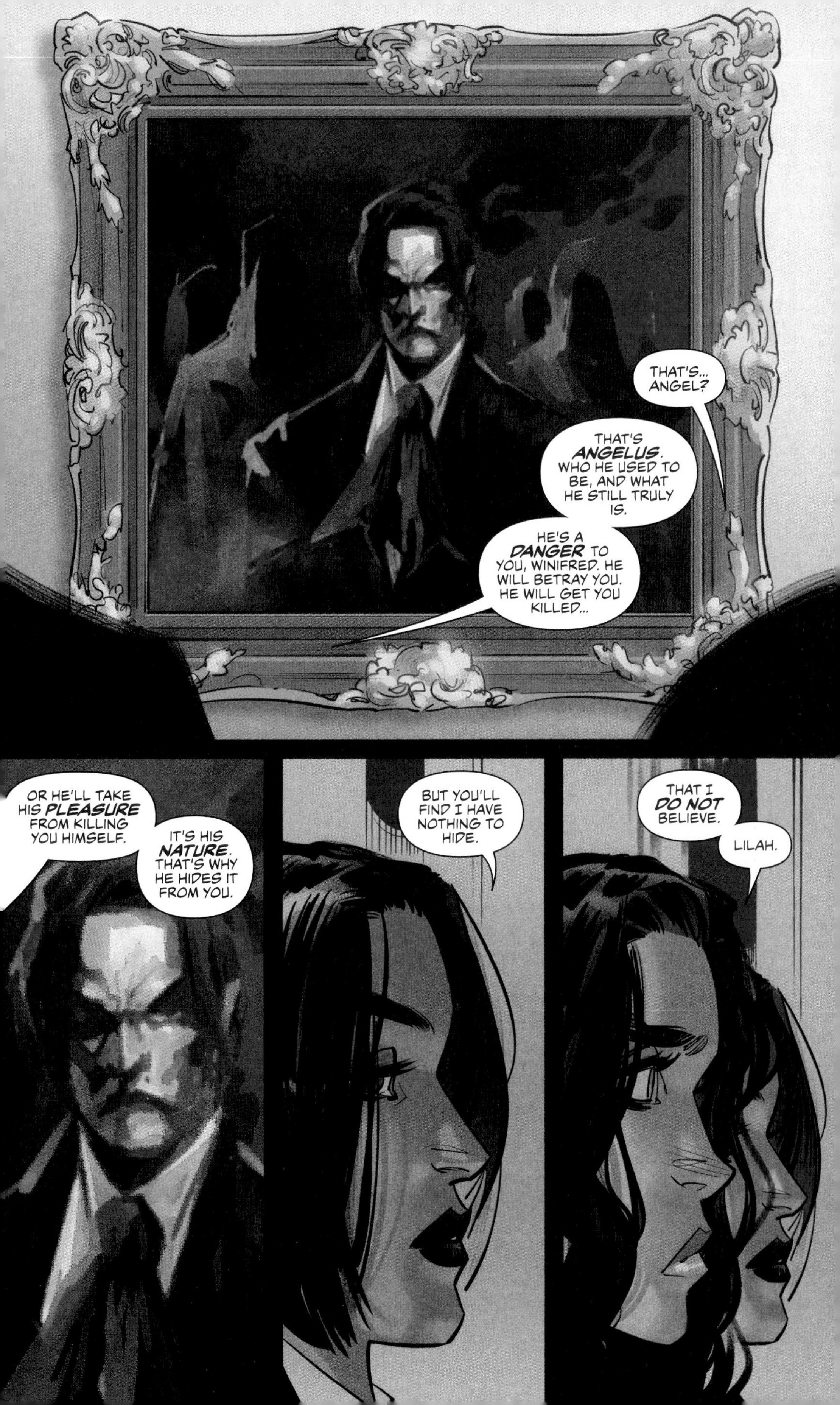

THAT'S... ANGEL?
THAT'S ANGELUS. WHO HE USED TO BE, AND WHAT HE STILL TRULY IS.
HE'S A DANGER TO YOU, WINIFRED. HE WILL BETRAY YOU. HE WILL GET YOU KILLED...
OR HE'LL TAKE HIS PLEASURE FROM KILLING YOU HIMSELF.
IT'S HIS NATURE. THAT'S WHY HE HIDES IT FROM YOU.
BUT YOU'LL FIND I HAVE NOTHING TO HIDE.
THAT I DO NOT BELIEVE.
LILAH.

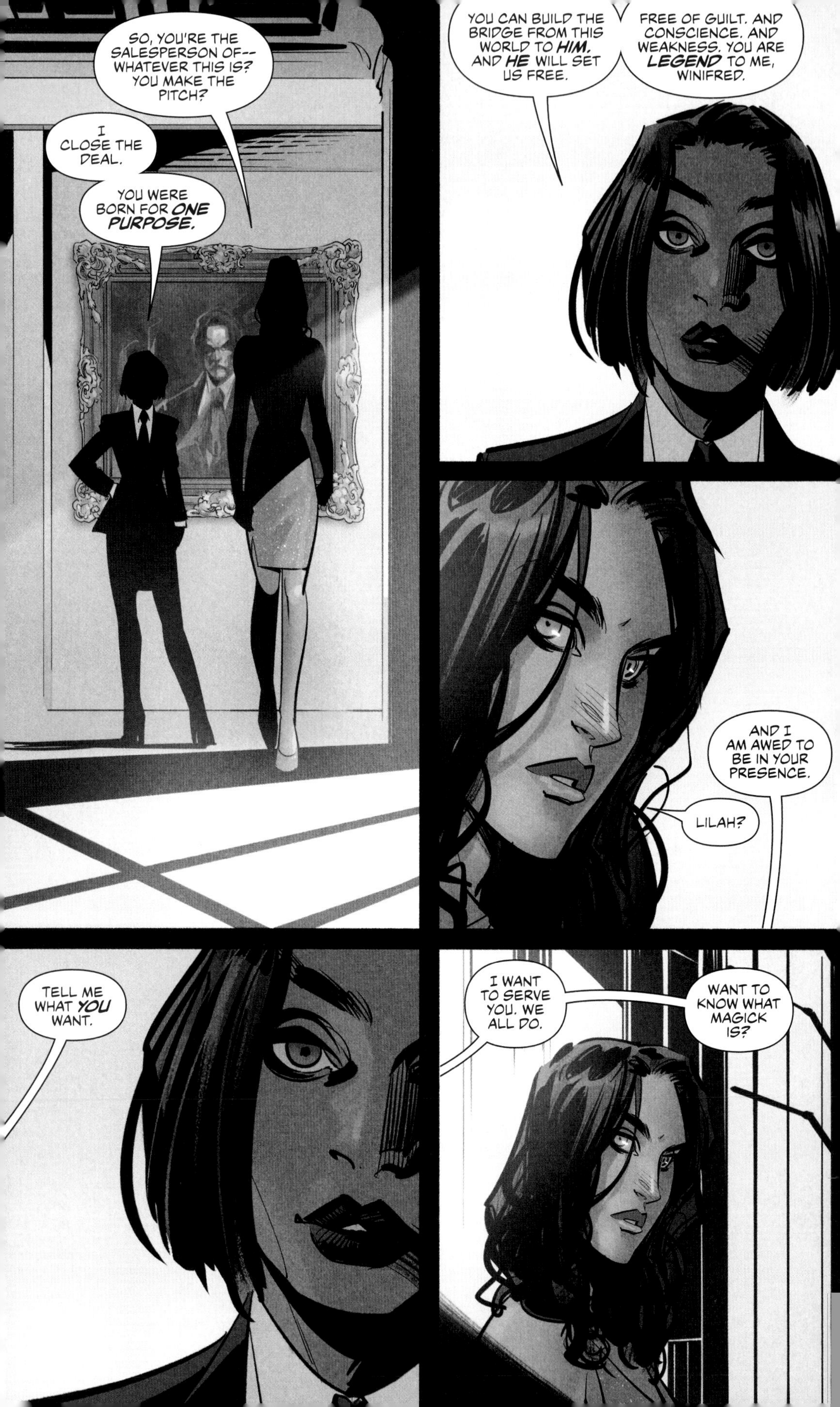
SO, YOU'RE THE SALESPERSON OF-- WHATEVER THIS IS? YOU MAKE THE PITCH?
I CLOSE THE DEAL.
YOU WERE BORN FOR ONE PURPOSE.
YOU CAN BUILD THE BRIDGE FROM THIS WORLD TO HIM. AND HE WILL SET US FREE.
FREE OF GUILT. AND CONSCIENCE. AND WEAKNESS. YOU ARE LEGEND TO ME, WINIFRED.
AND I AM AWED TO BE IN YOUR PRESENCE.
LILAH?
TELL ME WHAT YOU WANT.
I WANT TO SERVE YOU. WE ALL DO.
WANT TO KNOW WHAT MAGICK IS?

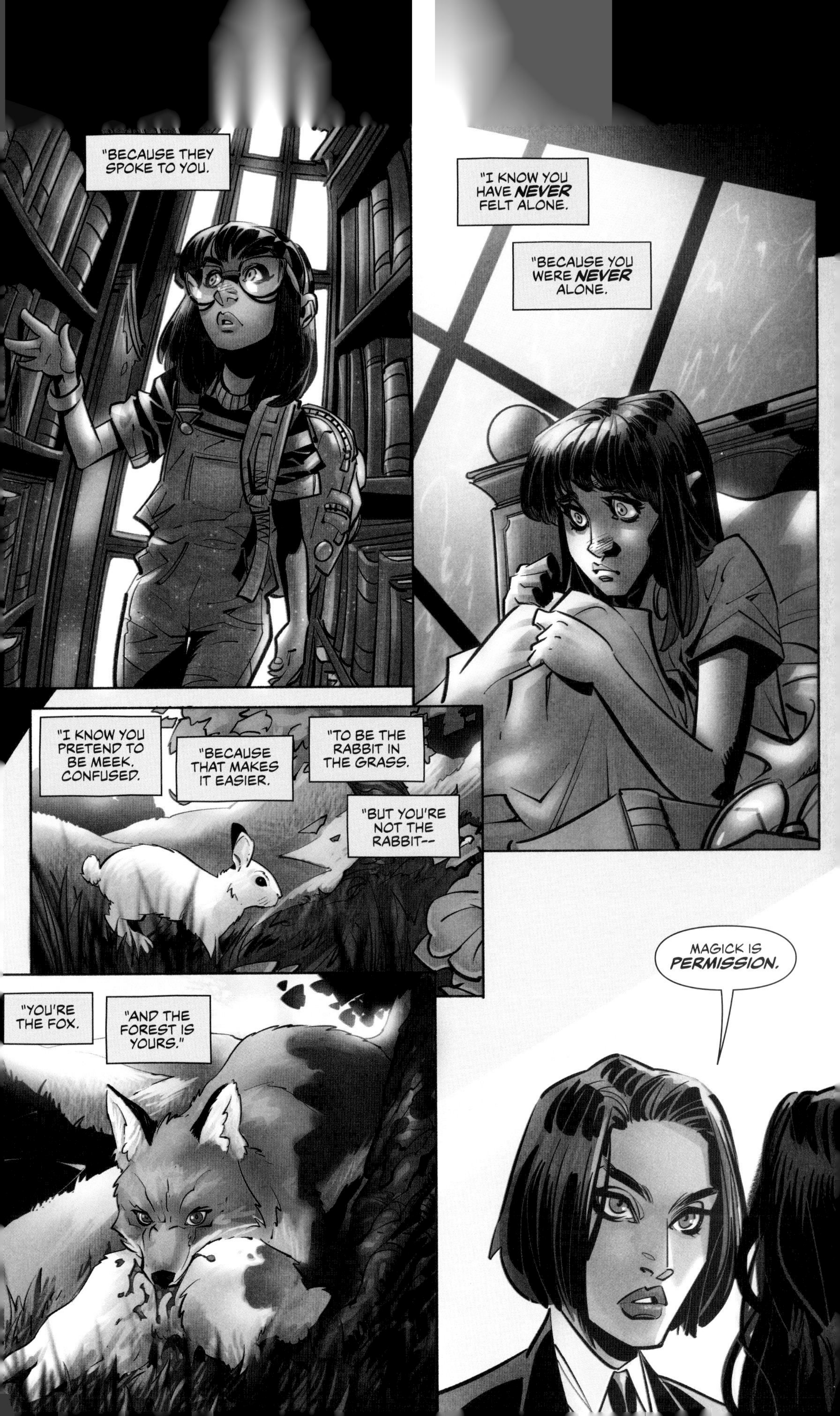
"BECAUSE THEY SPOKE TO YOU.
"I KNOW YOU HAVE NEVER FELT ALONE.
"BECAUSE YOU WERE NEVER ALONE.
"I KNOW YOU PRETEND TO BE MEEK. CONFUSED.
"BECAUSE THAT MAKES IT EASIER.
"TO BE THE RABBIT IN THE GRASS.
"BUT YOU'RE NOT THE RABBIT--
"YOU'RE THE FOX.
"AND THE FOREST IS YOURS."
MAGICK IS PERMISSION.

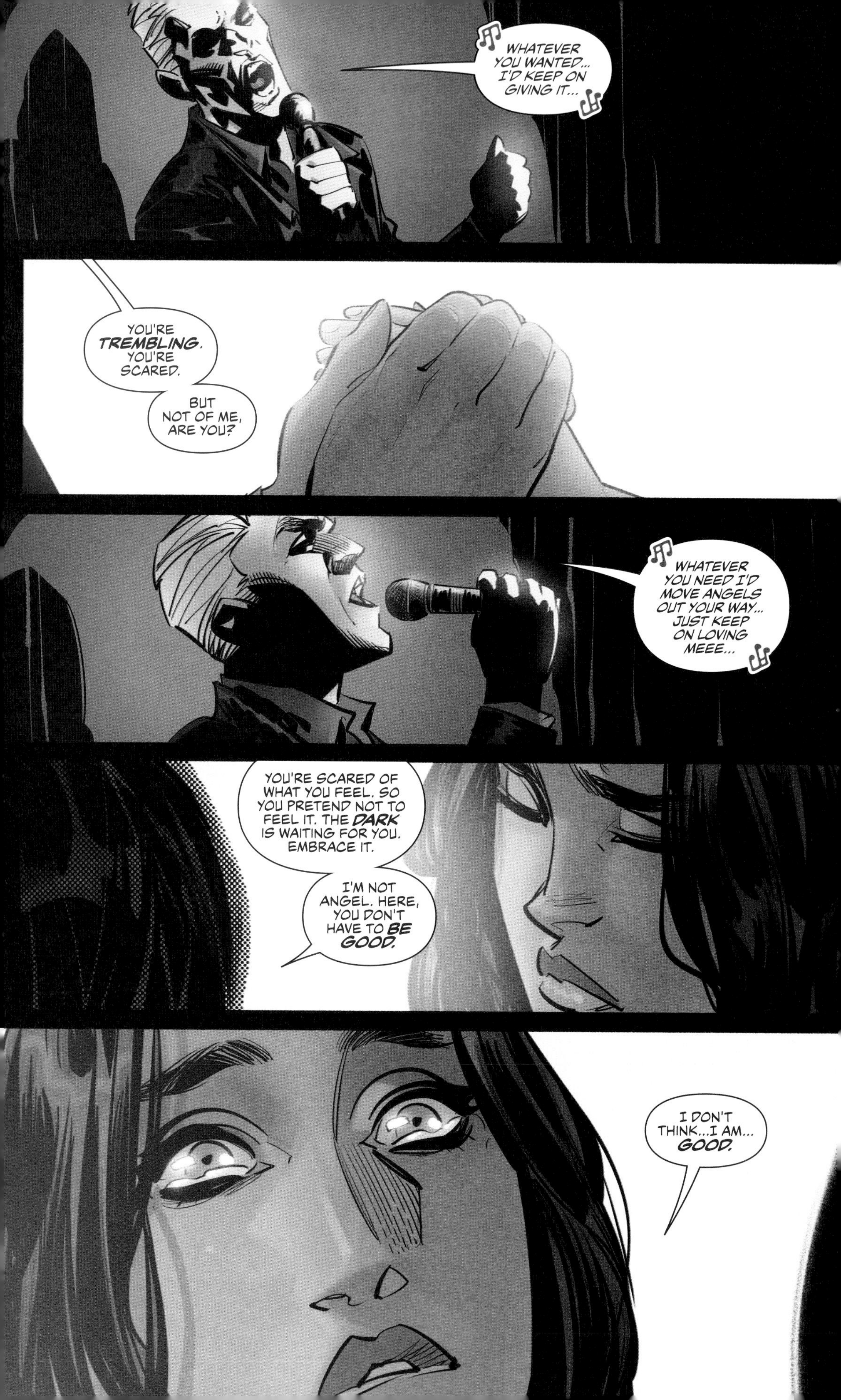
WHATEVER YOU WANTED... I'D KEEP ON GIVING IT...
YOU'RE TREMBLING. YOU'RE SCARED.
BUT NOT OF ME, ARE YOU?
WHATEVER YOU NEED I'D MOVE ANGELS OUT YOUR WAY... JUST KEEP ON LOVING MEEE...
YOU'RE SCARED OF WHAT YOU FEEL. SO YOU PRETEND NOT TO FEEL IT. THE DARK IS WAITING FOR YOU. EMBRACE IT.
I'M NOT ANGEL. HERE, YOU DON'T HAVE TO BE GOOD.
I DON'T THINK...I AM... GOOD.

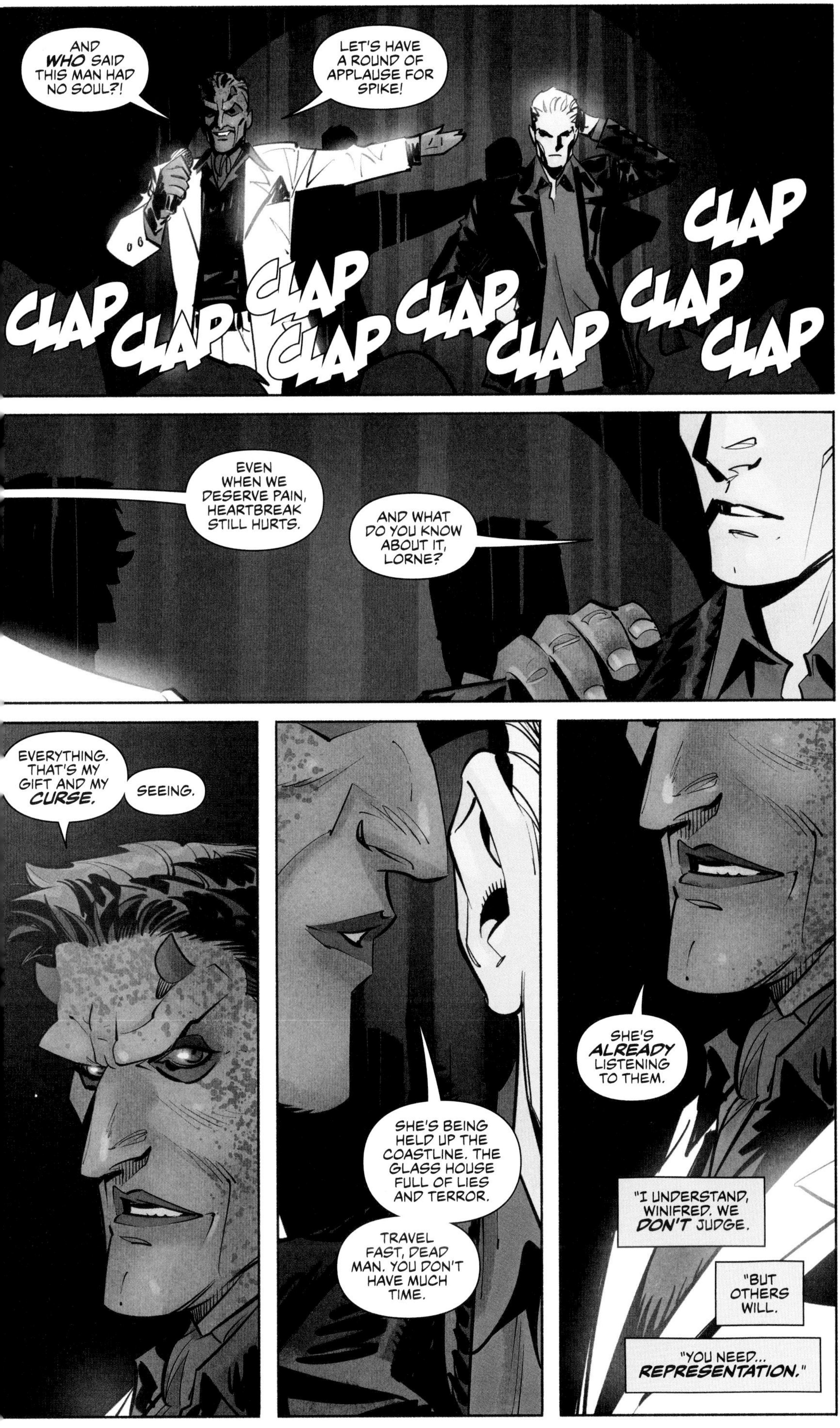
AND WHO SAID THIS MAN HAD NO SOUL?!
LET'S HAVE A ROUND OF APPLAUSE FOR SPIKE!
CLAP CLAP CLAP CLAP CLAP CLAP CLAP CLAP CLAP
EVEN WHEN WE DESERVE PAIN, HEARTBREAK STILL HURTS.
AND WHAT DO YOU KNOW ABOUT IT, LORNE?
EVERYTHING. THAT'S MY GIFT AND MY CURSE.
SEEING.
SHE'S BEING HELD UP THE COASTLINE. THE GLASS HOUSE FULL OF LIES AND TERROR.
TRAVEL FAST, DEAD MAN. YOU DON'T HAVE MUCH TIME.
SHE'S ALREADY LISTENING TO THEM.
"I UNDERSTAND, WINIFRED. WE DON'T JUDGE.
"BUT OTHERS WILL.
"YOU NEED... REPRESENTATION."

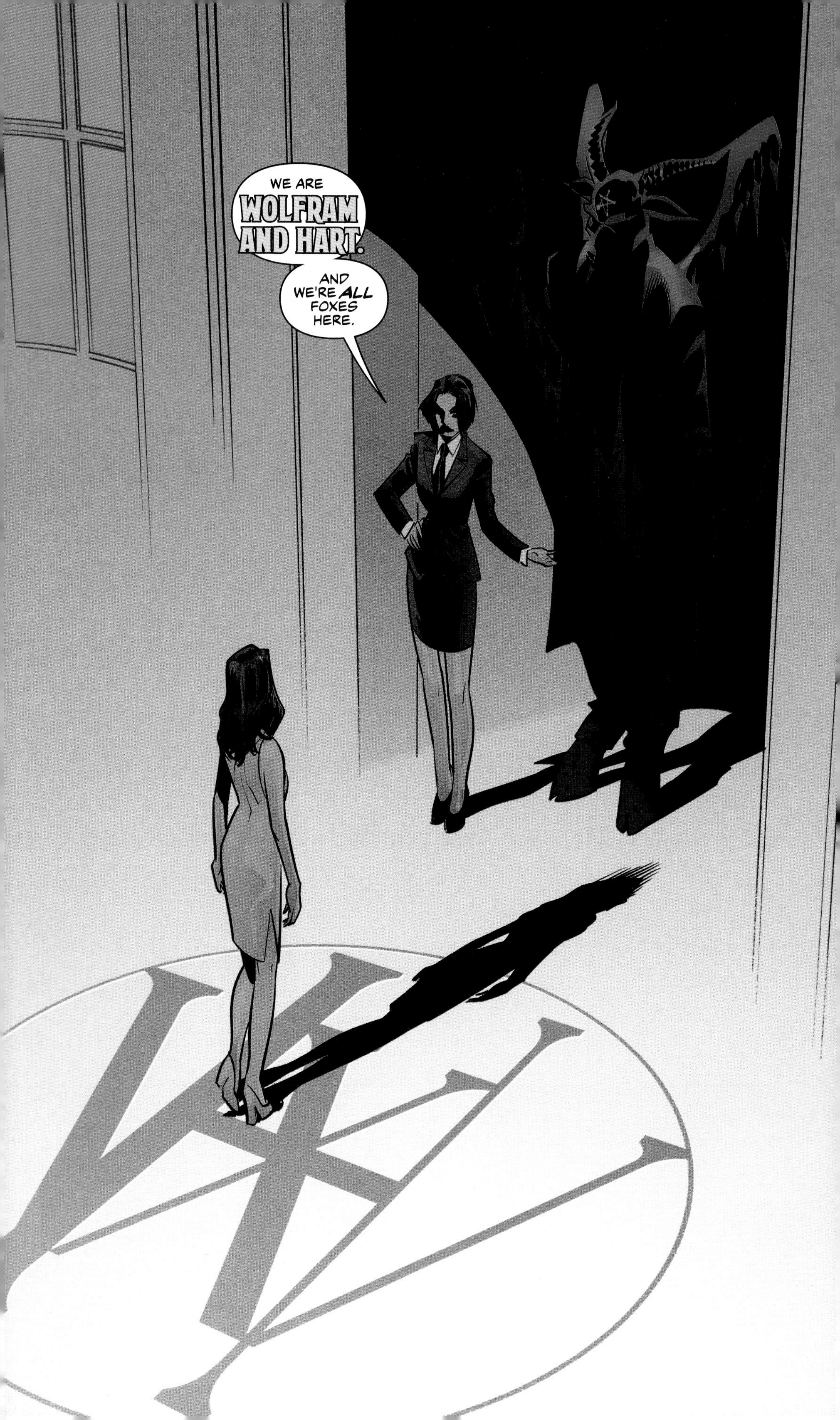
WE ARE WOLFRAM AND HART.
AND WE'RE ALL FOXES HERE.

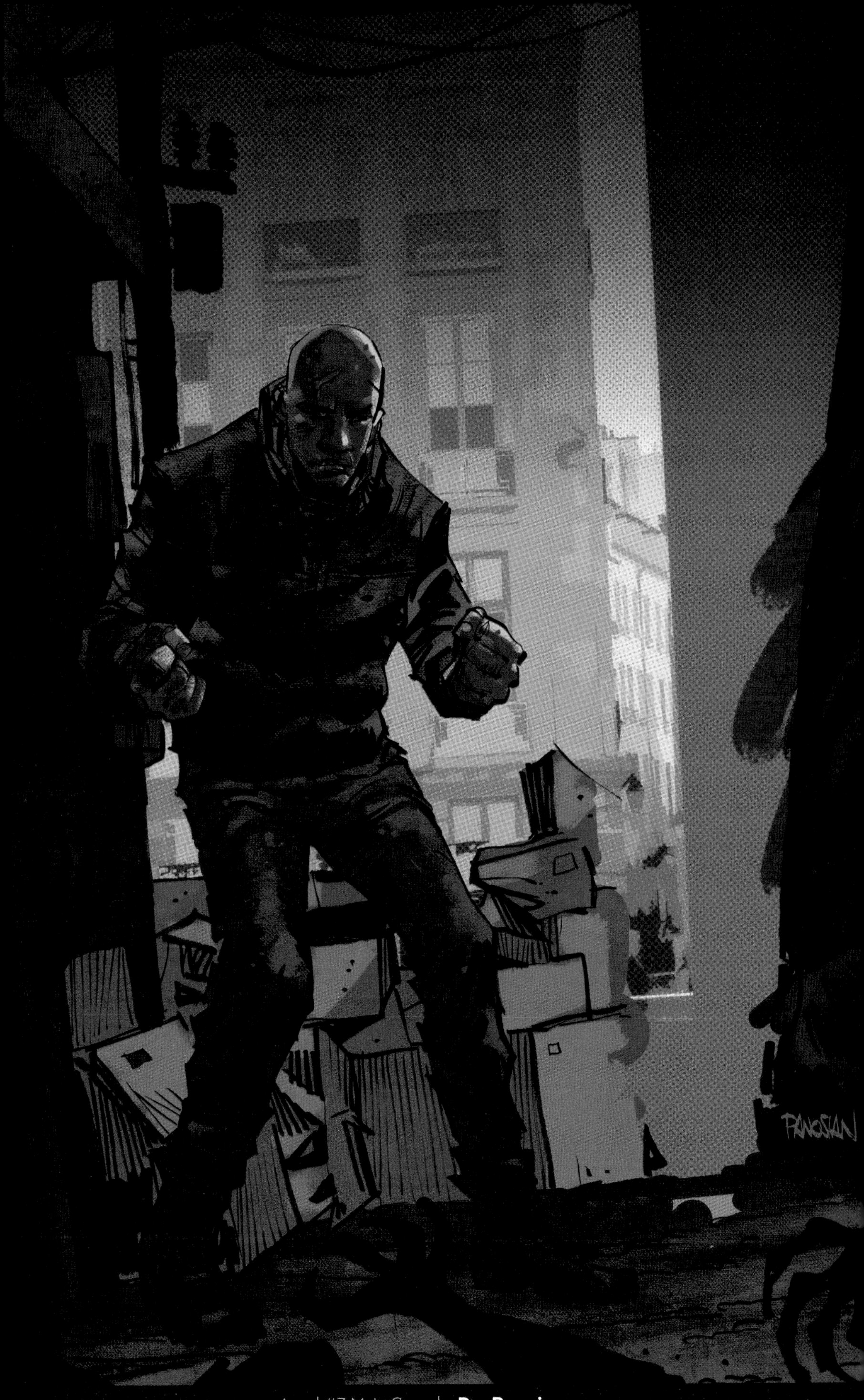
PANOSIAN

Angel #7 Main Cover by **Dan Panosian**

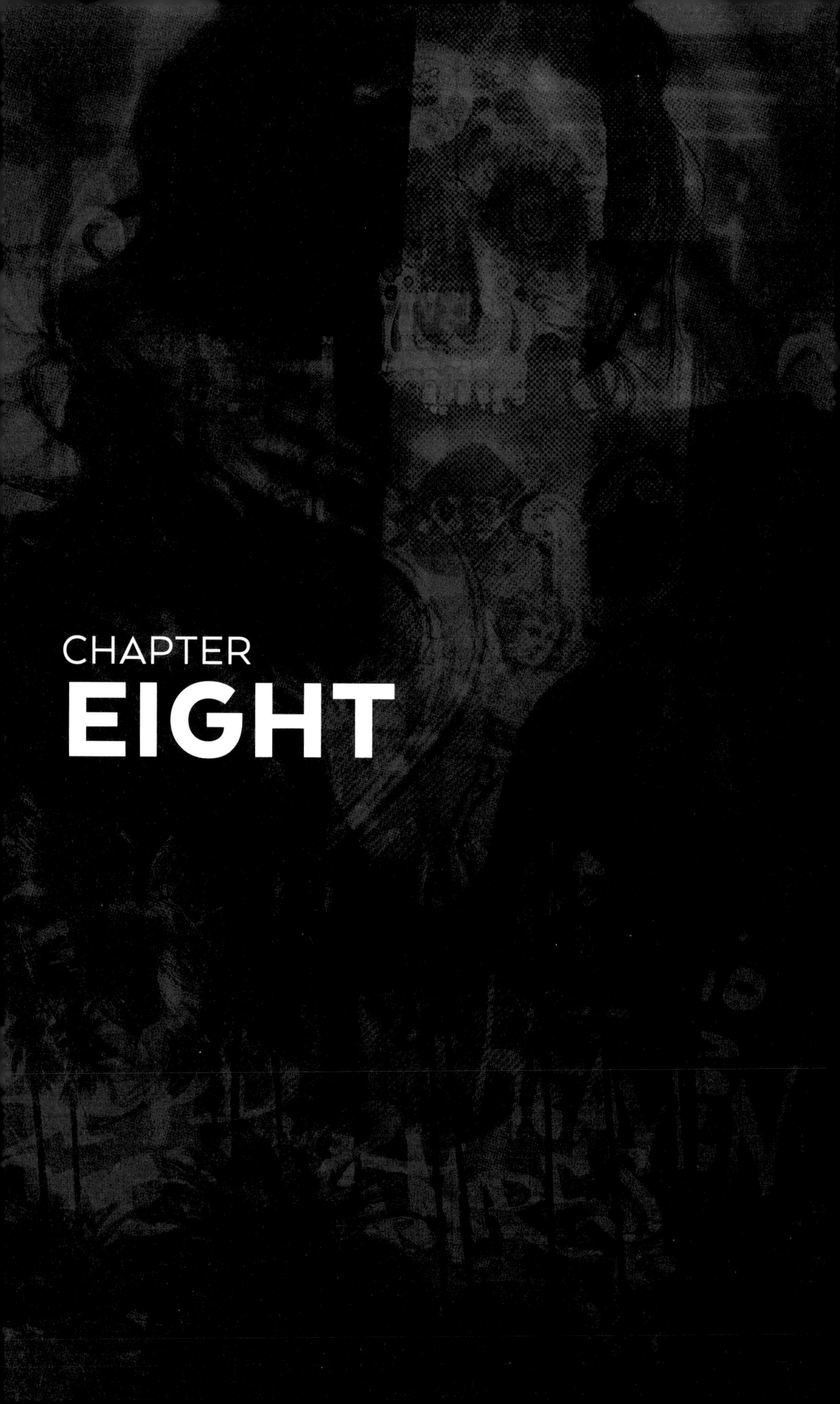

CHAPTER EIGHT

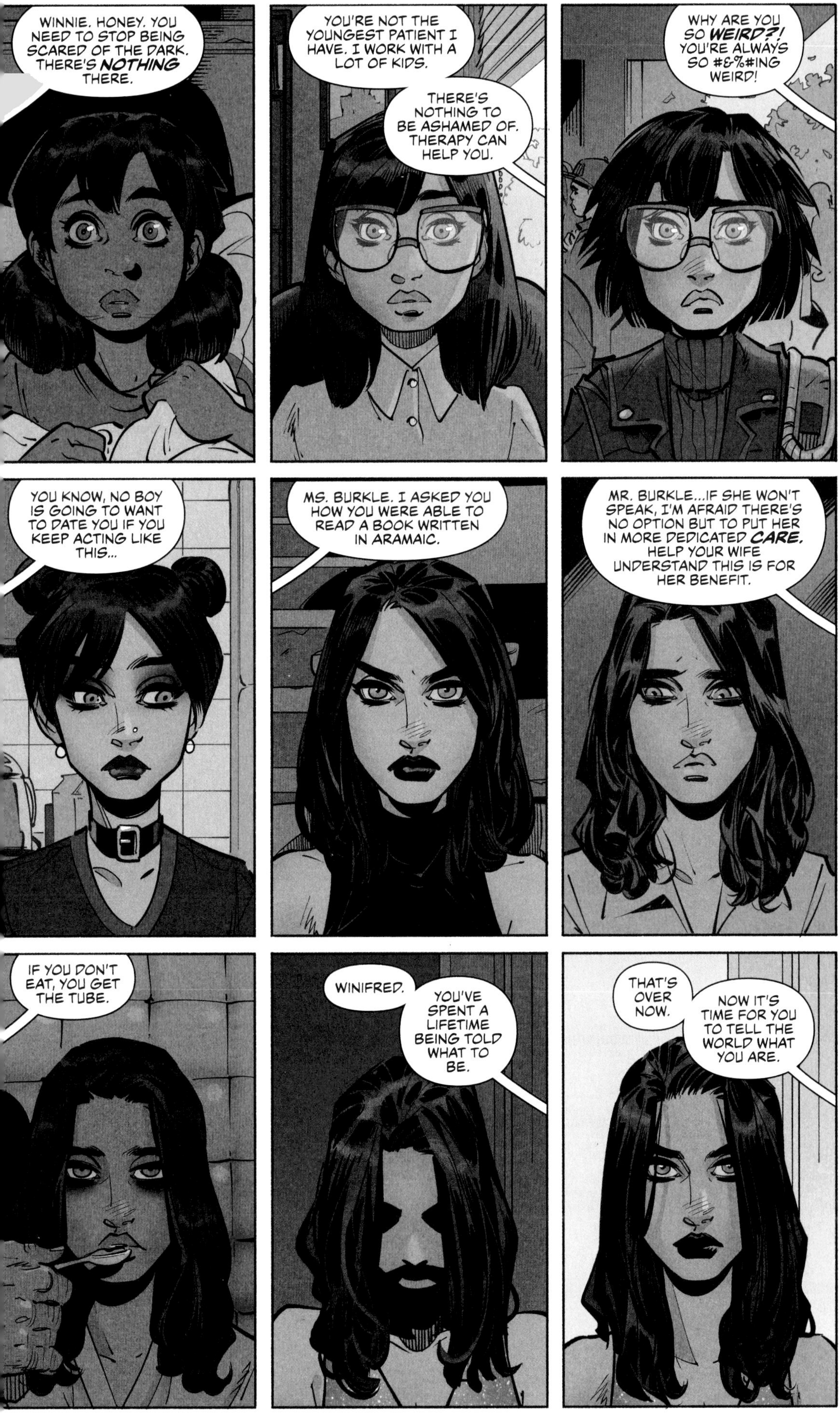
WINNIE. HONEY. YOU NEED TO STOP BEING SCARED OF THE DARK. THERE'S NOTHING THERE.
YOU'RE NOT THE YOUNGEST PATIENT I HAVE. I WORK WITH A LOT OF KIDS.
THERE'S NOTHING TO BE ASHAMED OF. THERAPY CAN HELP YOU.
WHY ARE YOU SO WEIRD?! YOU'RE ALWAYS SO #&%#ING WEIRD!
YOU KNOW, NO BOY IS GOING TO WANT TO DATE YOU IF YOU KEEP ACTING LIKE THIS...
MS. BURKLE. I ASKED YOU HOW YOU WERE ABLE TO READ A BOOK WRITTEN IN ARAMAIC.
MR. BURKLE...IF SHE WON'T SPEAK, I'M AFRAID THERE'S NO OPTION BUT TO PUT HER IN MORE DEDICATED CARE. HELP YOUR WIFE UNDERSTAND THIS IS FOR HER BENEFIT.
IF YOU DON'T EAT, YOU GET THE TUBE.
WINIFRED.
YOU'VE SPENT A LIFETIME BEING TOLD WHAT TO BE.
THAT'S OVER NOW.
NOW IT'S TIME FOR YOU TO TELL THE WORLD WHAT YOU ARE.

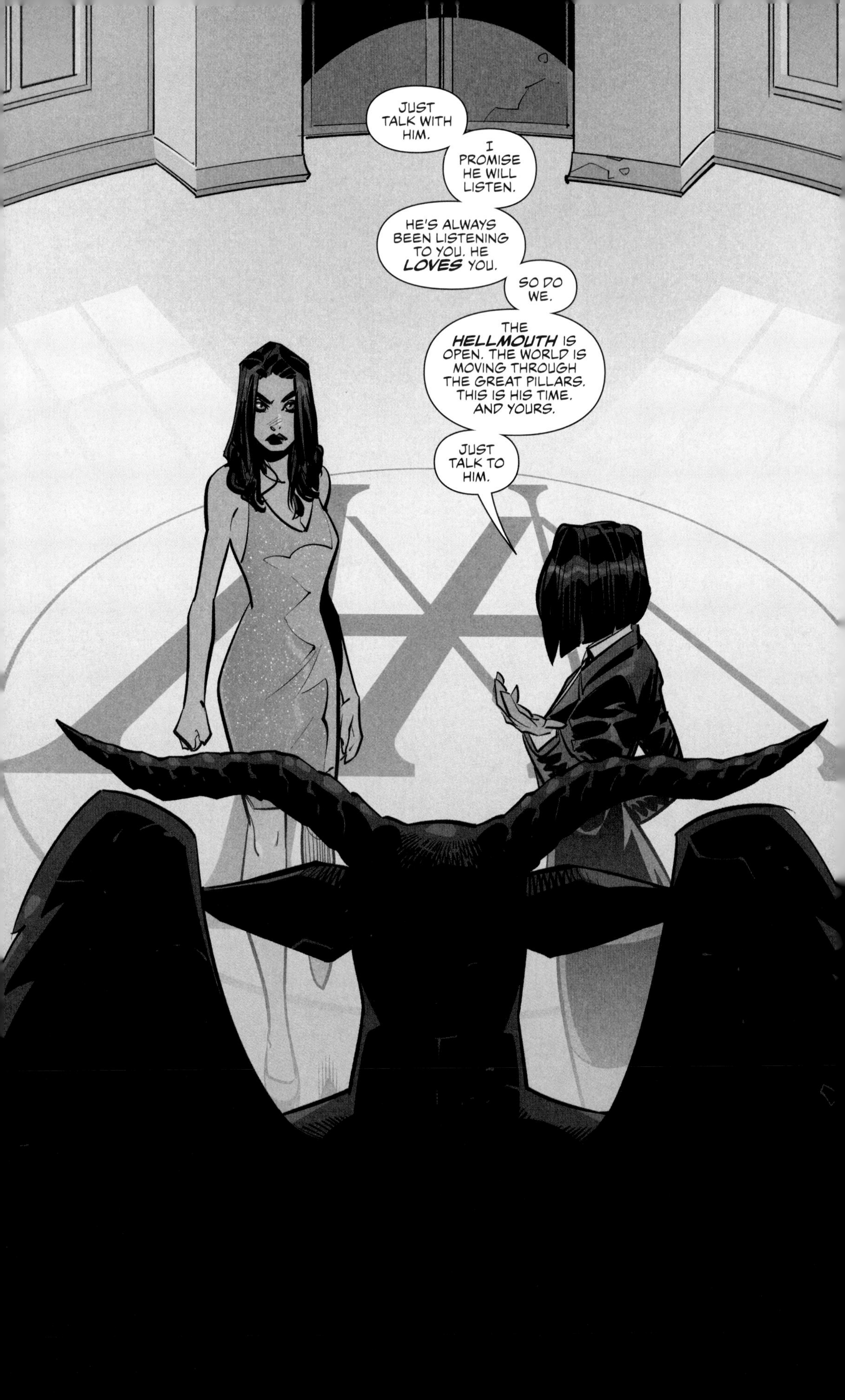
JUST TALK WITH HIM.
I PROMISE HE WILL LISTEN.
HE'S ALWAYS BEEN LISTENING TO YOU. HE LOVES YOU.
SO DO WE.
THE HELLMOUTH IS OPEN. THE WORLD IS MOVING THROUGH THE GREAT PILLARS. THIS IS HIS TIME. AND YOURS.
JUST TALK TO HIM.

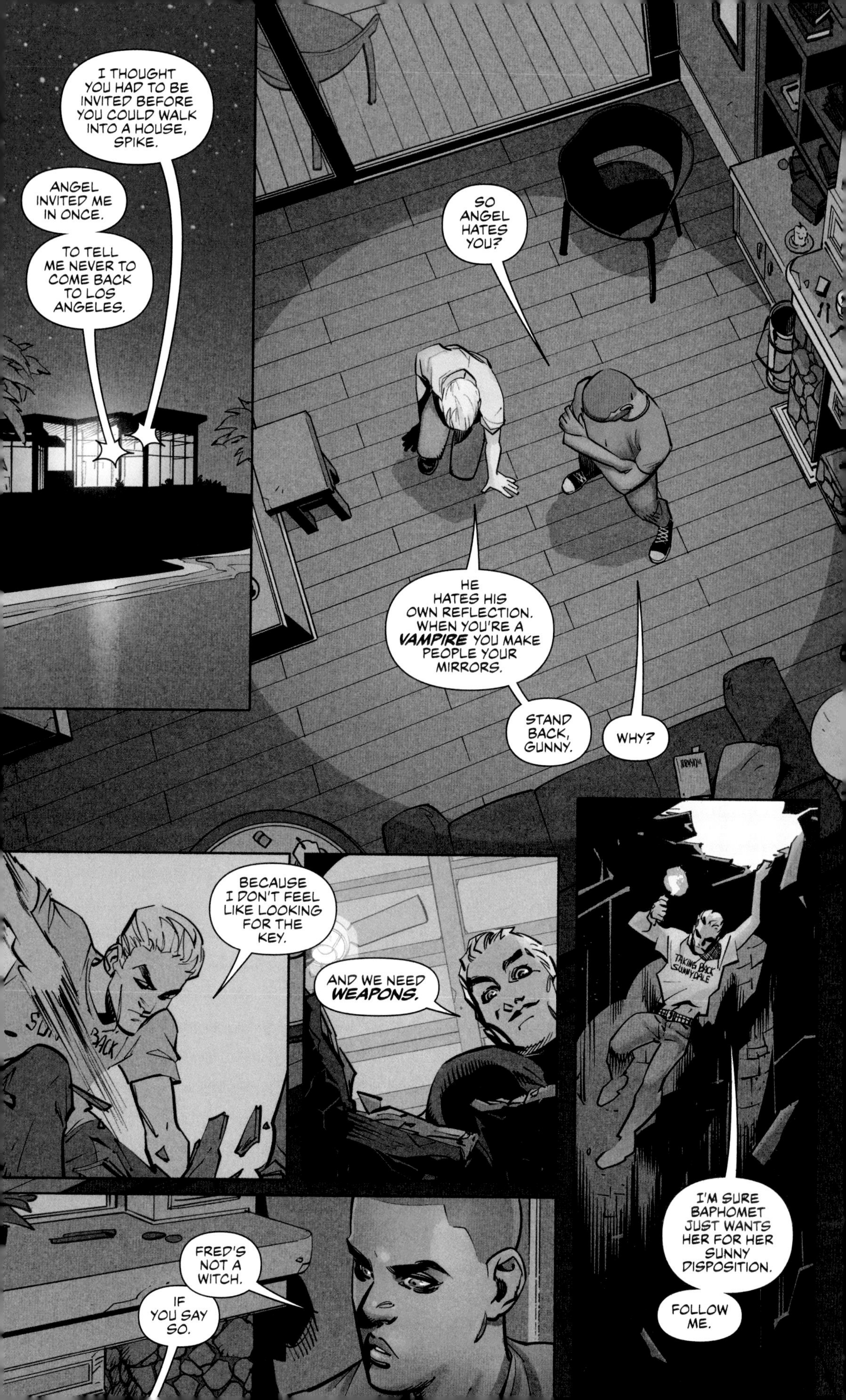
I THOUGHT YOU HAD TO BE INVITED BEFORE YOU COULD WALK INTO A HOUSE, SPIKE.
ANGEL INVITED ME IN ONCE.
TO TELL ME NEVER TO COME BACK TO LOS ANGELES.
SO ANGEL HATES YOU?
HE HATES HIS OWN REFLECTION. WHEN YOU'RE A VAMPIRE YOU MAKE PEOPLE YOUR MIRRORS.
STAND BACK, GUNNY.
WHY?
BECAUSE I DON'T FEEL LIKE LOOKING FOR THE KEY.
AND WE NEED WEAPONS.
TAKING BACK SUNNYDALE
FRED'S NOT A WITCH.
IF YOU SAY SO.
I'M SURE BAPHOMET JUST WANTS HER FOR HER SUNNY DISPOSITION.
FOLLOW ME.

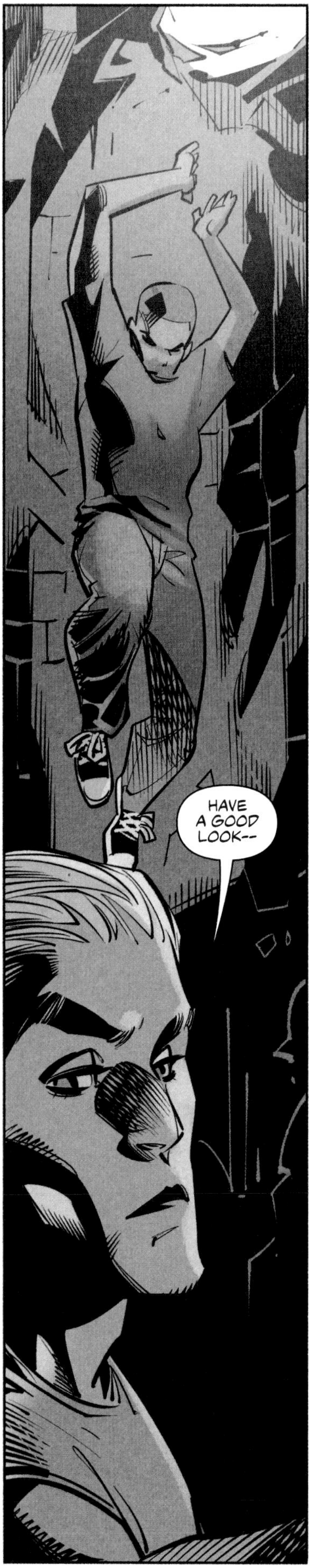
HAVE A GOOD LOOK--

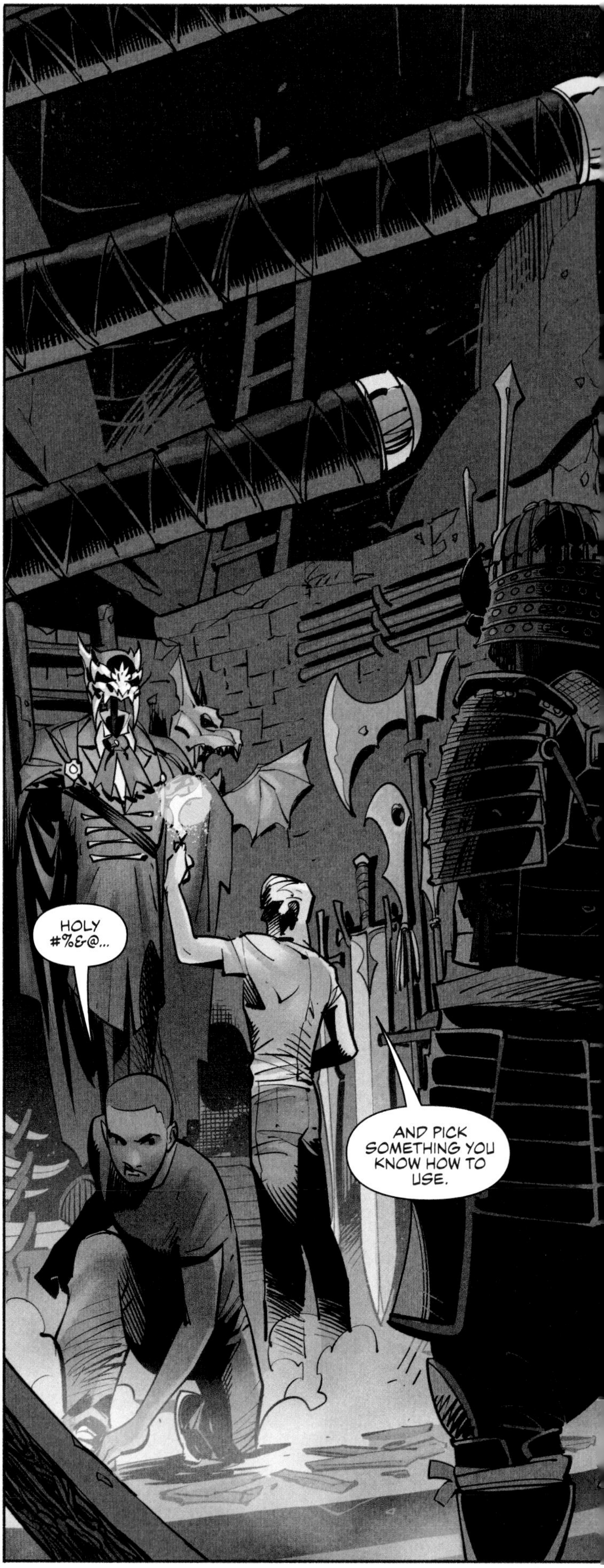
HOLY #%&@...
AND PICK SOMETHING YOU KNOW HOW TO USE.

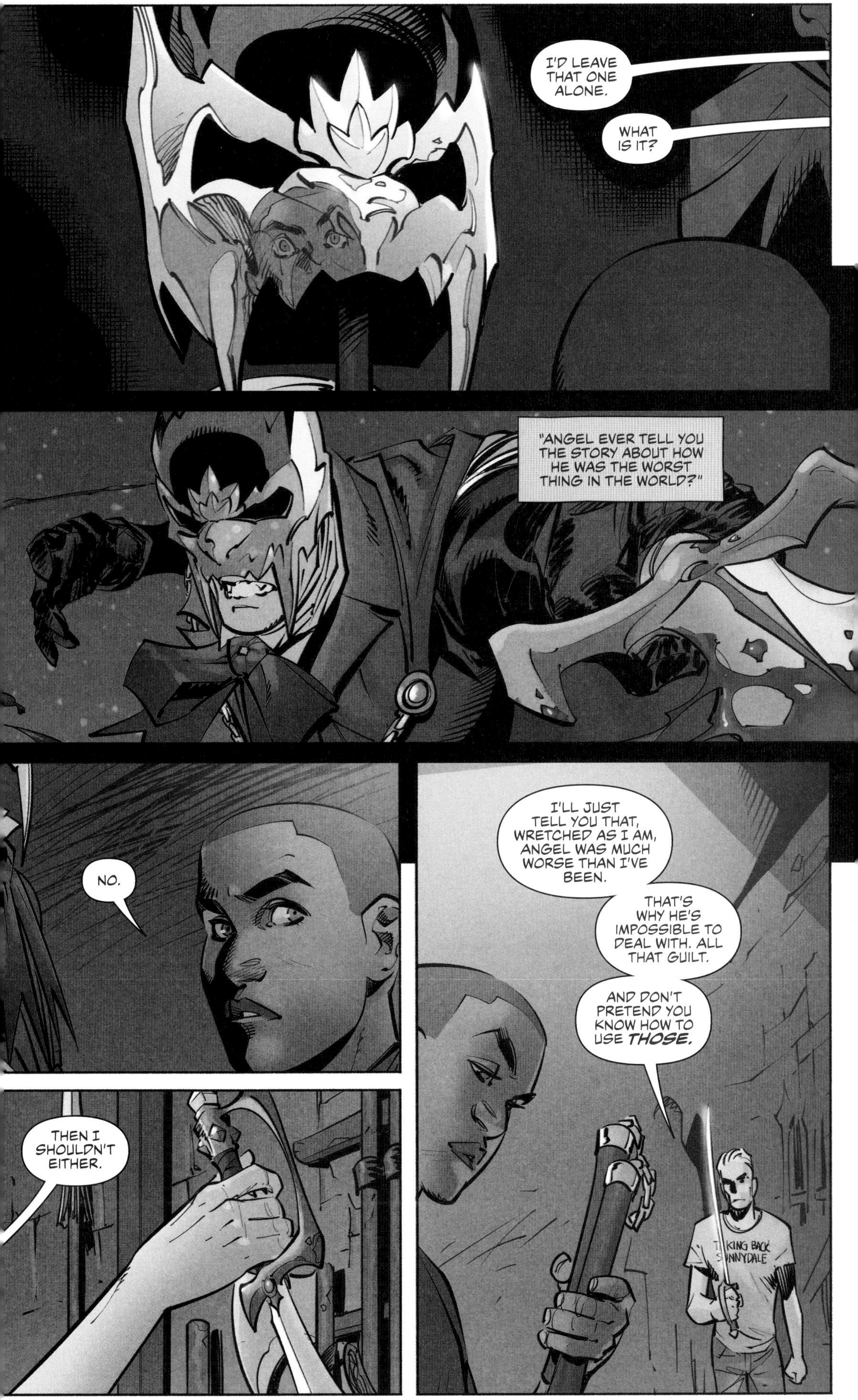
I'D LEAVE THAT ONE ALONE.
WHAT IS IT?
"ANGEL EVER TELL YOU THE STORY ABOUT HOW HE WAS THE WORST THING IN THE WORLD?"
NO.
I'LL JUST TELL YOU THAT, WRETCHED AS I AM, ANGEL WAS MUCH WORSE THAN I'VE BEEN.
THAT'S WHY HE'S IMPOSSIBLE TO DEAL WITH. ALL THAT GUILT.
AND DON'T PRETEND YOU KNOW HOW TO USE ***THOSE.***
THEN I SHOULDN'T EITHER.

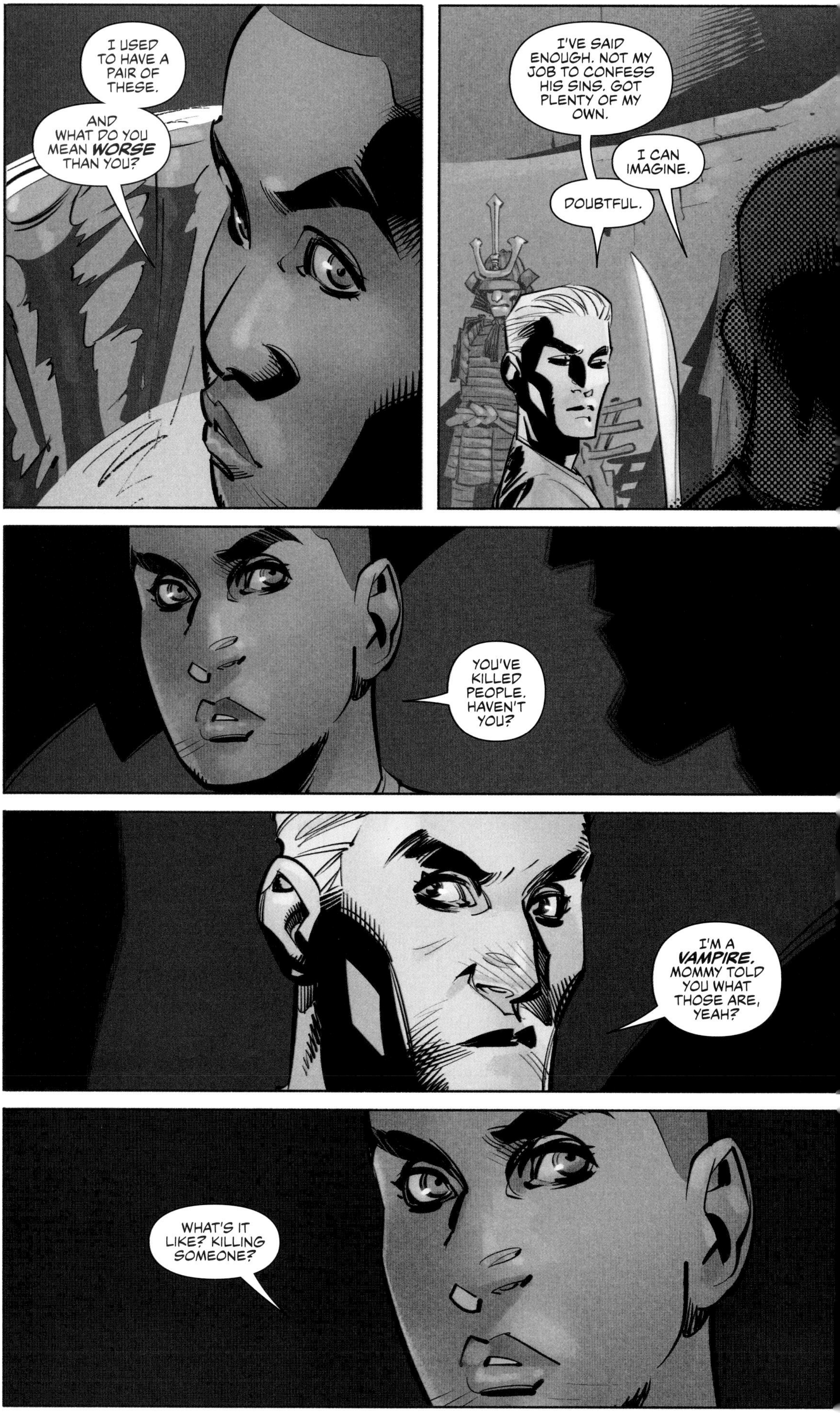
I USED TO HAVE A PAIR OF THESE.
AND WHAT DO YOU MEAN **WORSE** THAN YOU?
I'VE SAID ENOUGH. NOT MY JOB TO CONFESS HIS SINS. GOT PLENTY OF MY OWN.
I CAN IMAGINE.
DOUBTFUL.
YOU'VE KILLED PEOPLE. HAVEN'T YOU?
I'M A ***VAMPIRE.*** MOMMY TOLD YOU WHAT THOSE ARE, YEAH?
WHAT'S IT LIKE? KILLING SOMEONE?

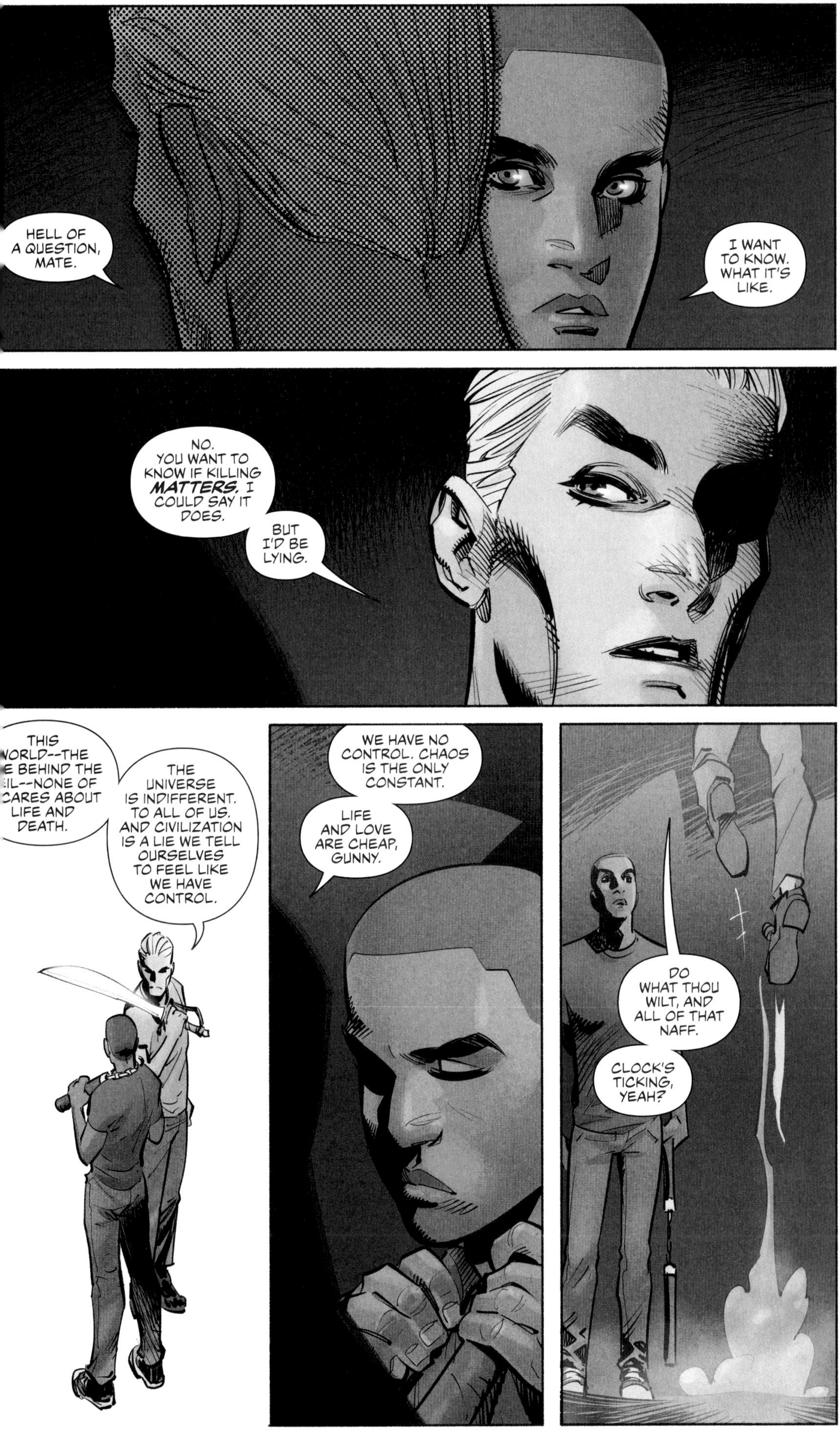

HELL OF A QUESTION, MATE.
I WANT TO KNOW. WHAT IT'S LIKE.
NO. YOU WANT TO KNOW IF KILLING **MATTERS.** I COULD SAY IT DOES.
BUT I'D BE LYING.
THIS ORLD--THE E BEHIND THE IL--NONE OF CARES ABOUT LIFE AND DEATH.
THE UNIVERSE IS INDIFFERENT. TO ALL OF US. AND CIVILIZATION IS A LIE WE TELL OURSELVES TO FEEL LIKE WE HAVE CONTROL.
WE HAVE NO CONTROL. CHAOS IS THE ONLY CONSTANT.
LIFE AND LOVE ARE CHEAP, GUNNY.
DO WHAT THOU WILT, AND ALL OF THAT NAFF.
CLOCK'S TICKING, YEAH?

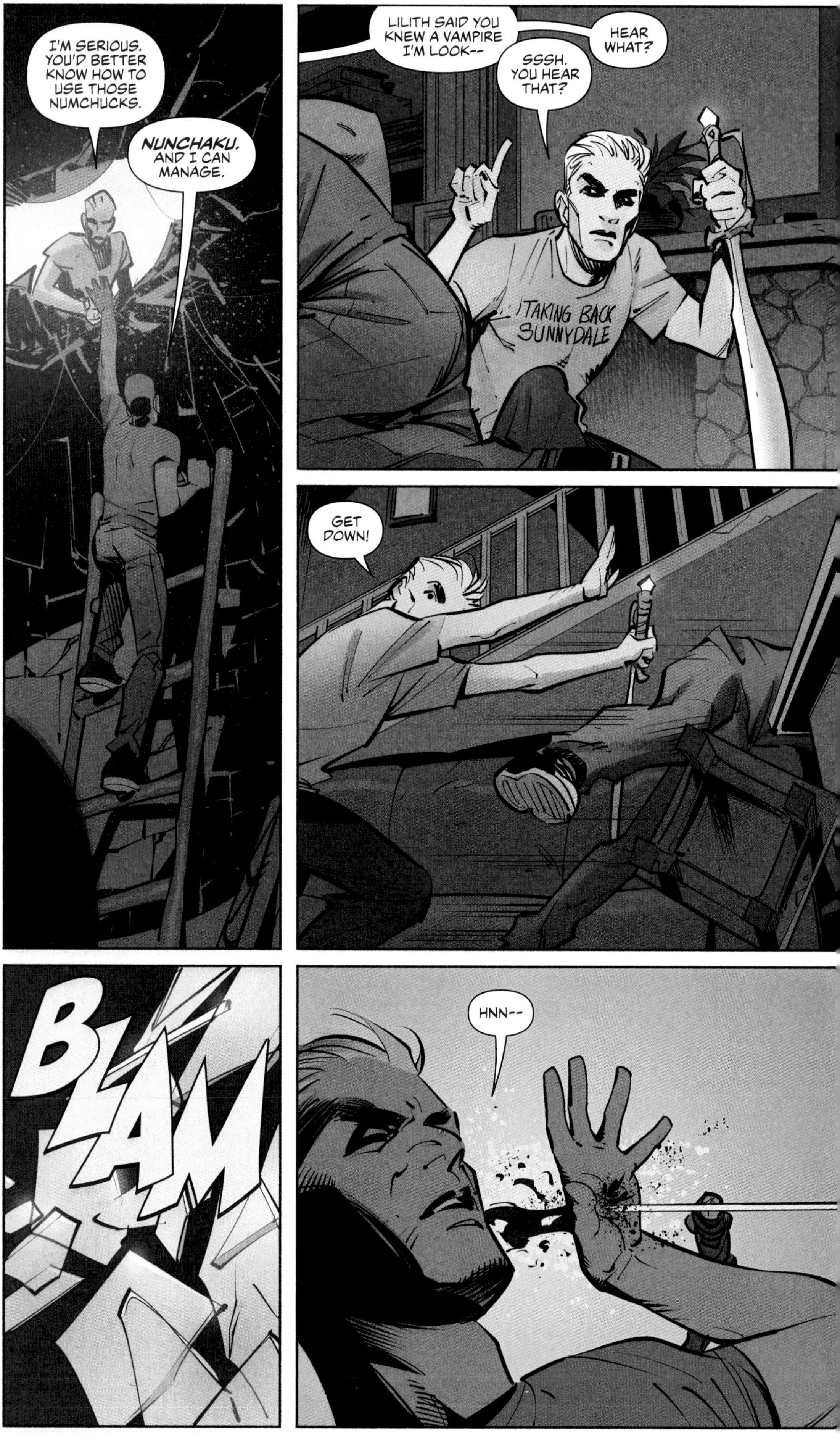
I'M SERIOUS. YOU'D BETTER KNOW HOW TO USE THOSE NUMCHUCKS.
NUNCHAKU. AND I CAN MANAGE.
LILITH SAID YOU KNEW A VAMPIRE I'M LOOK--
SSSH. YOU HEAR THAT?
HEAR WHAT?
TAKING BACK SUNNYDALE
GET DOWN!
BLAM
HNN--

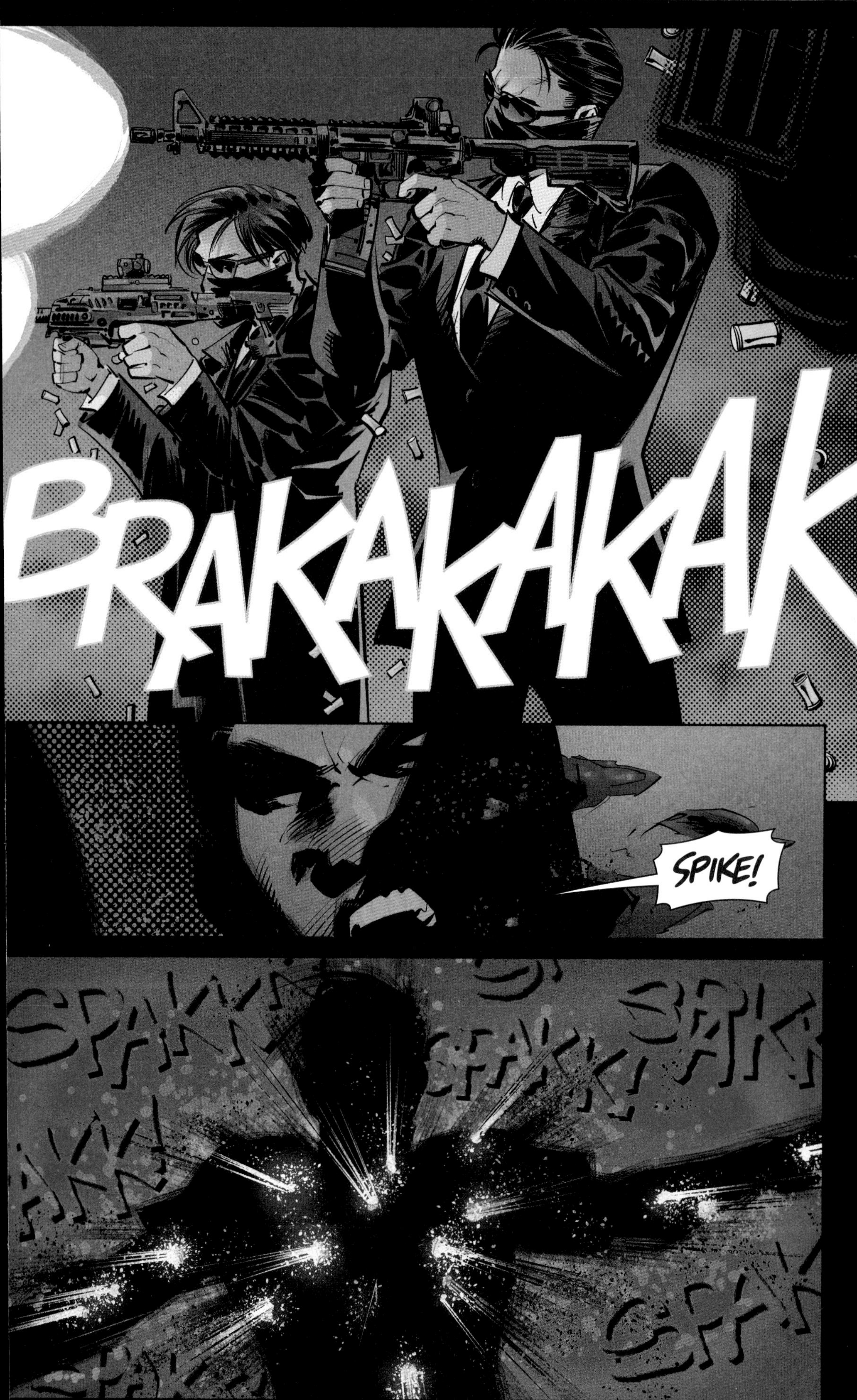
BRAKAKAKAK
SPIKE!

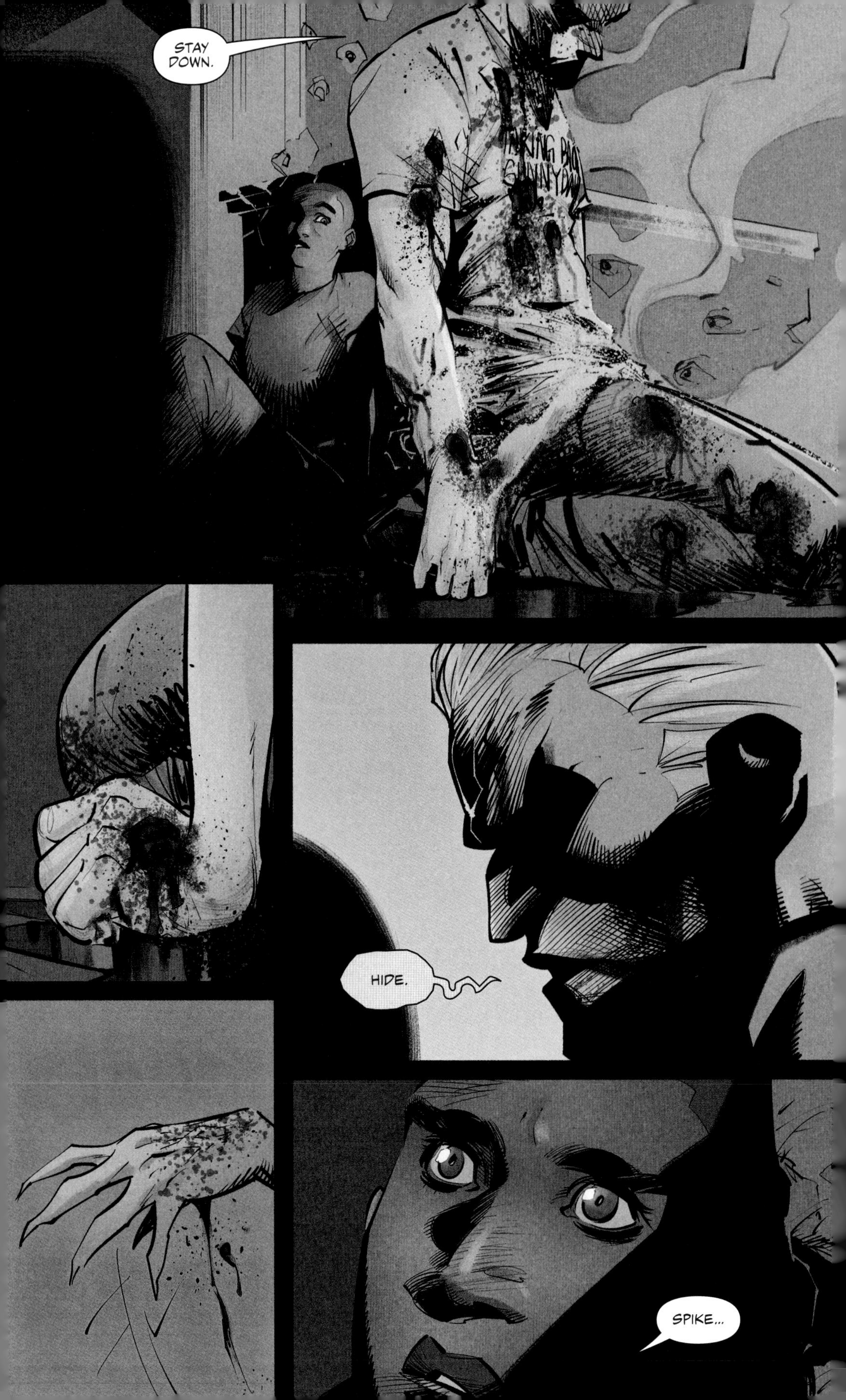
STAY DOWN.
HIDE.
SPIKE...

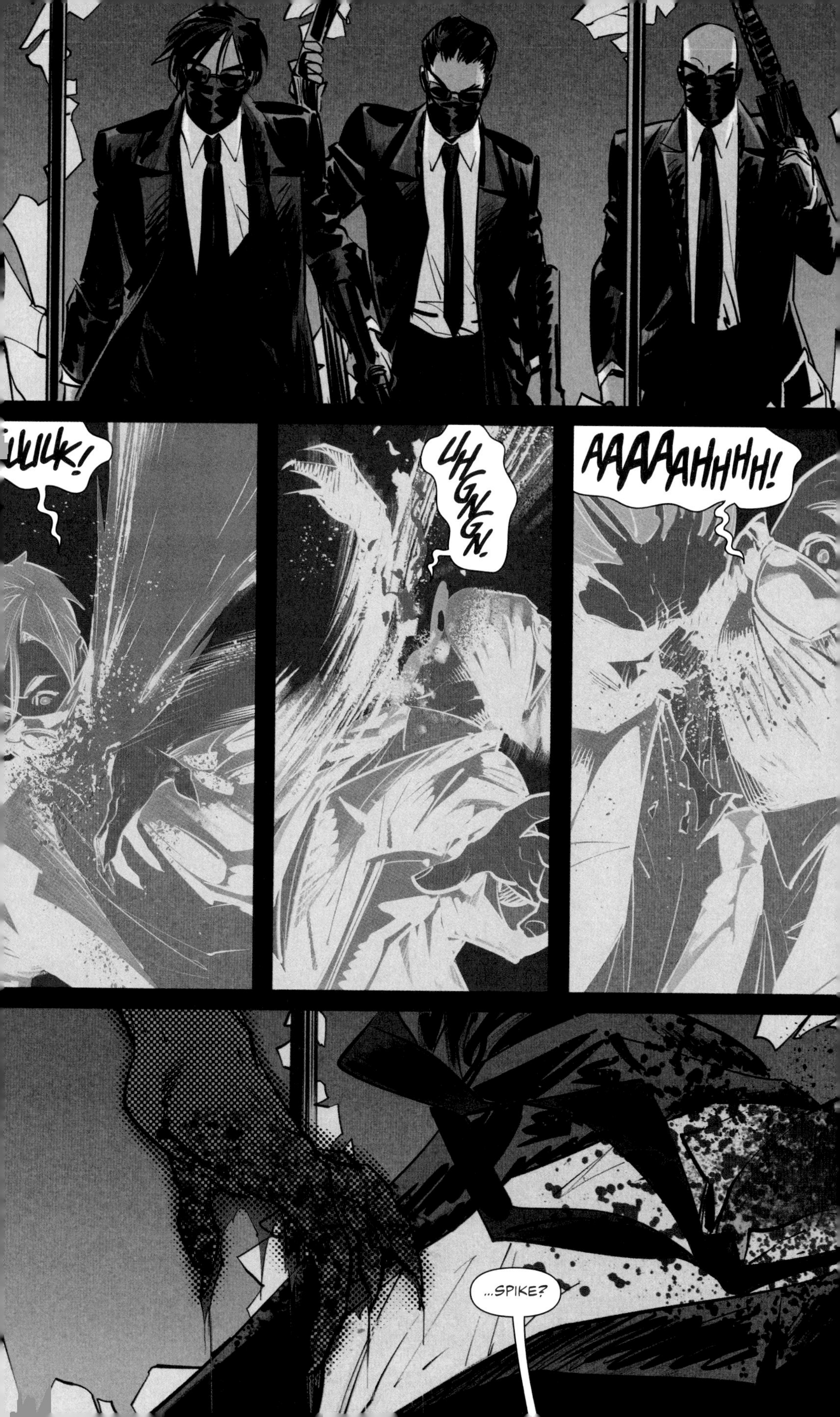
UULK!
UHGNGN!
AAAAAHHHH!
...SPIKE?

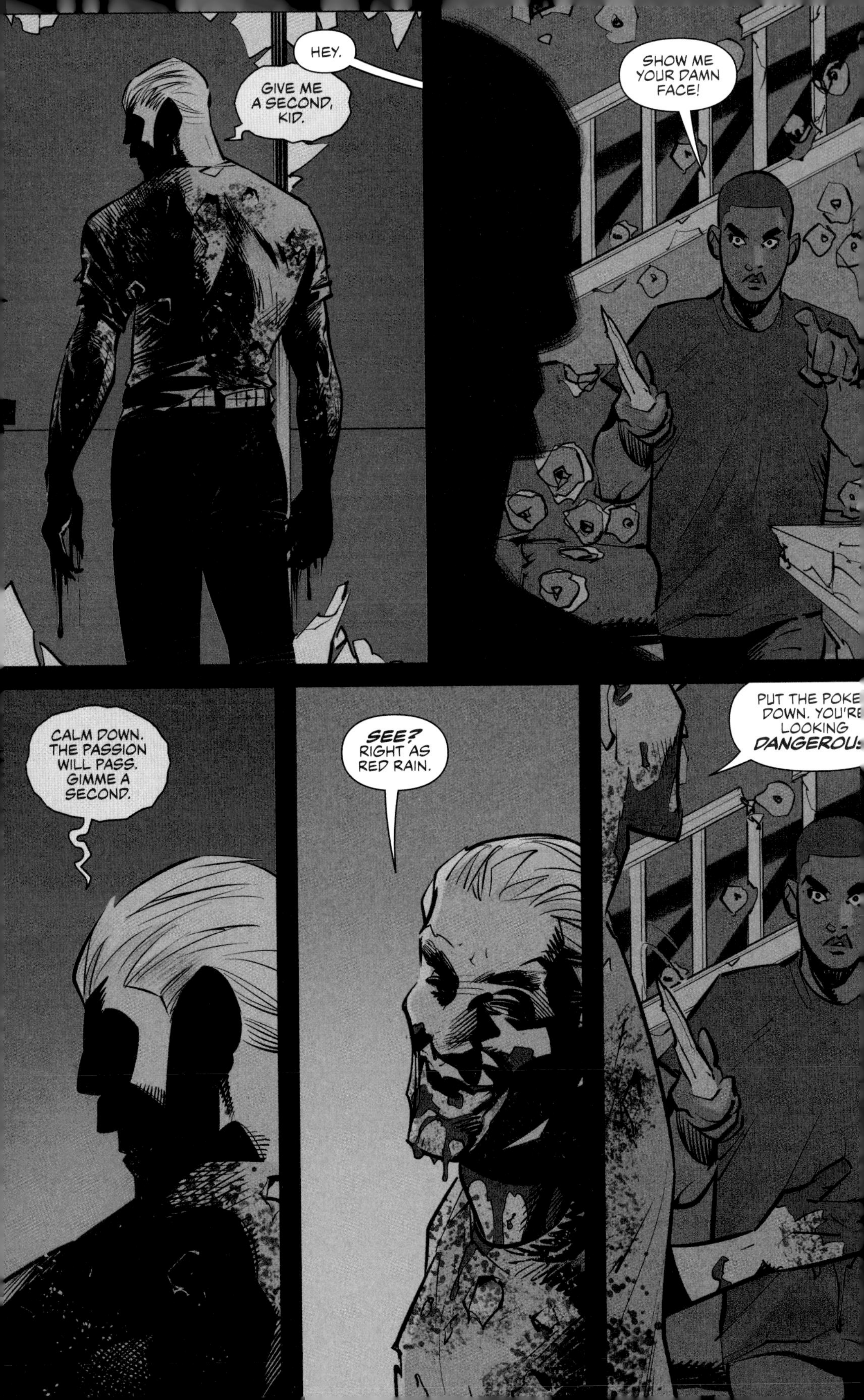
HEY.
GIVE ME A SECOND, KID.
SHOW ME YOUR DAMN FACE!
CALM DOWN. THE PASSION WILL PASS. GIMME A SECOND.
SEE? RIGHT AS RED RAIN.
PUT THE POKE DOWN. YOU'RE LOOKING DANGEROU

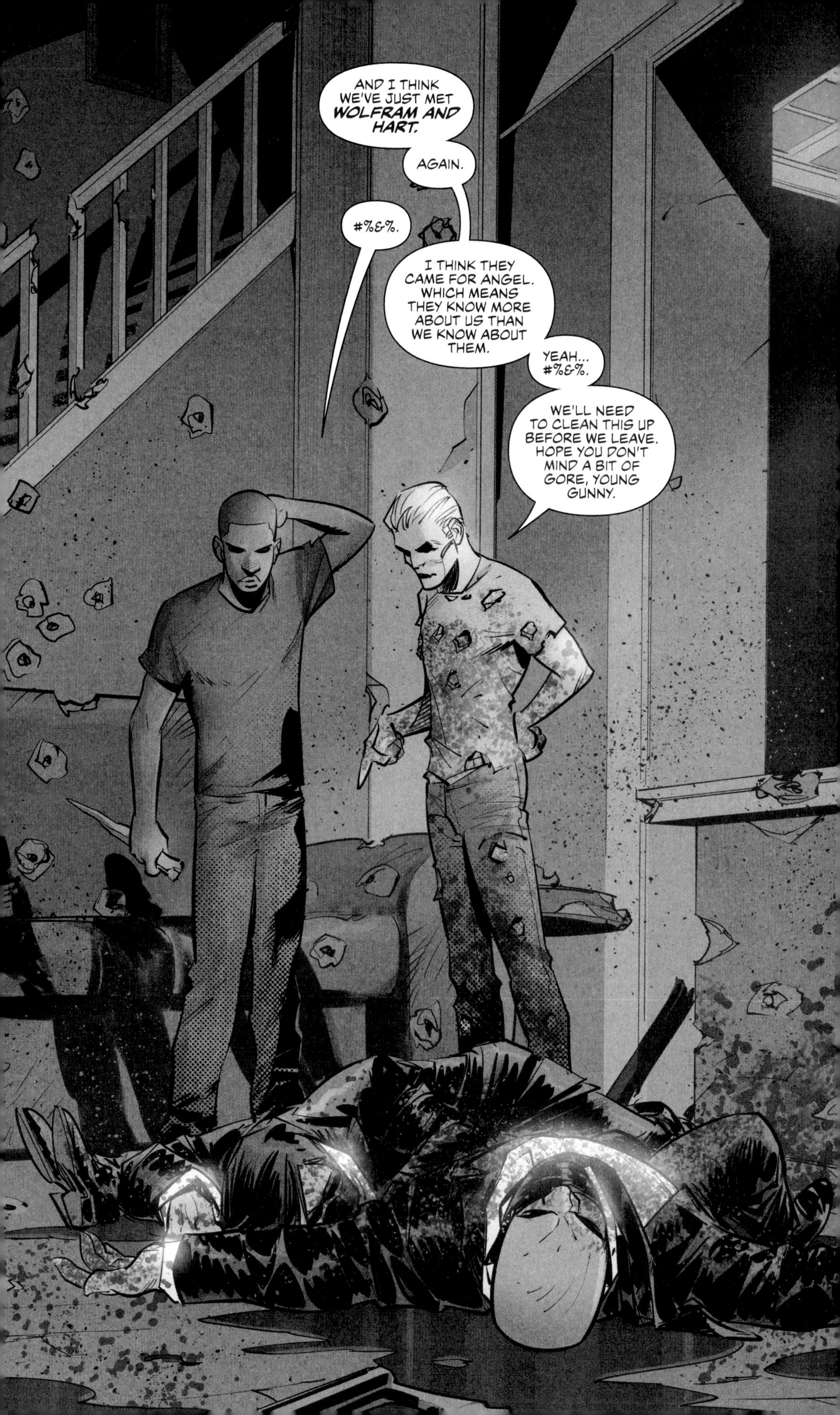
AND I THINK WE'VE JUST MET *WOLFRAM AND HART.*
AGAIN.
#%&%.
I THINK THEY CAME FOR ANGEL. WHICH MEANS THEY KNOW MORE ABOUT US THAN WE KNOW ABOUT THEM.
YEAH... #%&%.
WE'LL NEED TO CLEAN THIS UP BEFORE WE LEAVE. HOPE YOU DON'T MIND A BIT OF GORE, YOUNG GUNNY.

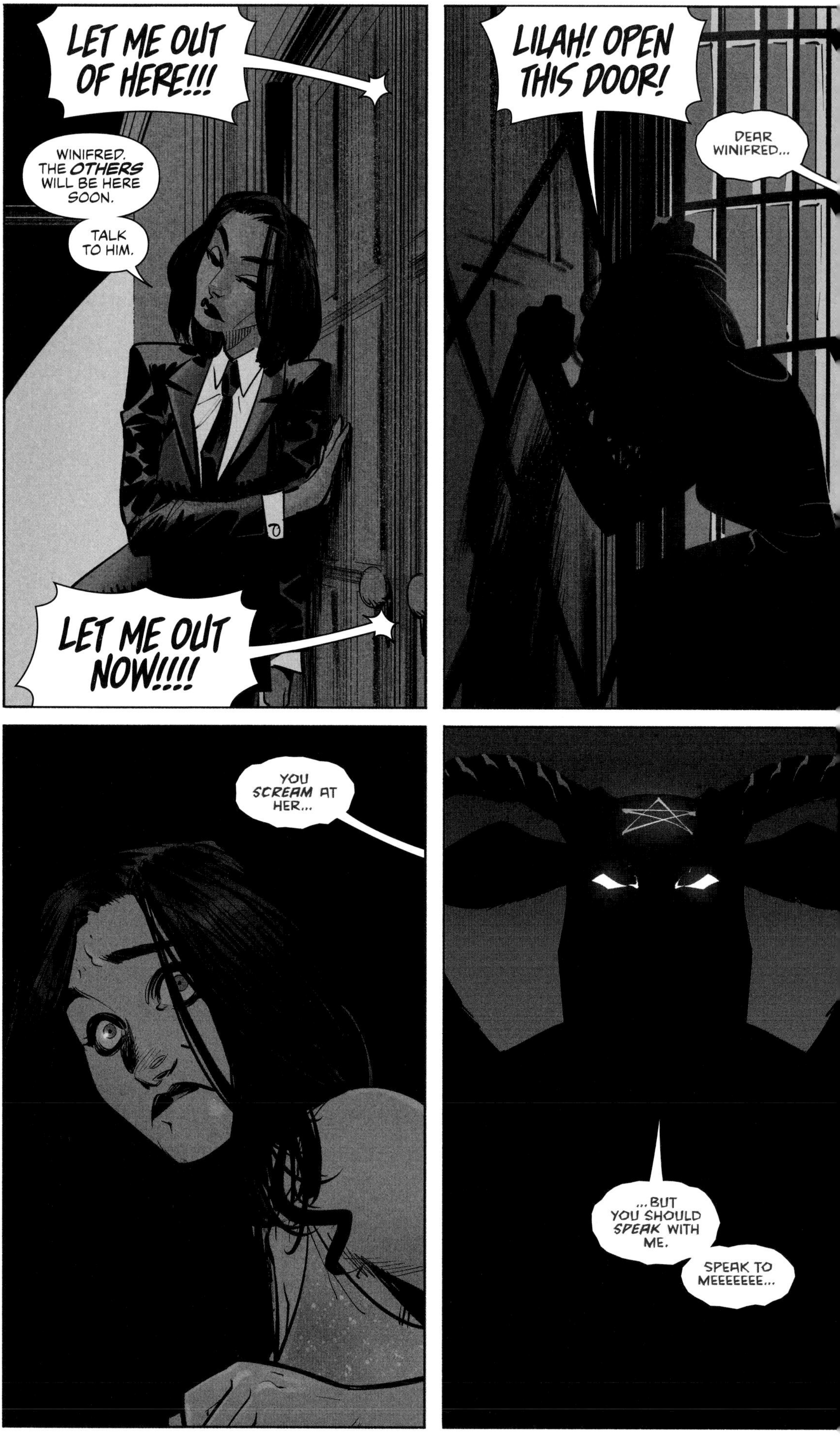
LET ME OUT OF HERE!!!
WINIFRED. THE *OTHERS* WILL BE HERE SOON.
TALK TO HIM.
LET ME OUT NOW!!!!
LILAH! OPEN THIS DOOR!
DEAR WINIFRED...
YOU *SCREAM* AT HER...
...BUT YOU SHOULD *SPEAK* WITH ME.
SPEAK TO MEEEEEEE...

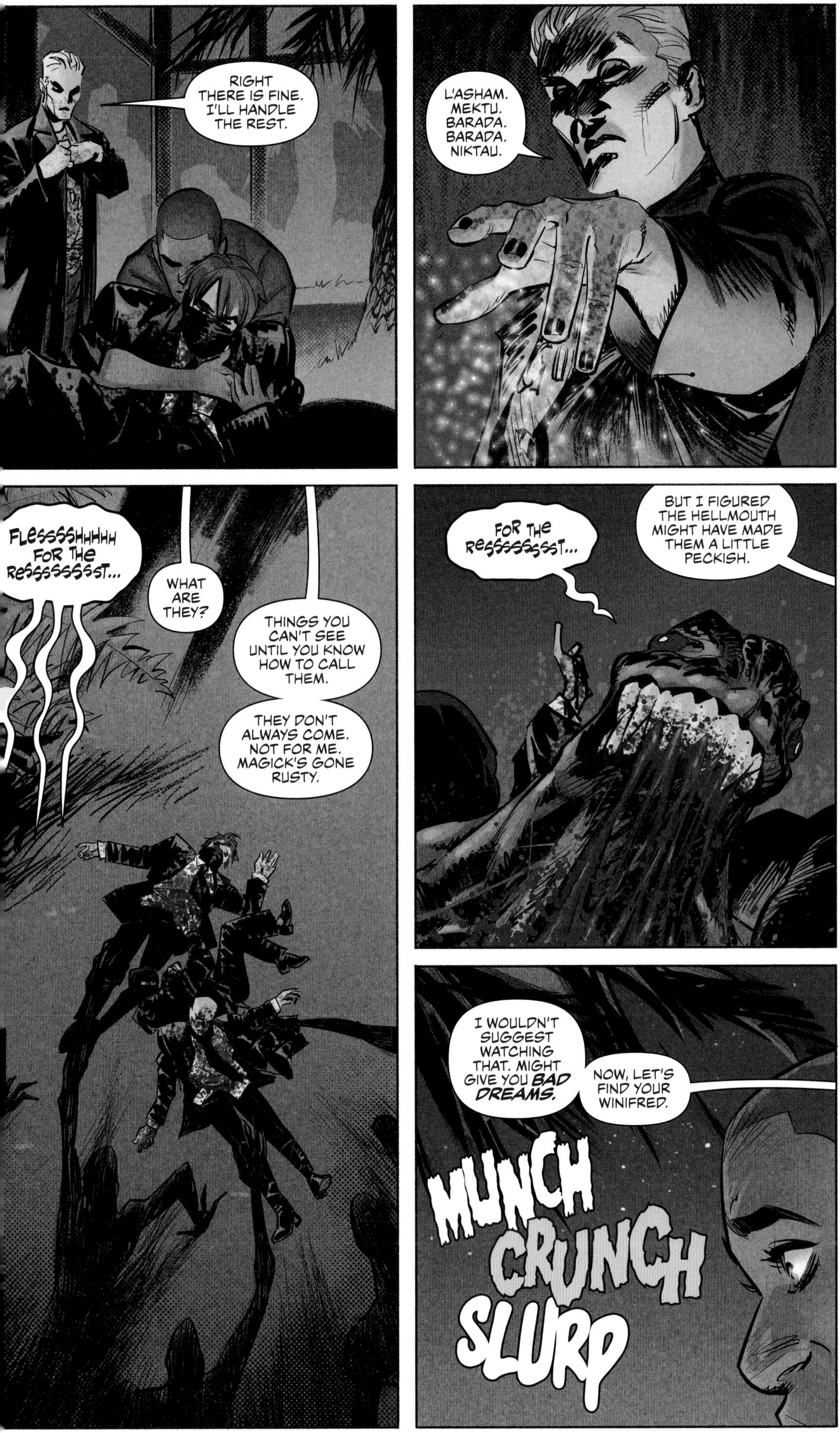
RIGHT THERE IS FINE. I'LL HANDLE THE REST.
L'ASHAM. MEKTU. BARADA. BARADA. NIKTAU.
FLESSSSHHHHH FOR THE RESSSSSSSST...
WHAT ARE THEY?
THINGS YOU CAN'T SEE UNTIL YOU KNOW HOW TO CALL THEM.
THEY DON'T ALWAYS COME. NOT FOR ME. MAGICK'S GONE RUSTY.
FOR THE RESSSSSSSST...
BUT I FIGURED THE HELLMOUTH MIGHT HAVE MADE THEM A LITTLE PECKISH.
I WOULDN'T SUGGEST WATCHING THAT. MIGHT GIVE YOU *BAD DREAMS.*
NOW, LET'S FIND YOUR WINIFRED.
MUNCH
CRUNCH
SLURP

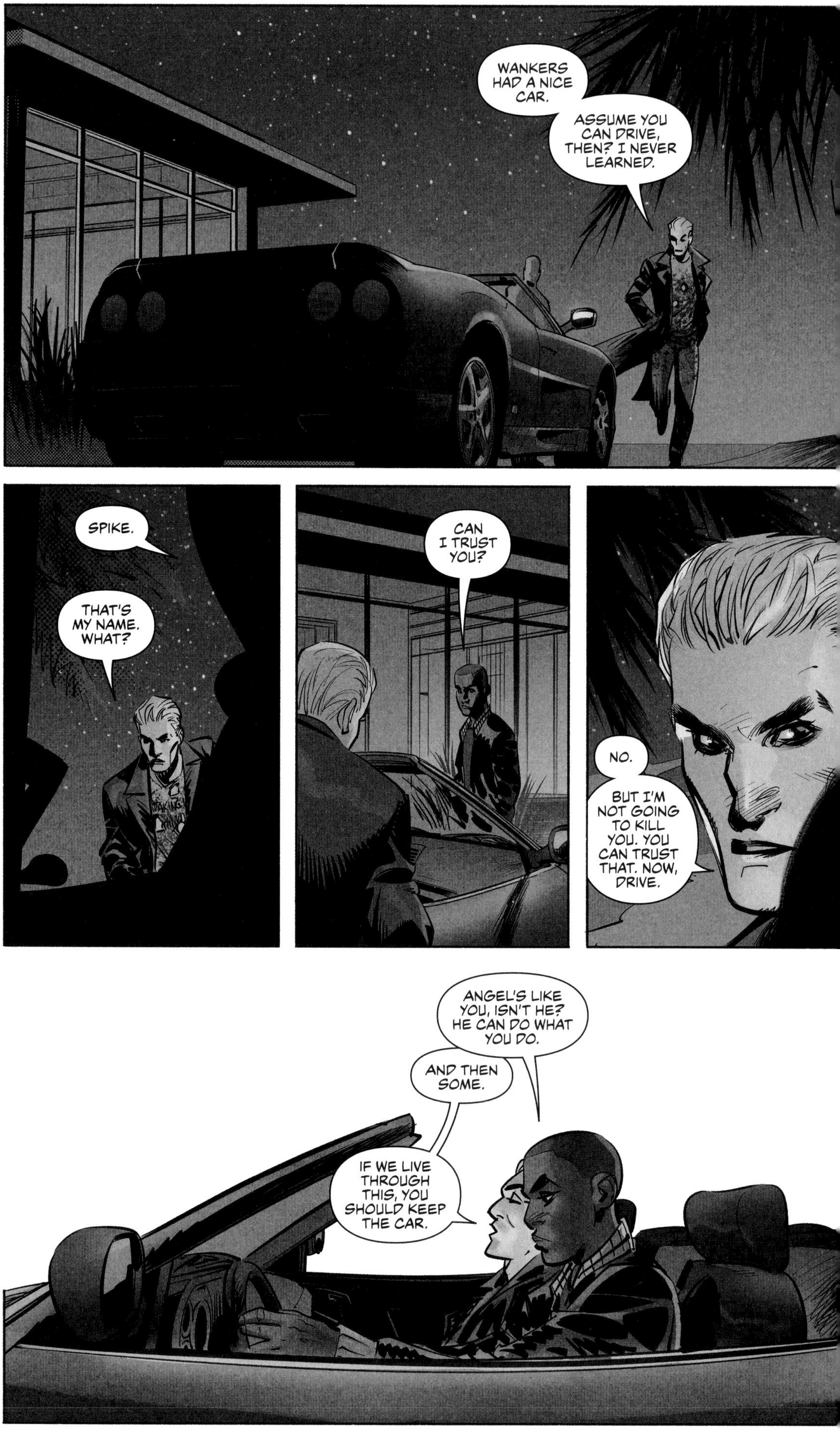
WANKERS HAD A NICE CAR.
ASSUME YOU CAN DRIVE, THEN? I NEVER LEARNED.
SPIKE.
THAT'S MY NAME. WHAT?
CAN I TRUST YOU?
NO.
BUT I'M NOT GOING TO KILL YOU. YOU CAN TRUST THAT. NOW, DRIVE.
ANGEL'S LIKE YOU, ISN'T HE? HE CAN DO WHAT YOU DO.
AND THEN SOME.
IF WE LIVE THROUGH THIS, YOU SHOULD KEEP THE CAR.

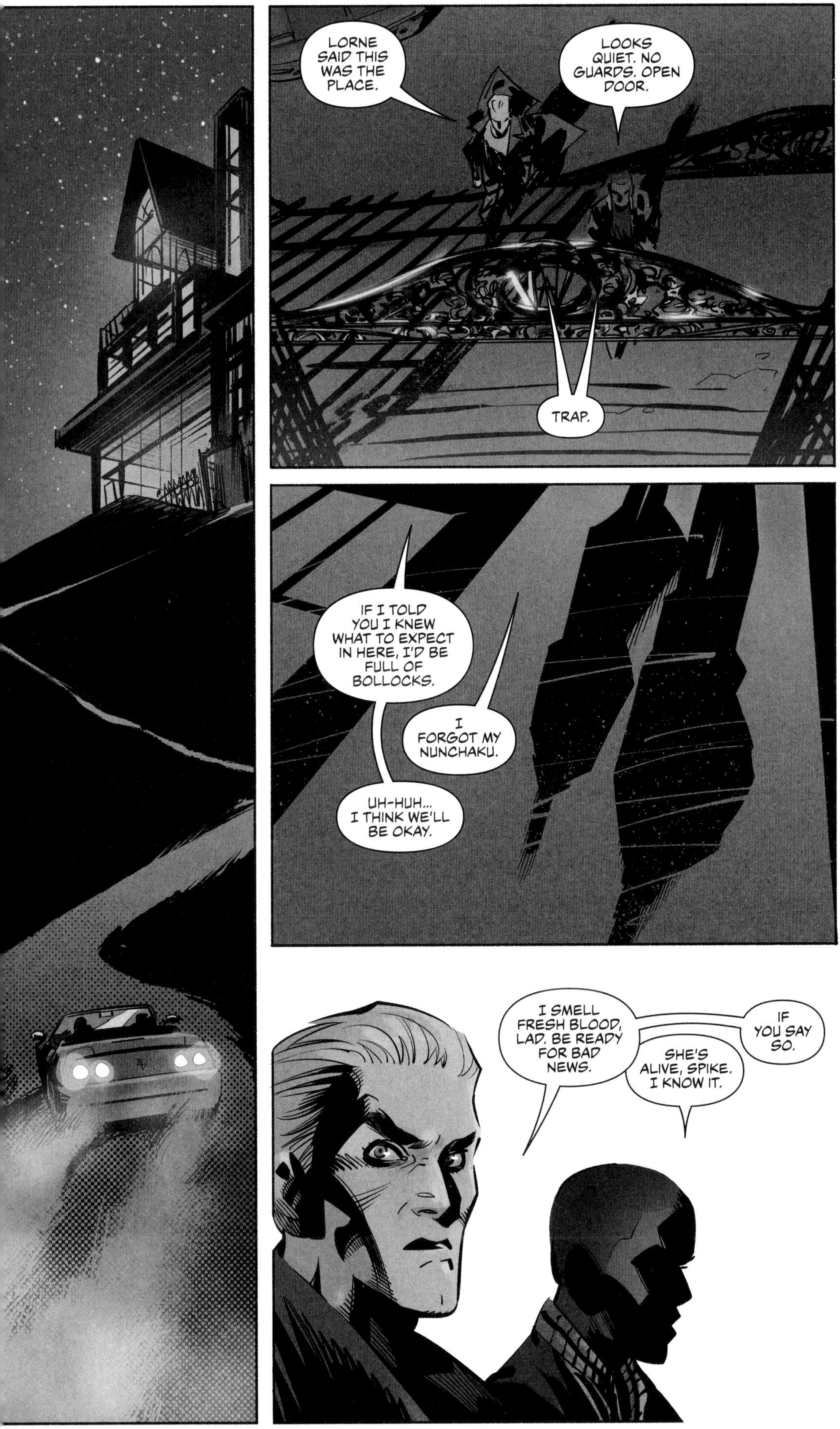
LORNE SAID THIS WAS THE PLACE.
LOOKS QUIET. NO GUARDS. OPEN DOOR.
TRAP.
IF I TOLD YOU I KNEW WHAT TO EXPECT IN HERE, I'D BE FULL OF BOLLOCKS.
I FORGOT MY NUNCHAKU.
UH-HUH... I THINK WE'LL BE OKAY.
I SMELL FRESH BLOOD, LAD. BE READY FOR BAD NEWS.
IF YOU SAY SO.
SHE'S ALIVE, SPIKE. I KNOW IT.

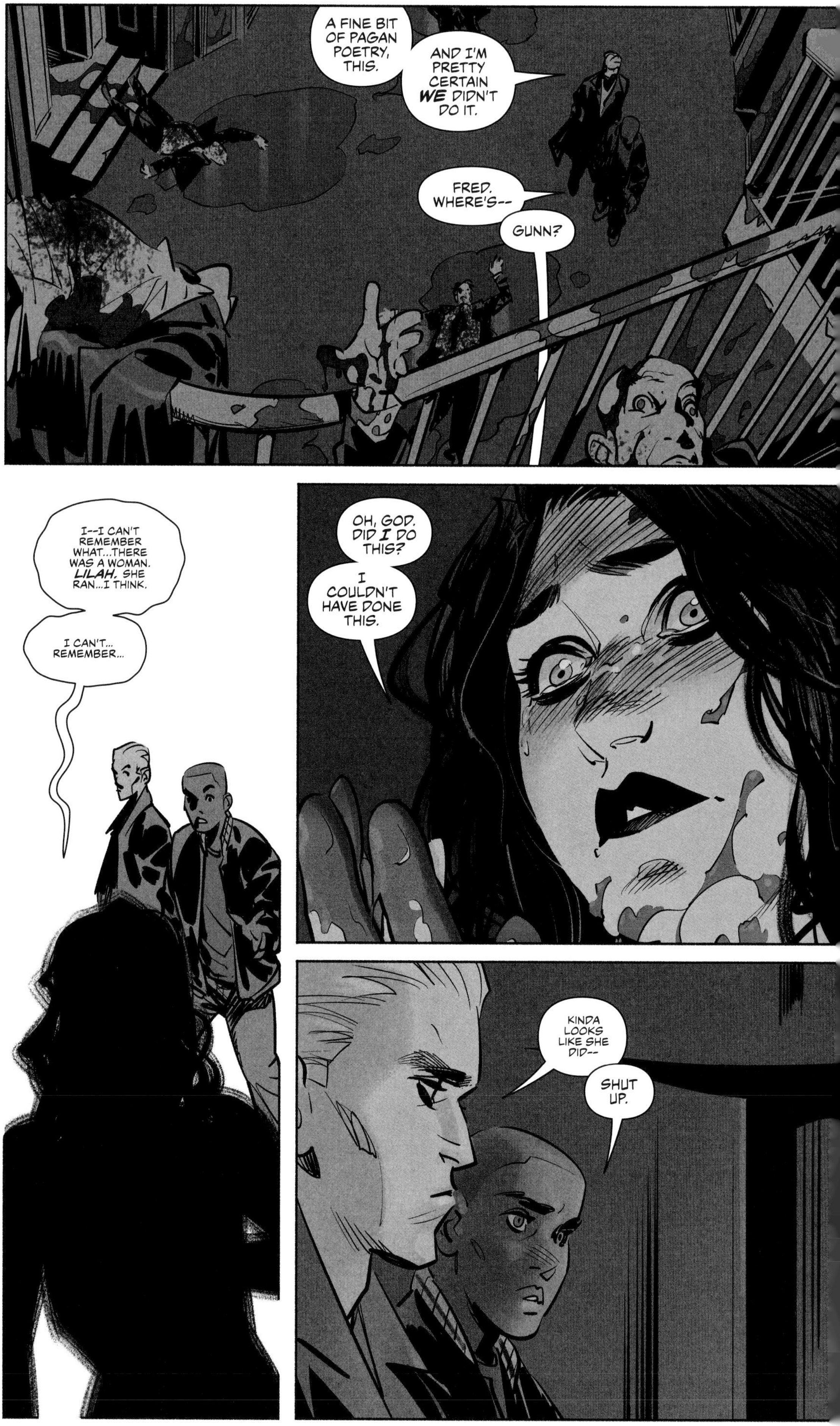
A FINE BIT OF PAGAN POETRY, THIS.
AND I'M PRETTY CERTAIN WE DIDN'T DO IT.
FRED. WHERE'S--
GUNN?
I--I CAN'T REMEMBER WHAT...THERE WAS A WOMAN. LILAH. SHE RAN...I THINK.
I CAN'T... REMEMBER...
OH, GOD. DID I DO THIS?
I COULDN'T HAVE DONE THIS.
KINDA LOOKS LIKE SHE DID--
SHUT UP.

GUNN...

...I TALKED TO *HIM*.

FRED... I...

WE'LL GET YOU OUT OF HERE.

GOOD RIDDANCE--

--TO BAD RUBBISH.

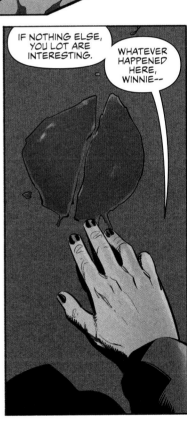

IF NOTHING ELSE, YOU LOT ARE INTERESTING.

WHATEVER HAPPENED HERE, WINNIE--

THE WORLD IS BETTER OFF.

BASED ON TONIGHT, MAYBE I SHOULD *STAY* IN LOS ANGELES. IT'S WHERE THE *FUN* IS.

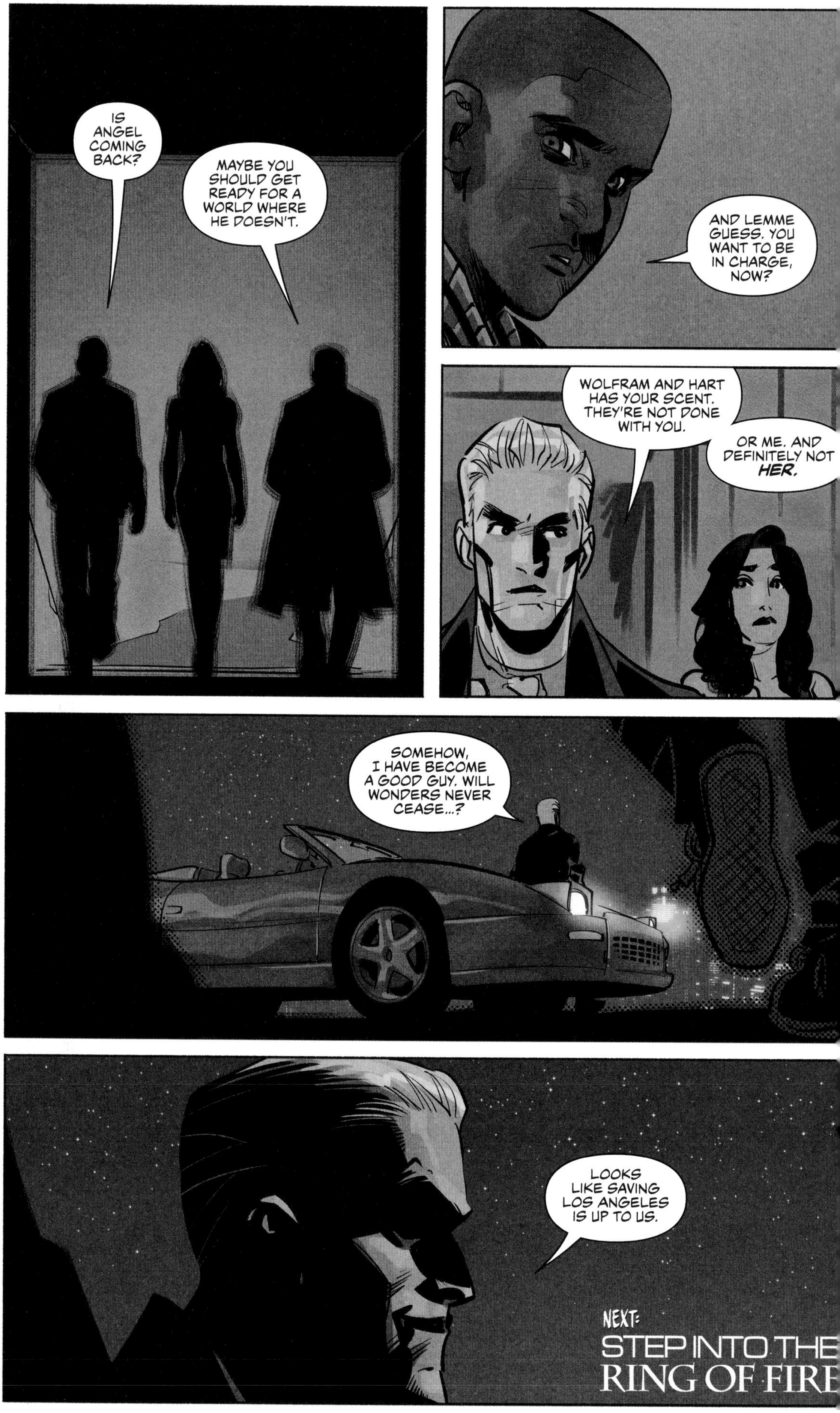
IS ANGEL COMING BACK?
MAYBE YOU SHOULD GET READY FOR A WORLD WHERE HE DOESN'T.
AND LEMME GUESS. YOU WANT TO BE IN CHARGE, NOW?
WOLFRAM AND HART HAS YOUR SCENT. THEY'RE NOT DONE WITH YOU.
OR ME. AND DEFINITELY NOT HER.
SOMEHOW, I HAVE BECOME A GOOD GUY. WILL WONDERS NEVER CEASE...?
LOOKS LIKE SAVING LOS ANGELES IS UP TO US.
NEXT:
STEP INTO THE
RING OF FIRE

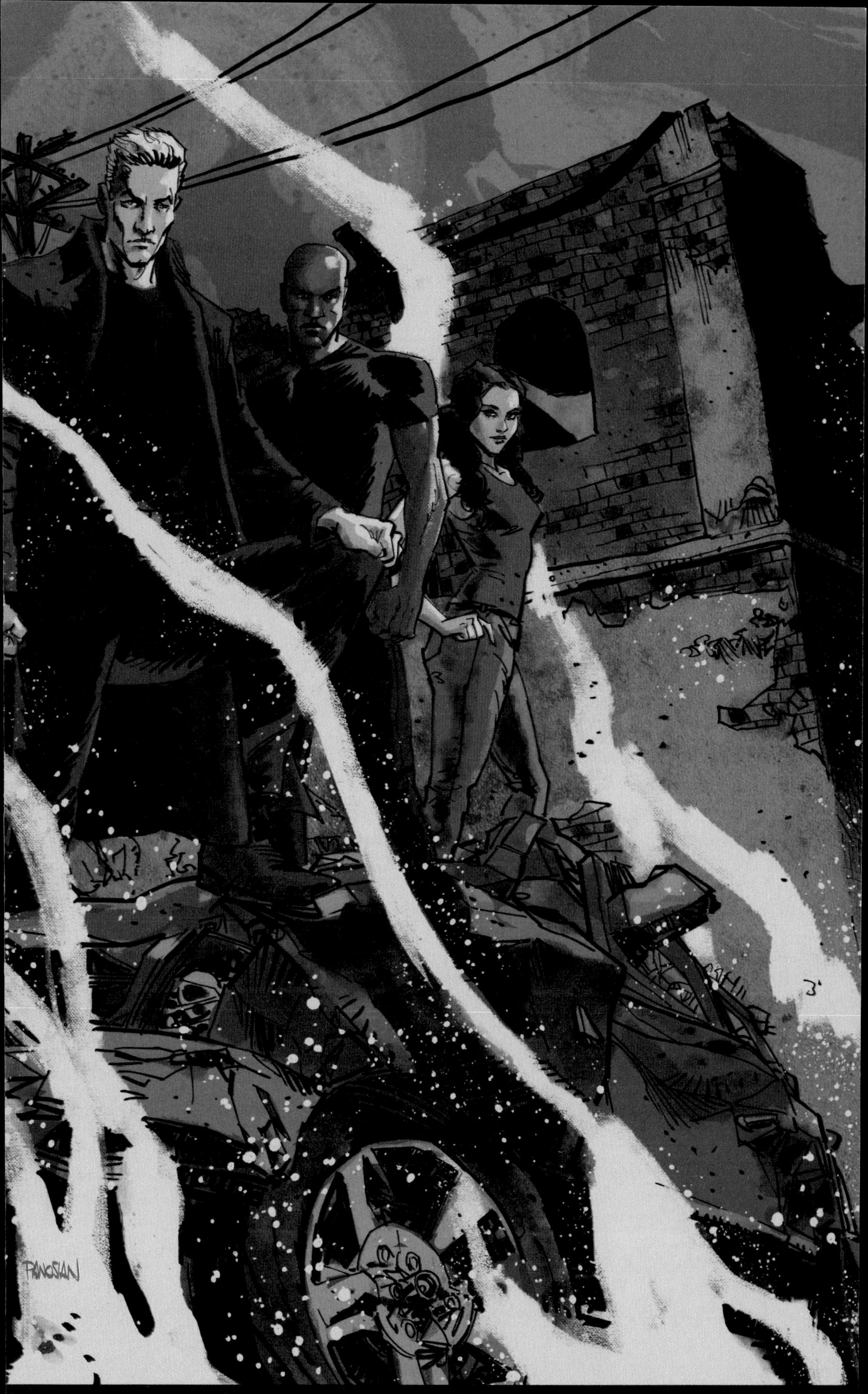
PANOSIAN

Angel #8 Main Cover by **Dan Panosian**

COVER
GALLERY

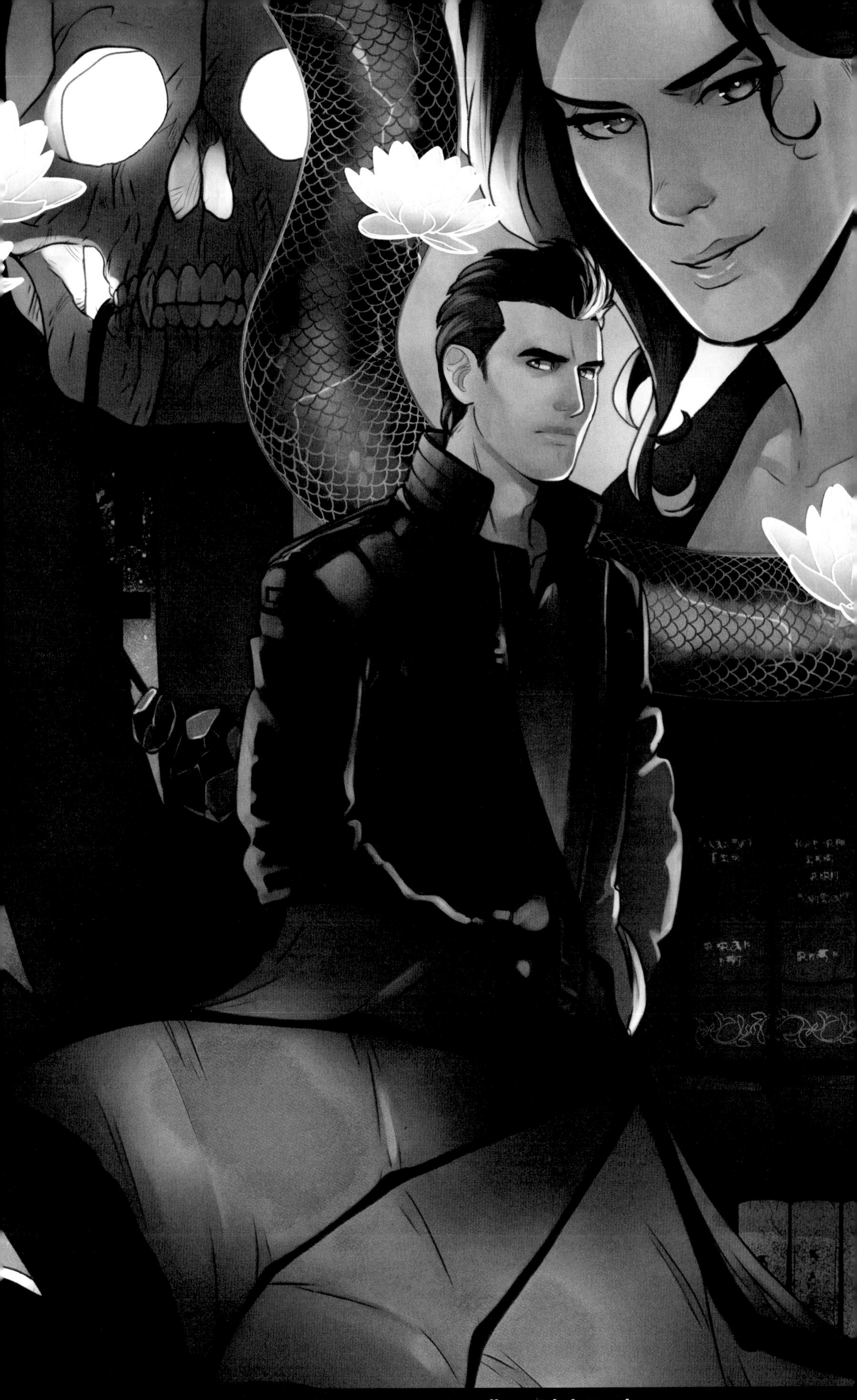

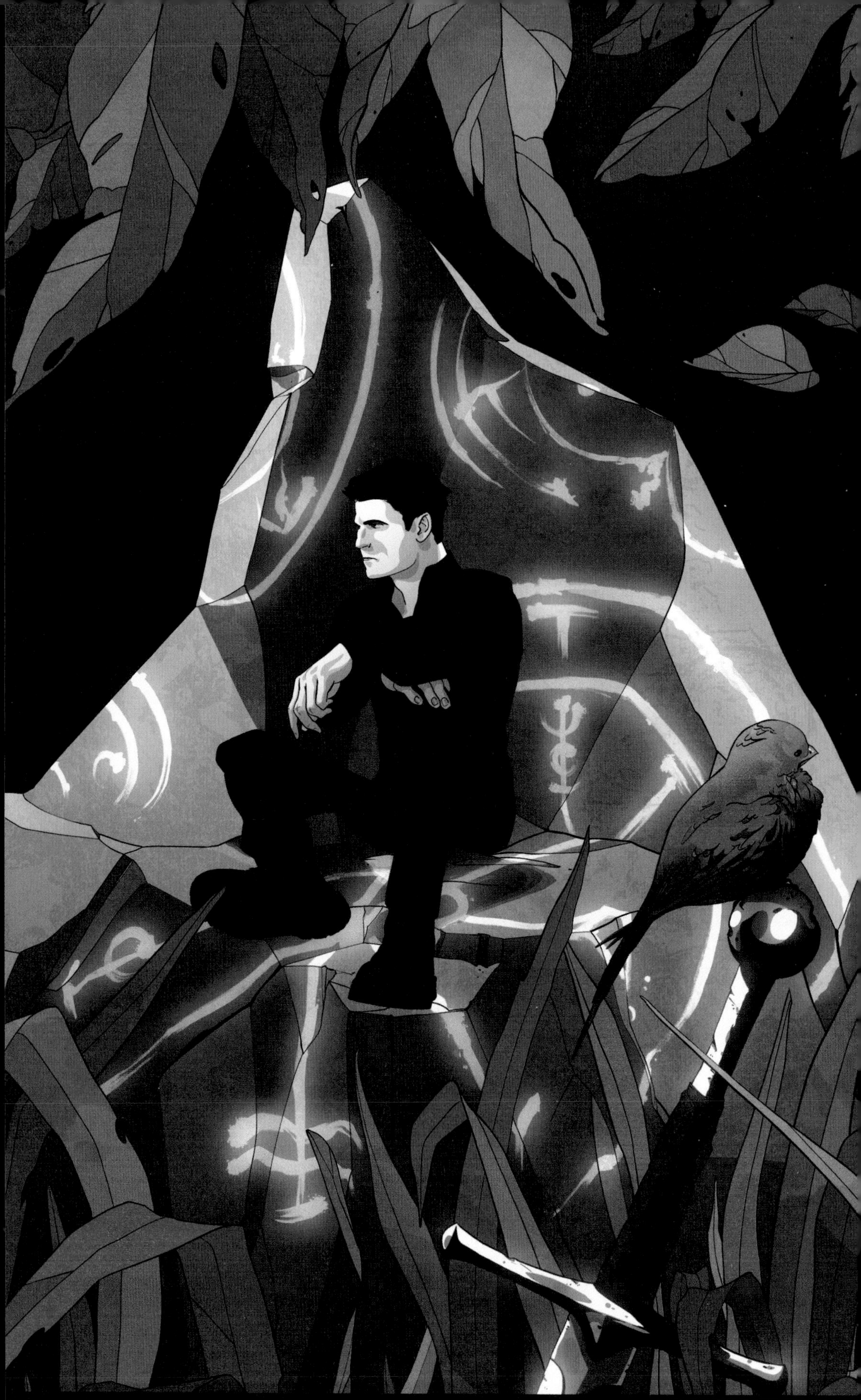

Angel #6 Hellmouth Connecting Cover by Goñi Montes

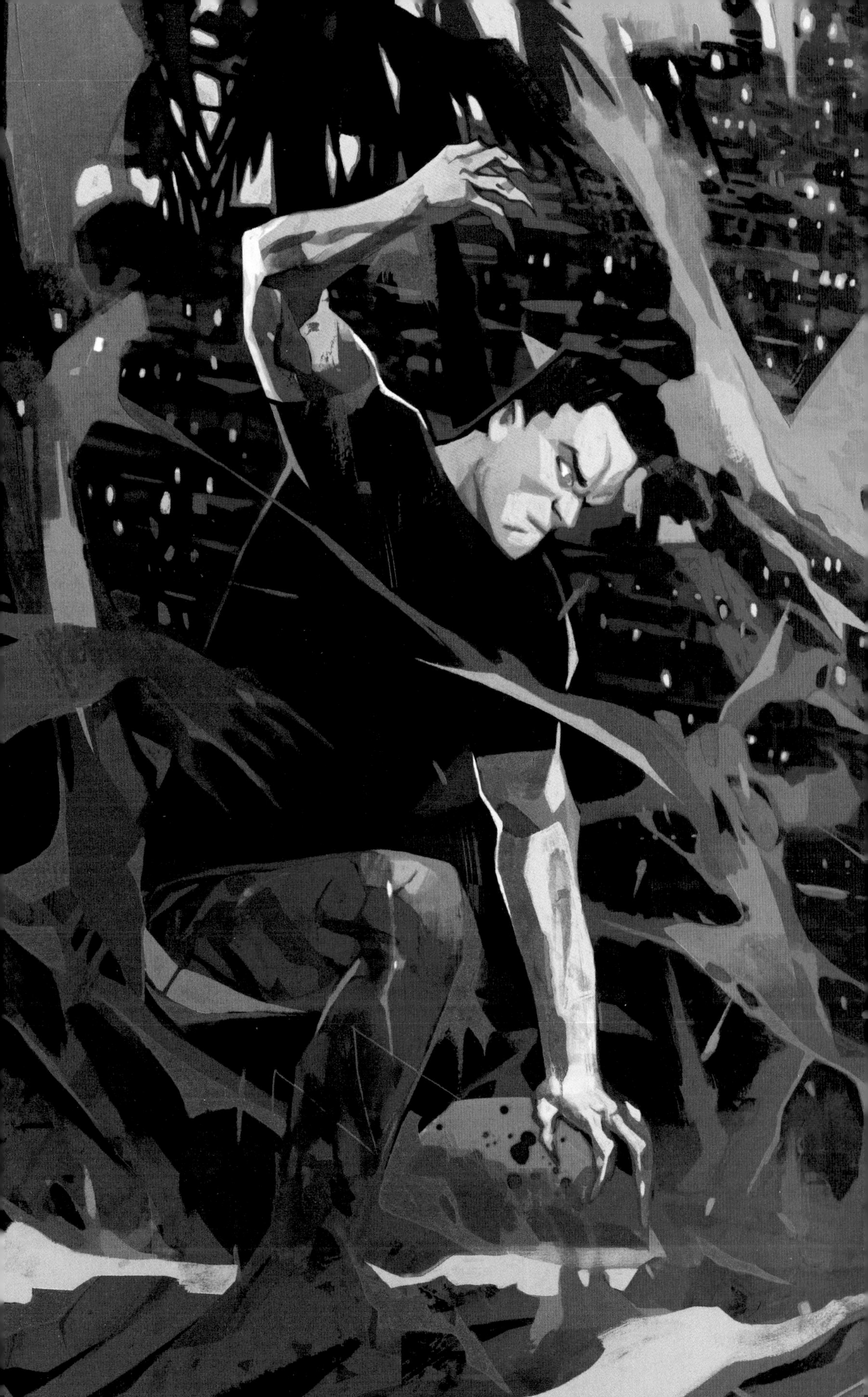

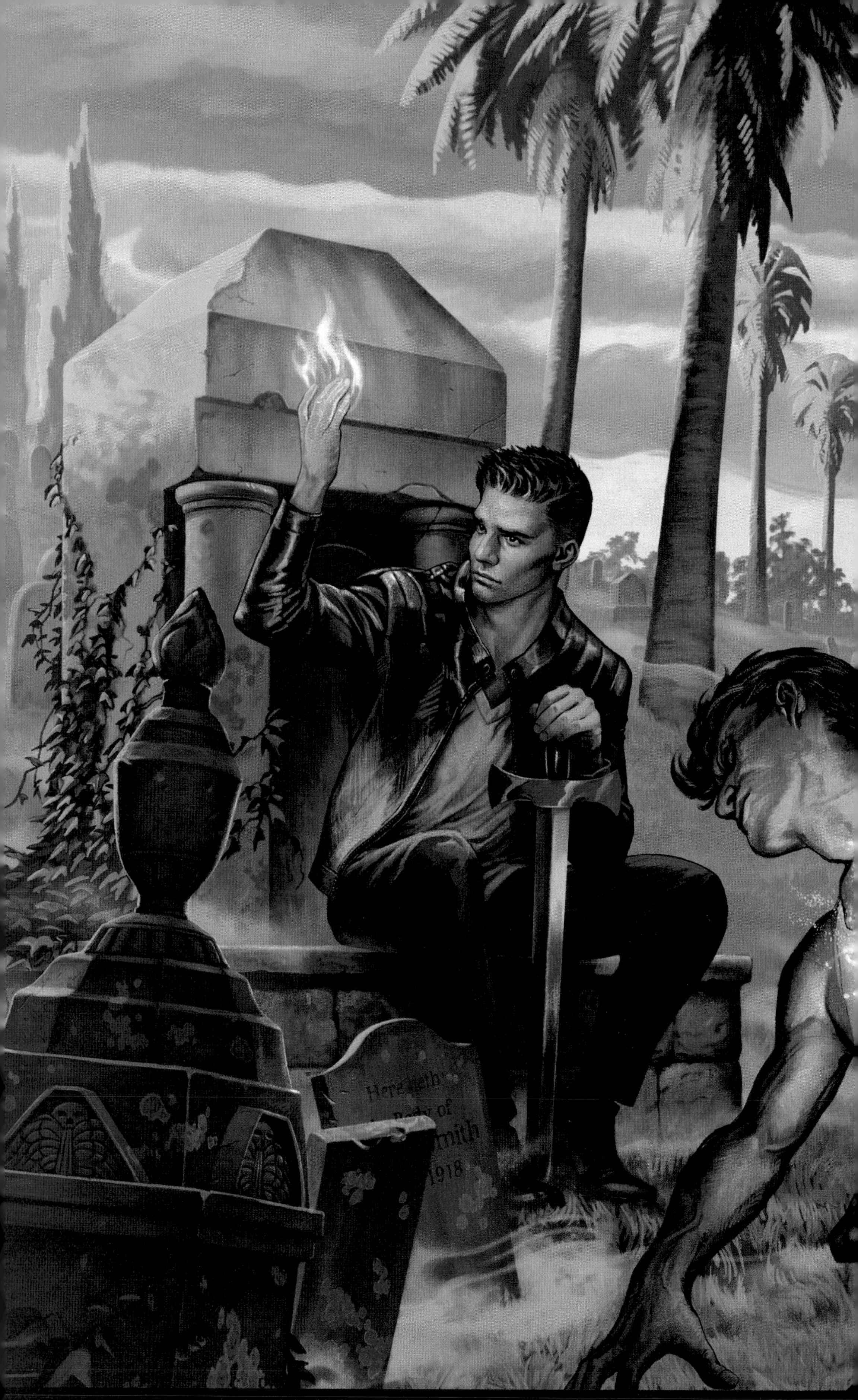

Here lieth
Body of
1918

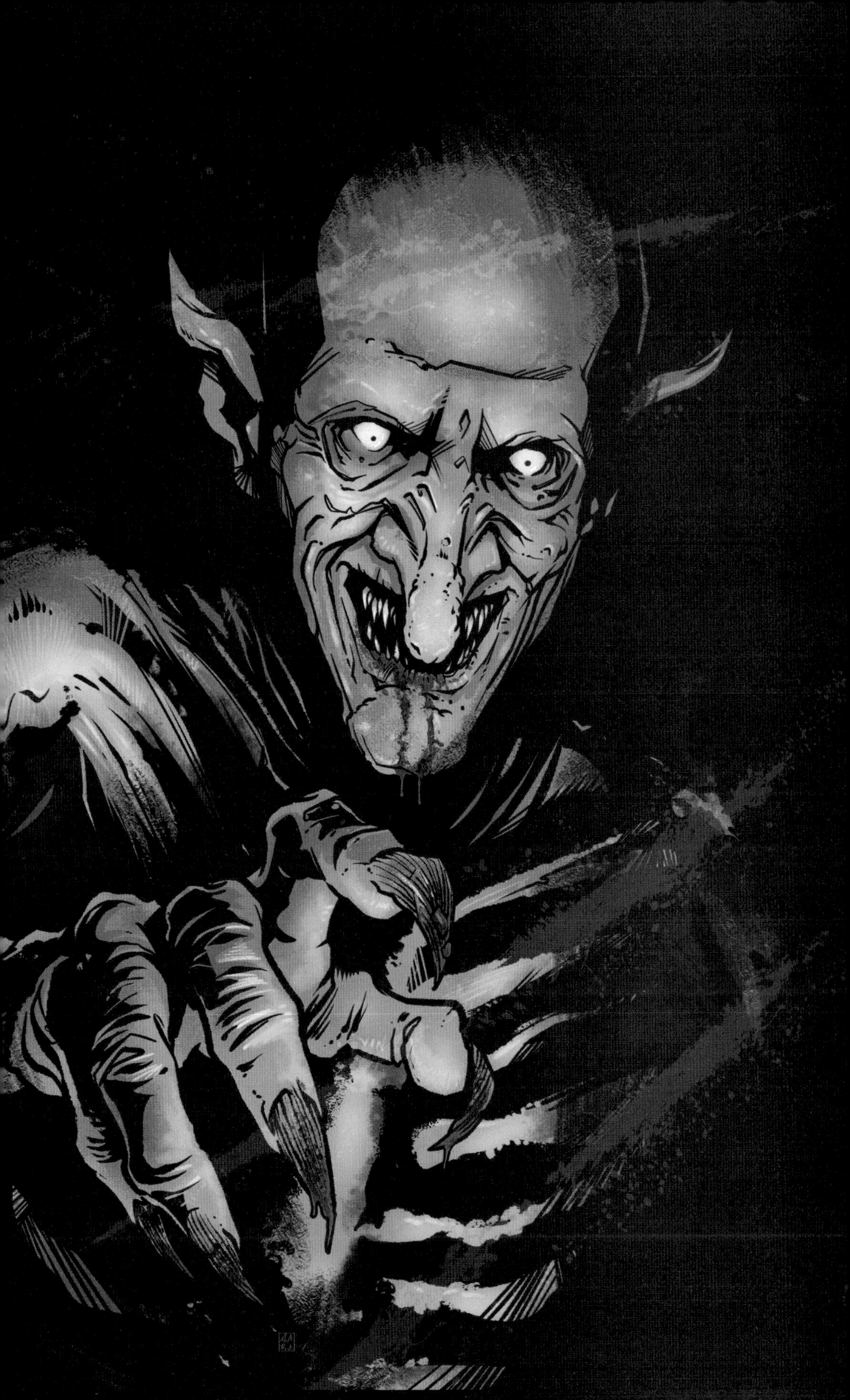

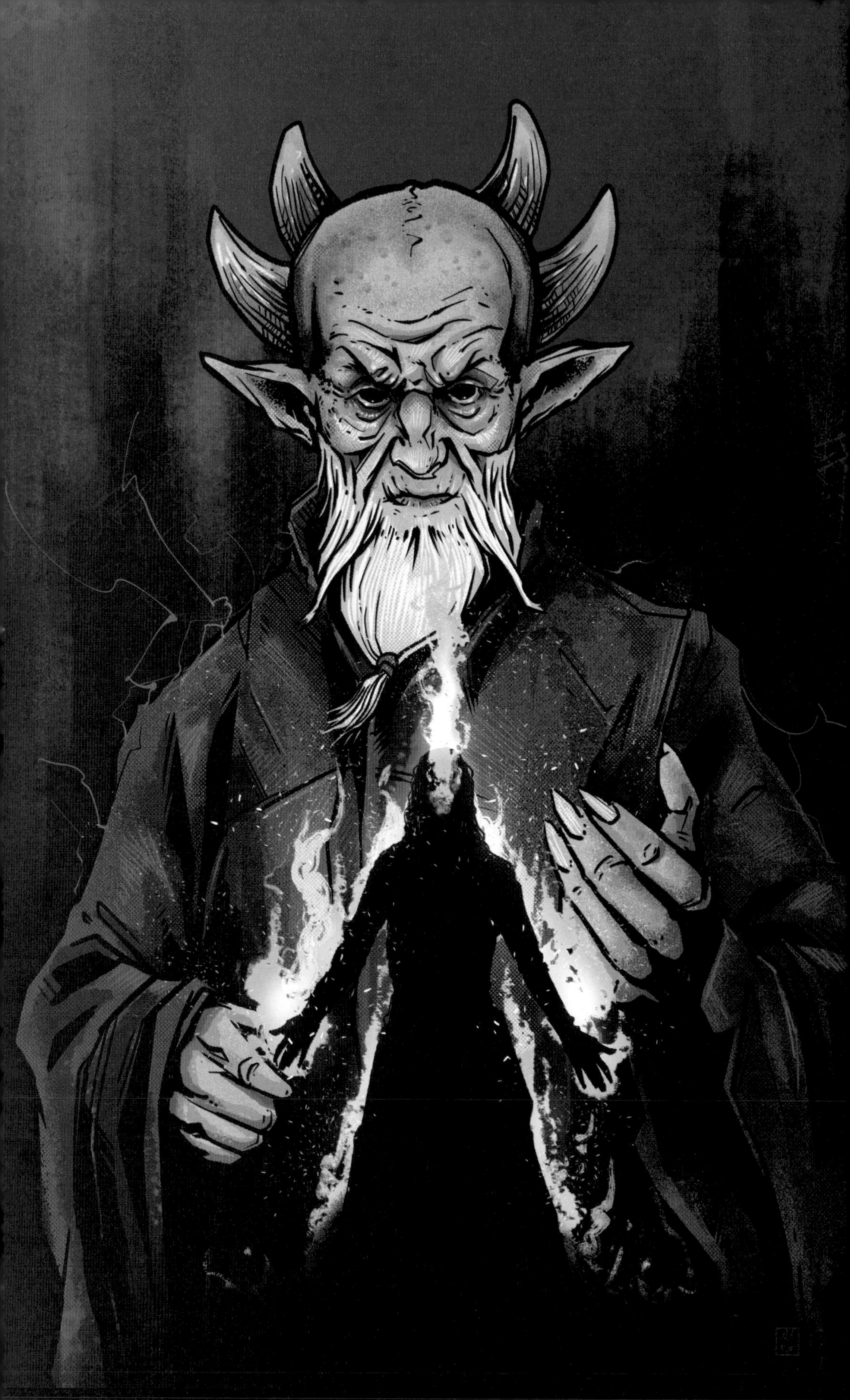

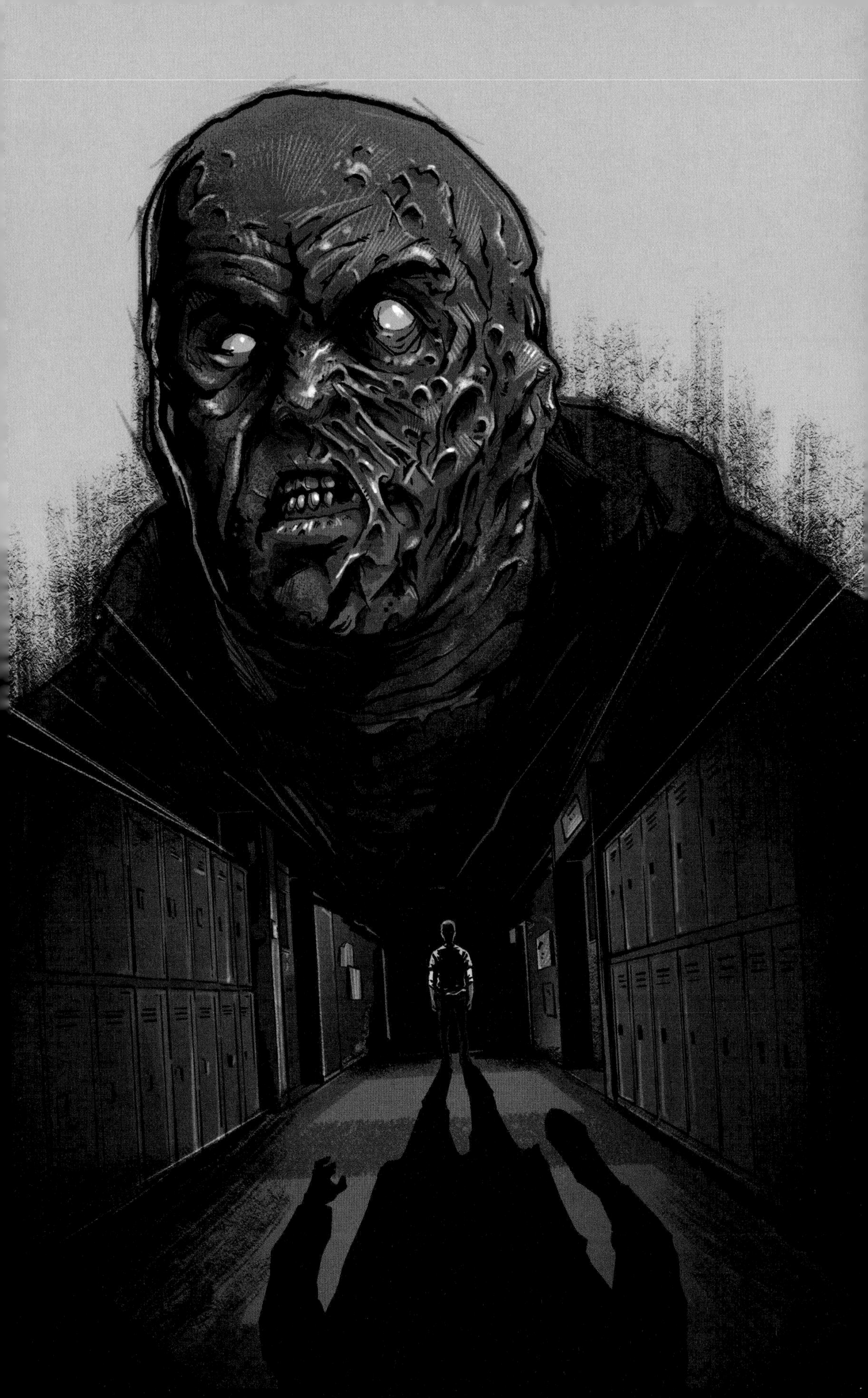

Angel #7 Preorder Cover by **Scott Buoncristiano**

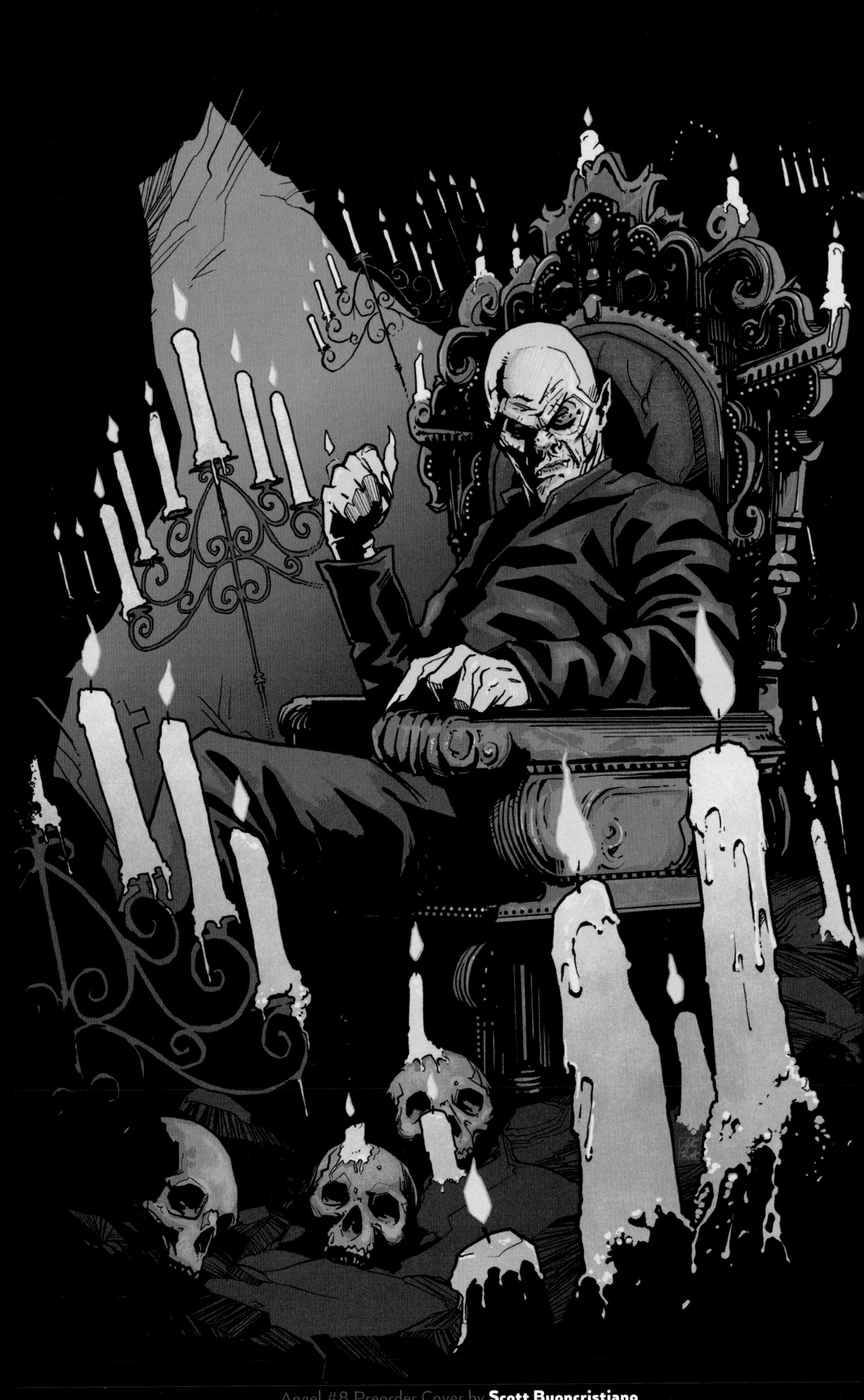

Angel #8 Preorder Cover by **Scott Buoncristiano**

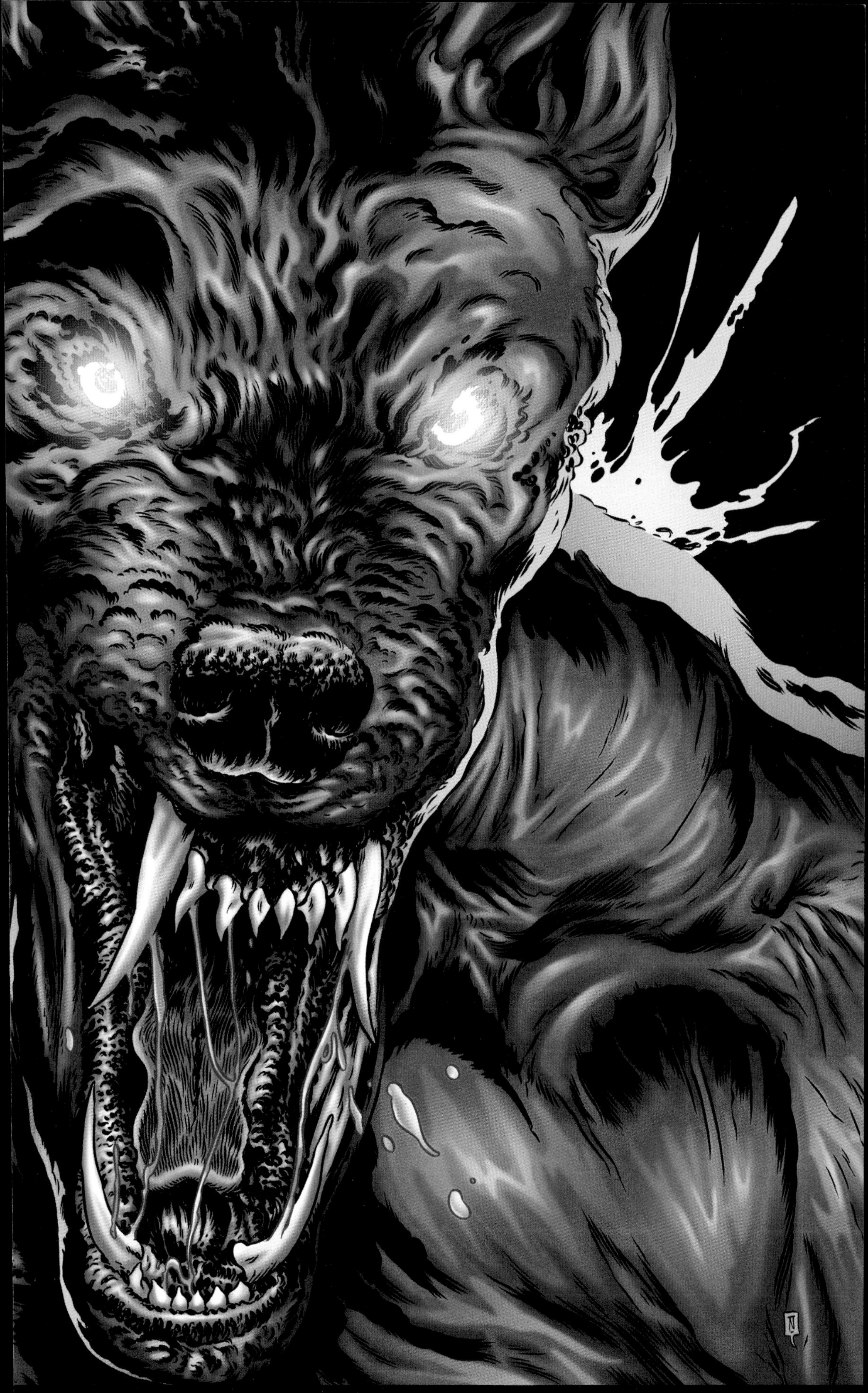

Angel #5 Variant Cover by **Troy Nixey**

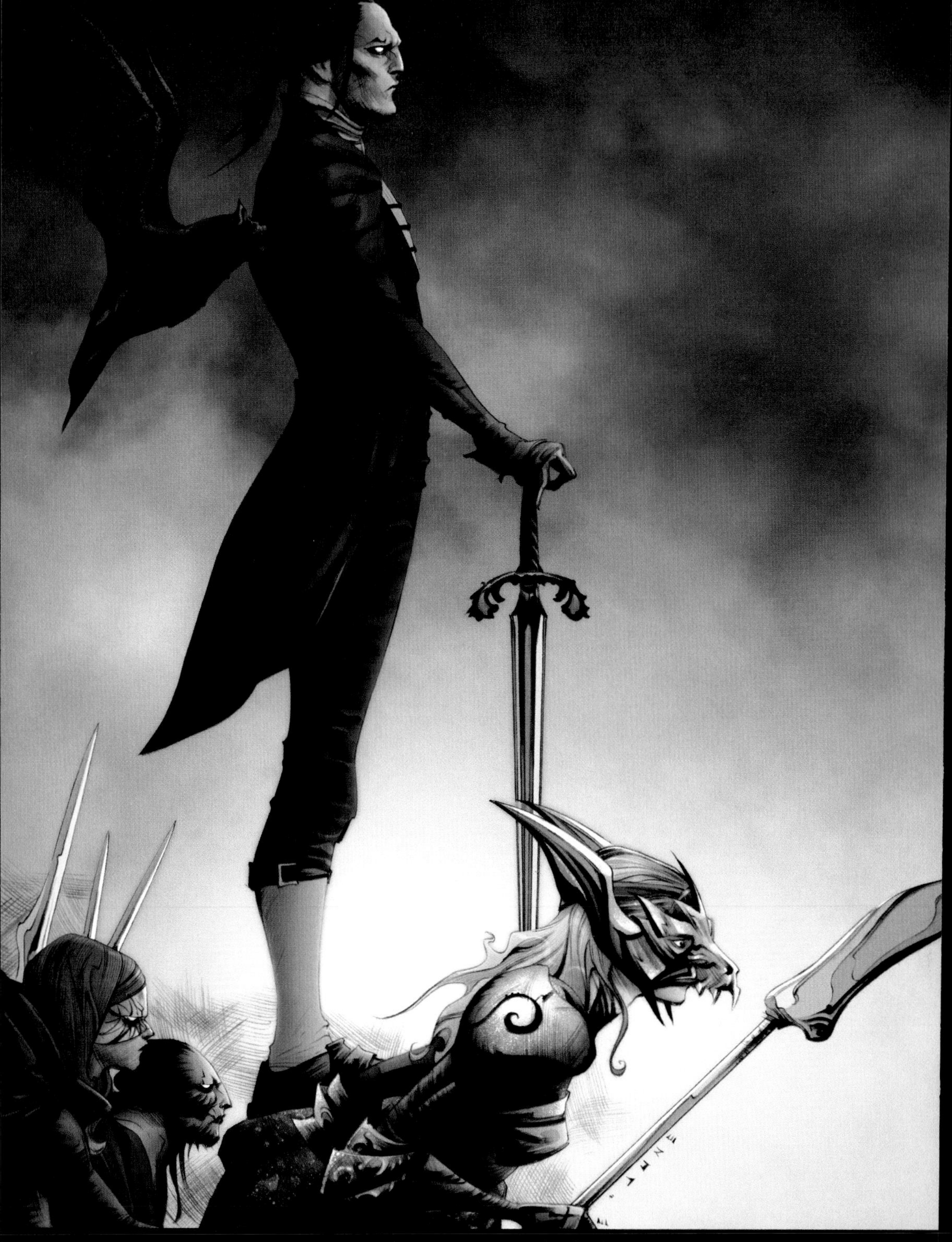

Angel #5 Variant Cover by **Jae Lee**

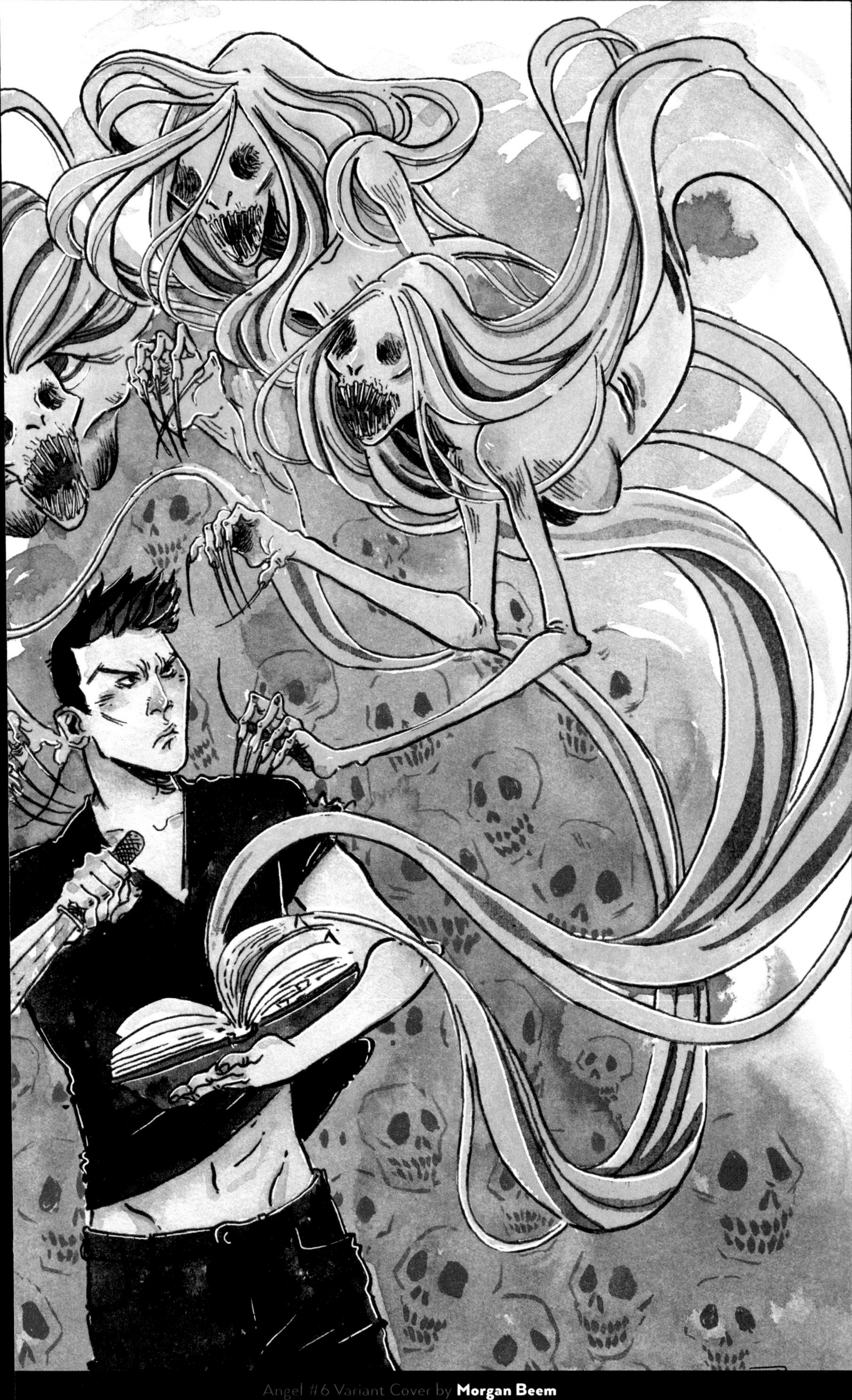

Angel #6 Variant Cover by **Morgan Beem**

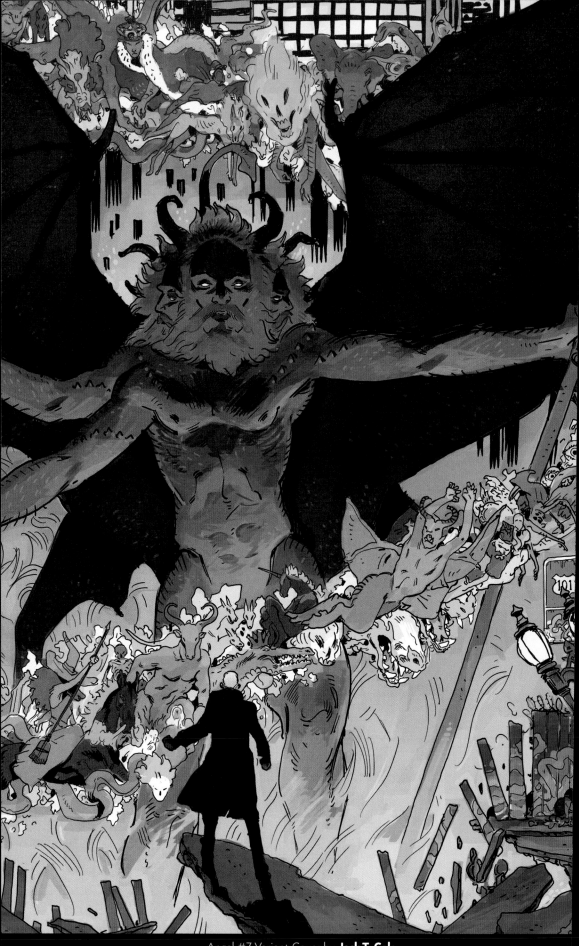

Angel #7 Variant Cover by **Jack T. Cole**

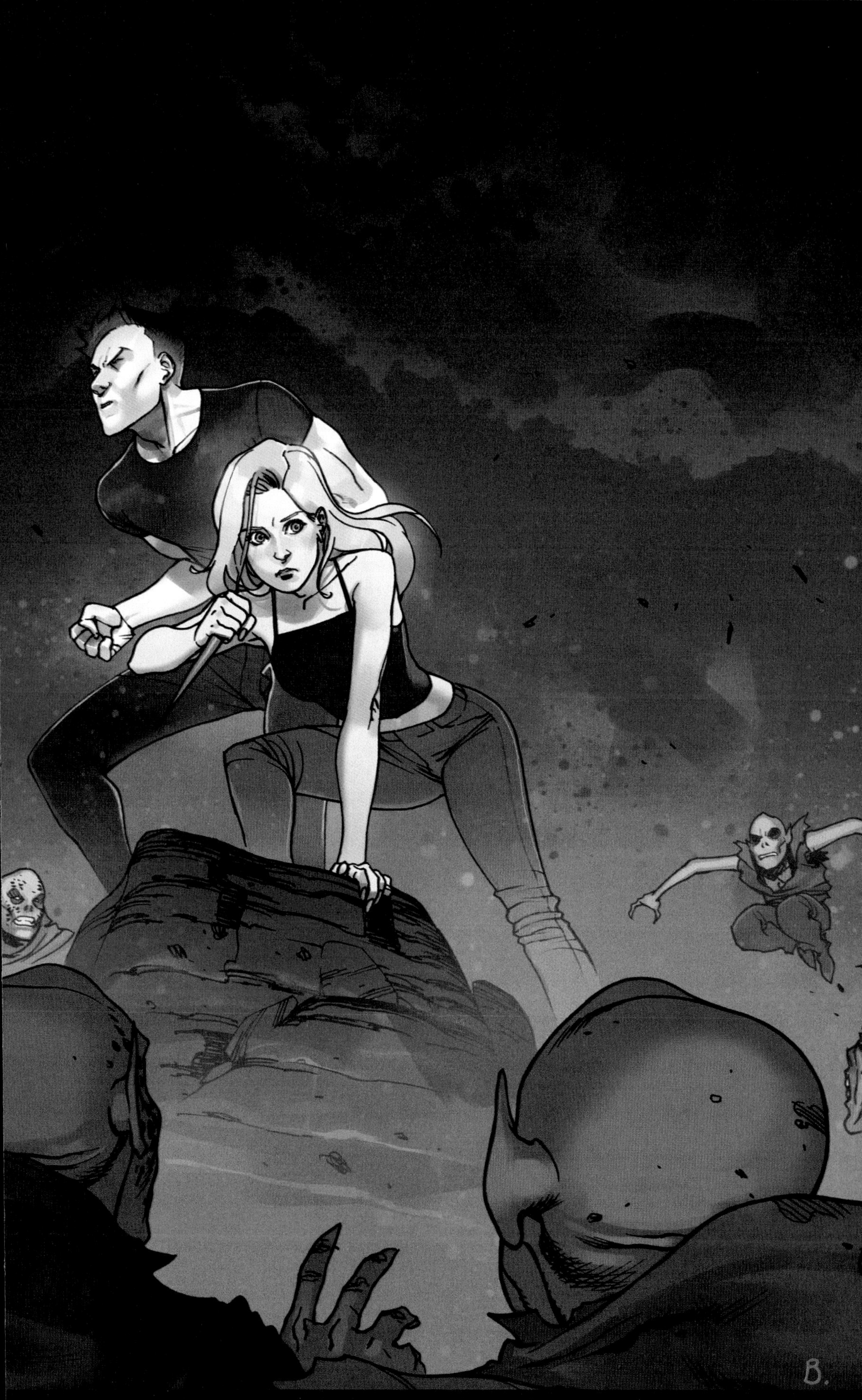
B.

Angel #8 Variant Cover by **Bengal**

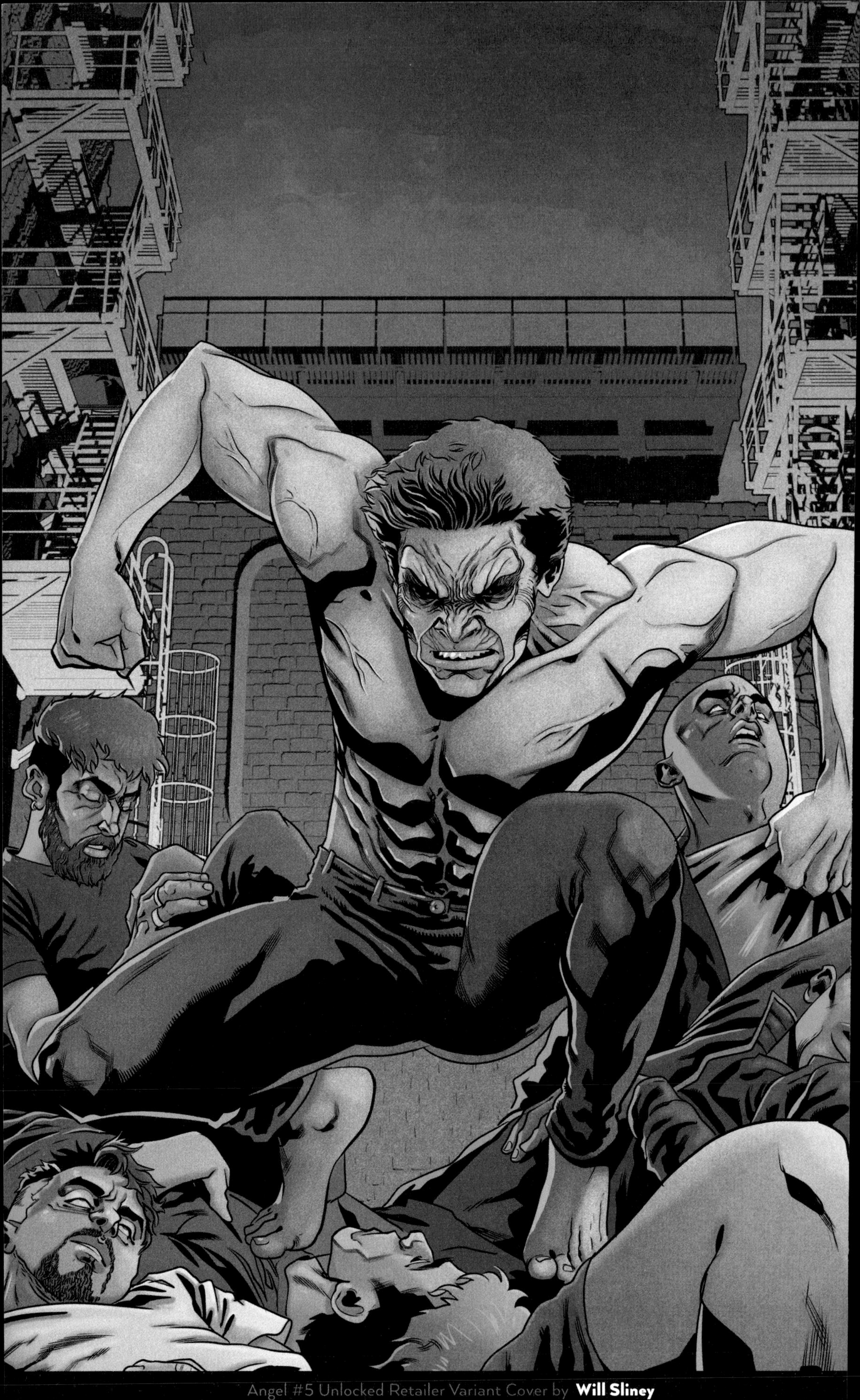

Angel #5 Unlocked Retailer Variant Cover by **Will Sliney**

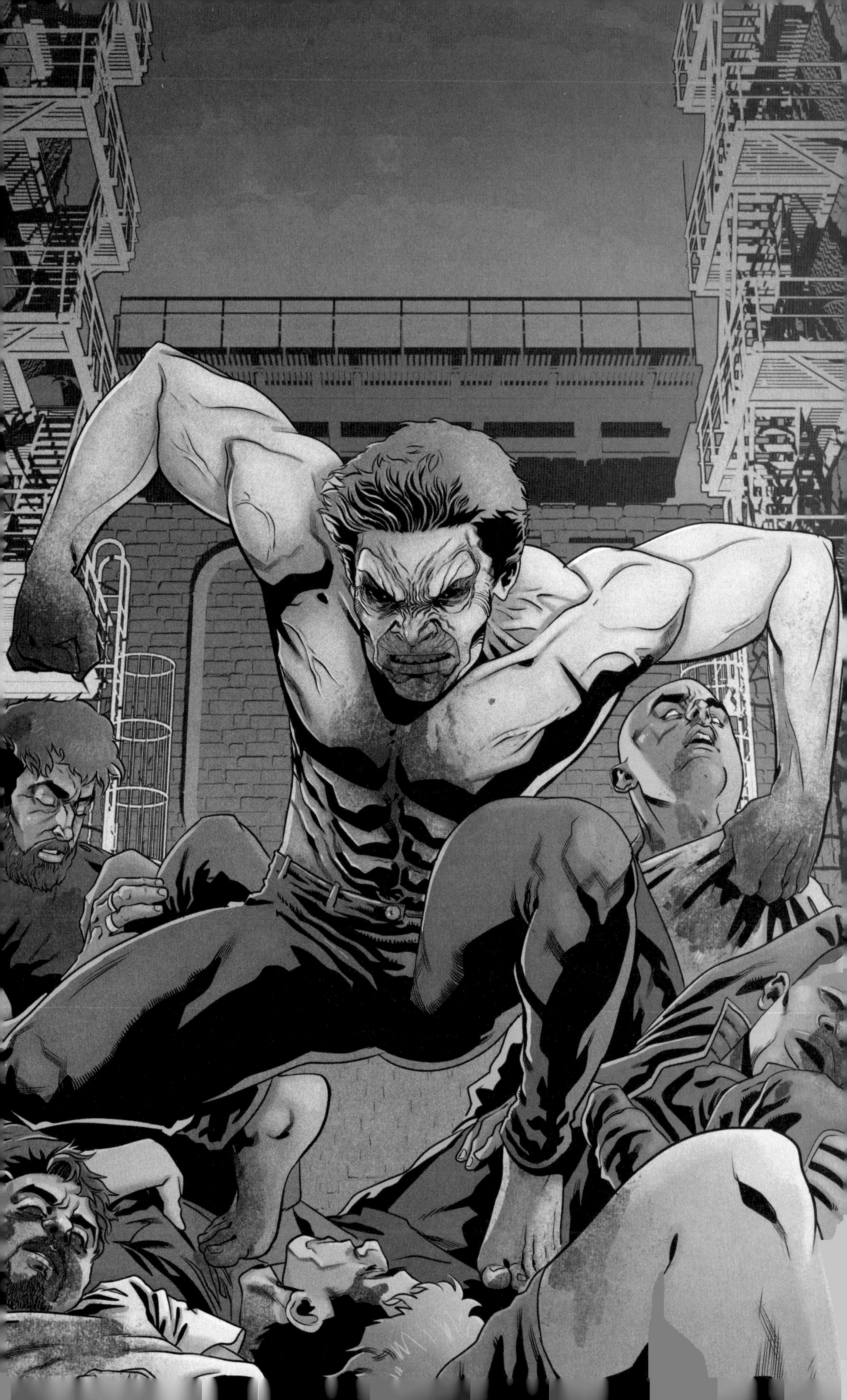

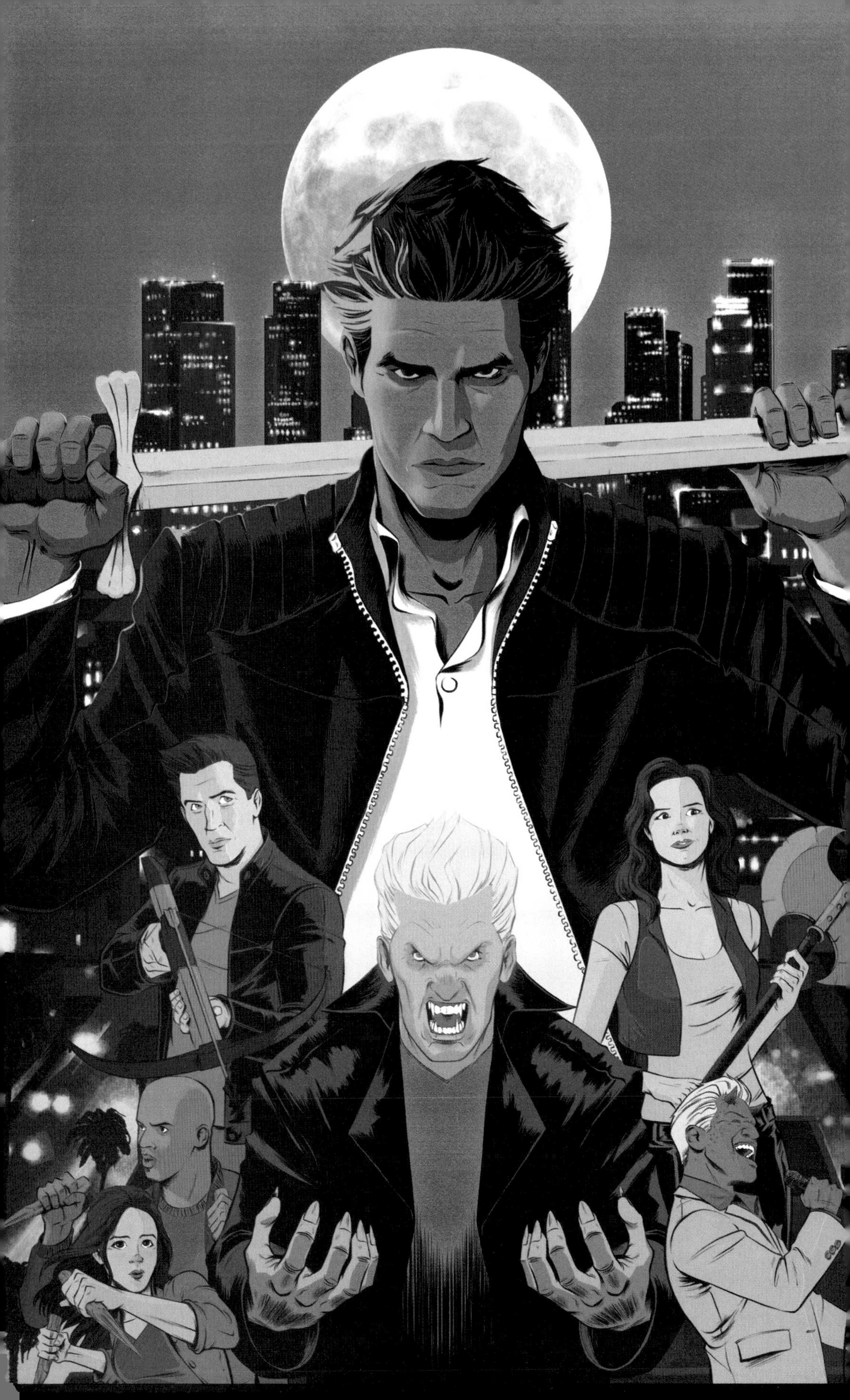

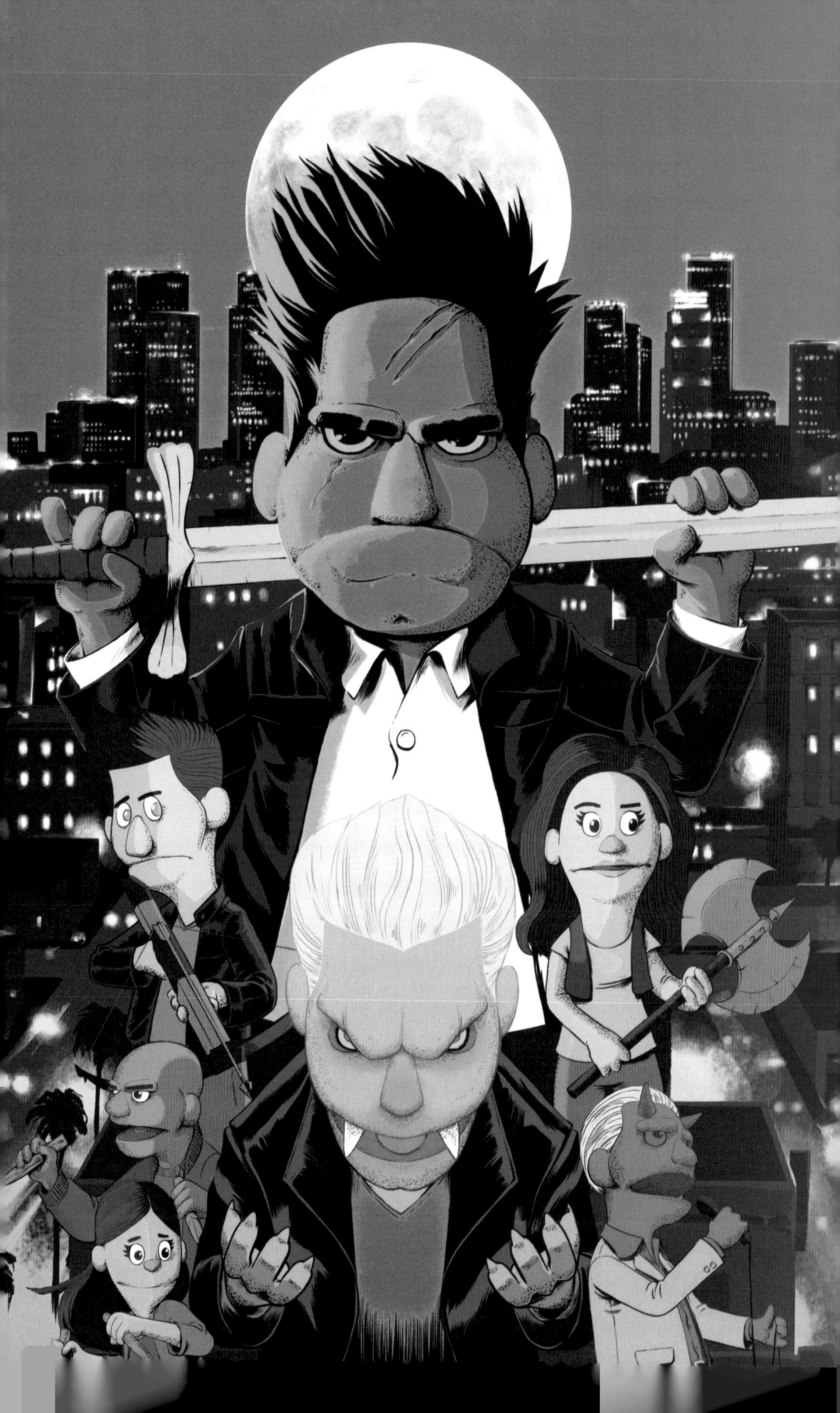

DISCOVER
VISIONARY CREATORS

THE
WOODS
JAMES TYNION IV • MICHAEL DIALYNAS
VOL. 1
THE ARROW

"The Spire is fantastic! My kind of genre free-for-all."
—BRIAN K. VAUGHAN
(Saga)
THE
SPIRE
SIMON SPURRIER
JEFF STOKELY
ANDRÉ MAY

MARK WAID · PETER KRAUSE
IRREDEEMABLE
AFTERWORD BY
GRANT MORRISON

MARK WAID · JEAN DIAZ
INCORRUPTIBLE

MICHAEL ALAN NELSON
DAN MORA
GABRIEL CASSATA
HEXED
THE HARLOT & THE THIEF VOLUME ONE

ABNETT · CULBARD
WILD'S
END
FIRST LIGHT
JEFF LEMIRE

James Tynion IV

The Woods

Volume 1
ISBN: 978-1-60886-454-6 | $9.99 US
Volume 2
ISBN: 978-1-60886-495-9 | $14.99 US
Volume 3
ISBN: 978-1-60886-773-8 | $14.99 US

The Backstagers

Volume 1
ISBN: 978-1-60886-993-0 | $14.99 US

Simon Spurrier

Six-Gun Gorilla

ISBN: 978-1-60886-390-7 | $19.99 US

The Spire

ISBN: 978-1-60886-913-8 | $29.99 US

Weavers

ISBN: 978-1-60886-963-3 | $19.99 US

Mark Waid

Irredeemable

Volume 1
ISBN: 978-1-93450-690-5 | $16.99 US
Volume 2
ISBN: 978-1-60886-000-5 | $16.99 US

Incorruptible

Volume 1
ISBN: 978-1-60886-015-9 | $16.99 US
Volume 2
ISBN: 978-1-60886-028-9 | $16.99 US

Michael Alan Nelson

Hexed The Harlot & The Thief

Volume 1
ISBN: 978-1-60886-718-9 | $14.99 US
Volume 2
ISBN: 978-1-60886-816-2 | $14.99 US

Day Men

Volume 1
ISBN: 978-1-60886-393-8 | $9.99 US
Volume 2
ISBN: 978-1-60886-852-0 | $9.99 US

Dan Abnett

Wild's End

Volume 1: First Light
ISBN: 978-1-60886-735-6 | $19.99 US
Volume 2: The Enemy Within
ISBN: 978-1-60886-877-3 | $19.99 US

Hypernaturals

Volume 1
ISBN: 978-1-60886-298-6 | $16.99 US
Volume 2
ISBN: 978-1-60886-319-8 | $19.99 US

AVAILABLE AT YOUR LOCAL COMICS SHOP AND BOOKSTORE

To find a comics shop in your area, visit www.comicshoplocator.com

WWW.**BOOM-STUDIOS**.COM

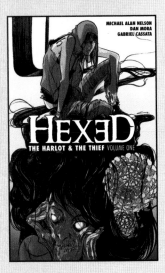

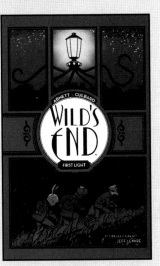